THE WORD IS ART

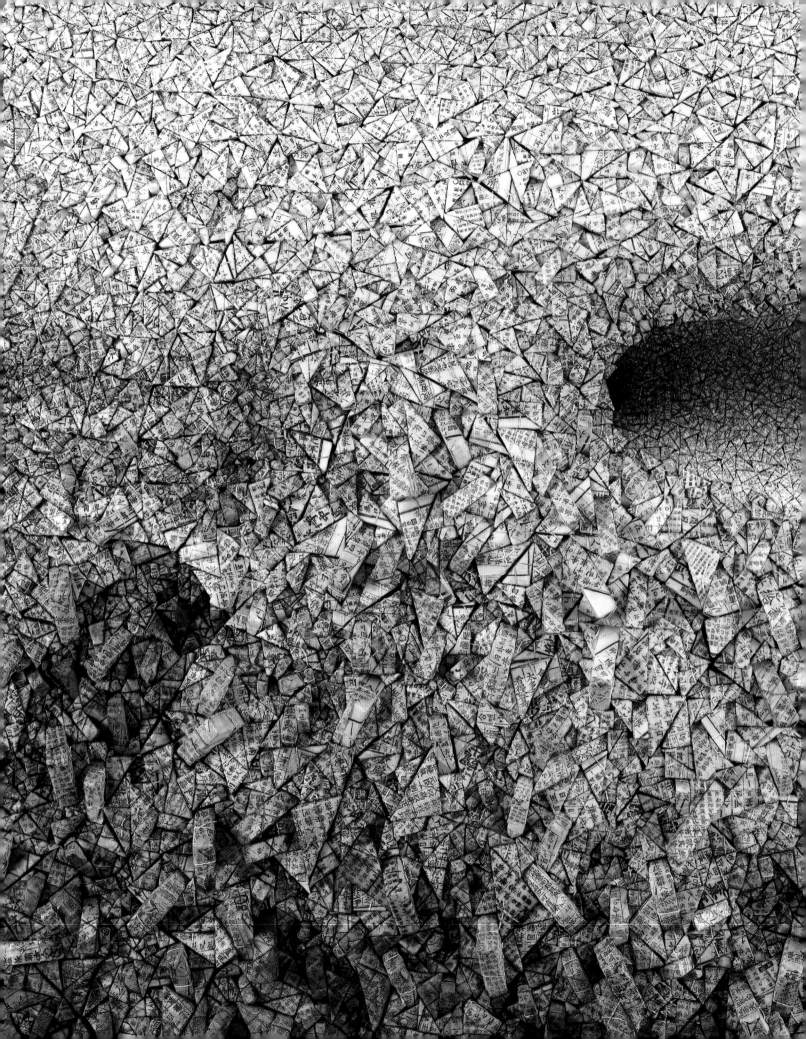

Michael Petry

THE WORD IS ART

T&H

6 Introduction

24 Installed Words

54 Three-Dimensional Words

88 Light

122 New Media

152 The Conceptual Word

184 Social Comment

220 The Drawn Word

258 Books

280 *Acknowledgments*

281 *Further Reading*

282 *Picture Credits*

284 *Index*

It should come as no surprise that *The Word is Art* is about words and books, and how they are used by contemporary artists. In the early years of the 21st century, there was a growing concern among some people that books would fall out of favour, with their digital equivalents taking their place. Similarly, some believed that young people would gradually start to shun writing. It was as if we were at a literary turning point – and in many ways we were, but it was not the one that many imagined. It could be argued that words and their very fluidity have become more important to people of all ages as this new century has progressed. Of course, we use words all the time in speech, but now we write – or rather, type – more than ever. While some people might not like the 'new writing' of textspeak, with its reliance on abbreviations, this development is entirely characteristic of language, which evolves continuously. The artists featured in this book have taken note of this phenomenon, and created work about words.

Any volume that claims to be a book of the word also references those other texts that profess to be books of the word, namely religious texts that have been revered for millennia. Followers of monotheistic religions – whether Judaism, Christianity or Islam – regard the book of their faith to be the word of their god. My book, in a way, is one that expounds a different kind of belief system – a belief in the power of art. The dramatic new museums that have opened across the globe in the last few decades – from the Guggenheim Museum in Bilbao to Tate Modern in London, to name only two – have become place-makers, even sites of pilgrimage, and have led to museums becoming the new churches of culture. Visitors may not worship the work they see, but they do seek it out, and it is no exaggeration to say that a type of enlightenment comes from the encounter. Words are often superfluous to the experience of looking at a painting or sculpture, but in many cases, as we shall see in this book, they are at the root of it.

We should begin by considering how contemporary works featuring words developed from the historic use of text in artworks. Words have found their way into art from the earliest times, and conceivably we could start with the ancient Greeks, who included inscriptions on sculptural works as a means of indicating who was depicted. Or we could race ahead to the Renaissance and the Dutch Golden Age, when artists added text to many paintings across different genres, and then there is the signature of the artist him- or herself. For many centuries, the signature has added a distinct commercial, if not artistic, value to works of art. Beyond painting and sculpture, examples of sophisticated calligraphy may be found in many cultures worldwide, from Chinese and Japanese scrolls to the illuminated manuscripts of north-western Europe, such as the Book of Kells. In the Islamic world in particular, where figural imagery in a religious context is rarely found, the written word developed into a dazzling art form, dating back to the 7th century.

My history of the word in art, however, focuses predominantly on work from the 20th century.

Of course, art has its own rich visual language that does not require the use of words. For example, in Western painting, an apple is often associated with Eve eating forbidden fruit from the Tree of Knowledge, which led to the Fall of Man. The depiction of an apple may, therefore, be a shorthand symbol for temptation or sin.

Contrast the familiar symbolism of an apple in a painting with the appearance of the word 'FÊTE' in stencil-type lettering across the top of the still life *Violin and Newspaper* (opposite) by the Cubist artist Georges Braque (1882–1963). We may understand that *fête* means 'party', but it has a seemingly untethered position on the canvas. This word is not a signature or description; it is an integral part of the image. It holds the composition together, yet simultaneously breaks out of the frame and into the everyday world. The viewer may feel that they are lacking vital information: what kind of party is it, where and when is it taking place? Are the missing details to be found in the newspaper also depicted in Braque's work, or the viewer's imagination alone? Anyone seeing the still life for the first time in the early 20th century could have been forgiven for believing that they were looking at an advertisement (albeit a very abstract one).

By the late 19th century, advertising was emerging as an art form in its own right, and well-known artists created posters that blurred the boundaries between fine art and advertising campaigns. For example, Henri de Toulouse-Lautrec (1864–1901) was commissioned to produce a series of powerfully graphic posters for the Parisian nightspot the Moulin Rouge, most famously *La Goulue at the Moulin Rouge* (opposite). The words on these posters are there to provide mundane information only (the name of the venue and the act), and while their colour and form help to create a cohesive

Henri de Toulouse-Lautrec · *La Goulue at the Moulin Rouge*, 1891
Poster lithograph printed in 4 colours
189 × 115.7 cm (74⅜ × 45½ in.)

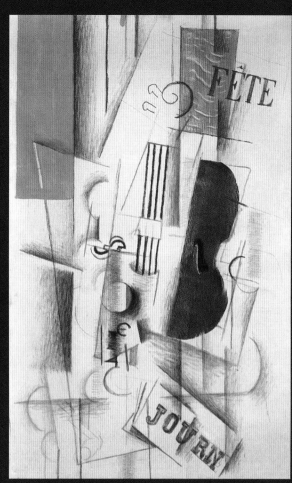

Georges Braque · *Violin and Newspaper*, 1912–13
Graphite, charcoal and oil on canvas
91.4 × 59.7 cm (36 × 23½ in.)

Juan Gris · *Still Life with Checked Tablecloth*, Paris, spring 1915
Oil and graphite on canvas
116.5 × 89.2 cm (45⅞ × 35⅛ in.)

Charles Demuth · *I Saw the Figure 5 in Gold*, 1928
Oil, graphite, ink and gold leaf on paperboard (Upson board)
90.2 × 76.2 cm (35½ × 30 in.)

whole, they nonetheless disrupt the sense of frivolity and flamboyance. By way of contrast, Cubism – one of the first abstract art styles of the 20th century – made text part of the image, frequently combining lettering and fractured motifs, such as musical instruments, on a canvas. Text was thus more than a sign, a symbol or a signifier; it had an importance equal to that of the painted or drawn object.

With the arrival of Cubism, the start of the 20th century witnessed a revolution in art-making practices. Braque, Pablo Picasso (1881–1973) and Juan Gris (1887–1927) began to introduce collage into their compositions, often experimenting with newspaper print; it was a means by which to incorporate elements of everyday life in art. Picasso's papier collé *Bottle of Vieux Marc, Glass, Guitar and Newspaper* (1913) features two pieces cut from *Le Figaro* newspaper, including the masthead, and the word 'VIEUX' is handwritten on the neck of the bottle. An outline of a guitar, rendered partly in ink and partly in white paper, occupies the centre of the blue paper ground. Braque offers a representation of a different stringed instrument in *Violin and Newspaper*. In graphite, in capital letters, he adds 'FÊTE' and 'JOURN', the latter indicating part of a newspaper masthead. Gris's *Still Life with Checked Tablecloth* (p. 9) is another work featuring hand-drawn text elements. By integrating text – including newspaper clippings documenting contemporary events – into their works, the Cubists brought together the art world and the outside world, speaking to viewers about their lives in the same way that artworks referencing our digital-based lives may do today. But whether analogue or digital, the text resonates as viewers read rather than just look at it. The text contains information, but it is a different type of information from, say, the depiction of an apple. There is a difference between the drawing of an object that has hidden, symbolic meaning and the rendering of a piece of text.

Artists of the Futurist movement, including Carlo Carrà, Gino Severini and Filippo Tommaso Marinetti, built on Cubism in the second decade of the 20th century, using text in their compositions to reflect the energy and dynamism of modern life. The influence of Futurism radiated towards Russia, especially the Suprematist works of Kazimir Malevich. The real breakthrough, the freeing of the word, came with the formation of the Dada movement in Zurich in 1916. The word in visual art took on new possibilities in the works of Tristan Tzara, Francis Picabia, Kurt Schwitters and, most importantly, Marcel Duchamp. Duchamp (1887–1968) had broken with Cubism by 1913 and instigated a rivalry with Picasso that had far-reaching effects on the course of modernism, to the extent that the art of the 20th century is sometimes considered to have been split into two main camps: those artists who, as in the case of Picasso, regarded the drawn image as pre-eminent; and those, like Duchamp, for whom the concept was paramount.

Dadaist works such as Picabia's (1879–1953) painting *Gabrielle Buffet, elle corrige les mœurs en riant* (Gabrielle Buffet, She Corrects Manners While Laughing, 1915) place text at odds with imagery: here, the words snake across two panes of clear glass, both attached by hinge to a black frame or stand. The viewer is left unsure what these words mean in themselves, let alone in relation to the object with which they appear. In his presentation of 'readymades' (the term he used to describe the artworks he made from manufactured objects), Duchamp often made verbal as well as visual puns. His *Comb* (1916), a steel dog-grooming comb, has an enigmatic inscription in white paint along its narrow edge: '3 OU 4 GOUTTES DE HAUTEUR N'ONT REIN A FAIRE AVEC LA SAUVAGERIE' (3 or 4 drops of height have nothing to do with savagery). Some critics have suggested that 'de hauteur' may be a play on 'd'auteur' (of the author), a reference to Duchamp's desire to move away from the 'savagery' of what he called 'retinal' – that is, purely visual – art.

One of Duchamp's most significant works is the 'rectified readymade' *L.H.O.O.Q.* (1919), a reproduction of Leonardo da Vinci's *Mona Lisa* to which he added a moustache, goatee and, beneath the portrait, a caption in capital letters that, when spoken aloud in French, sounds like a sentence that translates as 'She has a hot arse'. Two years earlier, Duchamp had purchased a porcelain urinal, signed it in black paint as 'R. Mutt' and submitted it, on its back, as a piece called *Fountain* to the Society of Independent Artists in New York. The board of directors excluded *Fountain* from the Society's inaugural exhibition, arguing that it could not be considered a work of art (and furthermore, was indecent). Duchamp later claimed that he had chosen to present a urinal because he believed it had the least chance of being liked, and in signing the piece with what he said was 'any old name' – although there is debate as to whether 'R. Mutt' is a pun on *Armut*, the German word for 'poverty', and it is also an adaptation of Mott, a manufacturer of sanitary ware – he concealed his identity as a well-known artist, so that the board members were not swayed by their knowledge of him. Here, the addition of text brings about a wholesale transformation, turning a mundane manufactured product into a piece that challenges the very concept of art.

In the 1920s such modernists as Alexander Rodchenko and El Lissitzky in Russia, Charles Demuth in the United States and László Moholy-Nagy, a Hungarian who taught at the Bauhaus in Germany and later founded the Institute of Design in Chicago, made works with a strong graphic quality that incorporated text. The Surrealist artist René Magritte (1898–1967) took things further in his series of word-image paintings. In *The Treachery of Images* (1929), he presents a painting of a pipe with the words 'Ceci n'est pas une pipe' painted beneath. Magritte's statement is one of plain fact: 'This is not a pipe'; it's a painted image of pipe, and in making this statement, the artist confronts the acceptance of an image of an object as being the object itself. This work calls into question the dominance of the optic (or the 'retinal', as Duchamp termed it) in art, and suggests that mimicry (or, in today's terms, photorealistic rendering) of the seen is as abstract an idea as anything else in the arts. More than twenty years after the creation of Cubism, it reconfirmed the written word as a fundamental aspect of art-making.

The devastation of the First World War elicited a different response from some artists, who rejected the avant-garde art forms of the early years of the century. Futurism, in particular, was discredited on account of its embrace of the machine age and implied enthusiasm for war. Picasso and Braque, the instigators of Cubism, both adopted a more traditional style of painting. In Germany, this so-called 'return to order' partly found its expression in the Neue Sachlichkeit (New Objectivity) movement, whose key artists Otto Dix and George Grosz sought to depict the reality of the human condition. The shift towards a more classical aesthetic was twisted by Mussolini's Fascists in Italy in the 1920s and especially by Hitler's National Socialist (Nazi) party in Germany in the 1930s, leading eventually to the Nazis' purge of modern, 'degenerate' art from German museums in 1937 and their promotion of idealized beauty and human perfection. It was only after the horrors of the Second World War that a new generation of artists was able to challenge notions of beauty and art. Artists such as Jean Dubuffet in France, Antoni Tàpies in Spain and Brion Gysin in England (working also in Paris and the US) took a deep interest in graffiti and calligraphy, incorporating them into their paintings. In the late 1950s, with the writer William S. Burroughs, Gysin (1916–1986) developed the cut-up (perhaps first used by Tzara in the 1920s) into a true art form. The idea of taking existing texts and then cutting them into pieces to be rearranged into a new text influenced a generation of artists in music, film and literature as well as fine art.

With the coming of the 1960s, the use of the word in art exploded as movements from Pop art to concrete poetry found ways to incorporate the signage of daily life. Pop took inspiration from the mass media and advertising, with *Campbell's Soup Cans* (1962) by Andy Warhol (1928–1987) – thirty-two canvases, each one depicting a different variety, with only the label on the front of each can distinguishing them – and *Green Coca-Cola Bottles* (1962) – seven rows of sixteen bottles, screenprinted above the company's logo – becoming emblematic of America's postwar consumerist culture. Warhol's romantic partner at the time, the poet/artist John Giorno (b. 1936), was inspired by Gysin and Burroughs to apply the cut-up technique, developing collages of texts borrowed from everyday signage and advertising. Dieter Roth, Dick Higgins, Ian Hamilton Finlay and Yoko Ono experimented with concrete poetry, which focuses as much on the shape of the poem on the printed page as on the language, rhythm and rhyme. In the mid-1960s, in a publishing programme developed by George Maciunas (1931–1978), the artists' collective Fluxus produced a series of Fluxus Editions, collaborative anthologies of items such as games, puzzles and documentations of artists' performances; printed materials often made up more than half of the contributions. Fluxus artists took an anti-capitalist stance, yet, in pioneering non-traditional art forms, produced works that were almost as throwaway as the advertisements they reflected.

Three of the most influential American artists of recent decades, Robert Rauschenberg, Cy Twombly and Jasper Johns, collectively had a significant effect on the word in art. After spending the first half of the decade studying, travelling and teaching (during which time he had a relationship with Rauschenberg),

Twombly (1928–2011) moved to Italy in 1957 and became enamoured with classical antiquity and mythology, scrawled references to which he incorporated in his paintings and drawings, including the *Poems to the Sea* series of 1959. In the late 1960s he developed his 'blackboard' paintings, waves of looping, illegible white script painted across a monochrome grey ground. Twombly worked within this style for several years before returning to classical themes in such pieces as *Apollo and the Artist* (opposite), in which the god's name stands out in blue among other inscriptions against a white ground.

Rauschenberg (1925–2008) and Johns (b. 1930) were in a relationship from 1954 to 1961, working closely together and also with the composer John Cage and his partner, the choreographer Merce Cunningham. All four were greatly influenced by Duchamp, and embraced his ideas of bringing art into life. In his 'Combines' (1954–64), hybrid works melding painting, collage and the assemblage of everyday objects, Rauschenberg incorporated advertisements and original and found texts from newspapers and magazines: for example, *Coca-Cola Plan* (1958) features the artist's notes on paper pasted on to a wooden structure that houses three Coca-Cola bottles, a newel cap and metal wings; *Black Market* (1961) combines many materials, including newsprint and a metal 'one way' street sign. The later 'Currents' series (1970), comprising collages and screenprints, utilizes headlines, texts and images found in such newspapers as the *New York Times*. Johns also turned to commonplace objects, as well as to depicting letters and numbers. *Gray Alphabets* (1956) is an imposing painting in the form of a rectangular grid, with boxes containing lower-case letters a–z, repeated in alphabetical order. *Map* (1961) is a painting of the United States with the names of the states added in stencil lettering. Johns challenges cartographic conventions by repeating names in various locations; 'Colorado', for example, appears in more than one state.

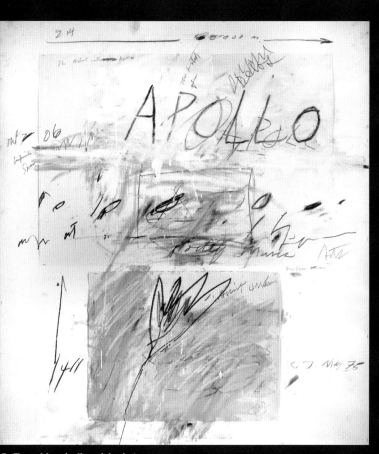

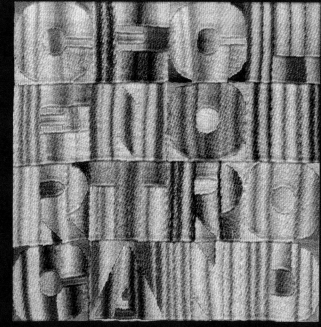

Alighiero Boetti · *Cercando il centro*, 1993
Embroidery on canvas
17 × 17 cm (6¾ × 6¾ in.)

Cy Twombly · *Apollo and the Artist*, 1975
Oil, wax crayon, pencil and collage on paper
142 × 128 cm (55⅞ × 50⅜ in.)

Ed Ruscha · *Large Trademark with Eight Spotlights*, 1962
Oil on canvas · 169.5 × 338.5 cm (66¾ × 133¼ in.)

Rauschenberg, Twombly and Johns were much feted in the art world, but it was a work by Robert Indiana (b. 1928) that became ubiquitous: originally designed in its red/blue/green colourway as a Christmas card for the Museum of Modern Art in 1965 and featuring on a US Postal Service stamp in 1973, Indiana's *LOVE* arranges the letters in a square, 'LO' (with a tilted 'O') stacked over 'VE'. Indiana had previously produced a series of paintings that referenced Demuth's *I Saw the Figure 5 in Gold* (p. 9), a tribute to William Carlos Williams's poem 'The Great Figure'. Indiana's work has a graphic quality that is also evident in the art of Ed Ruscha (b. 1937). Based in Los Angeles and with a background in graphic design and advertising, Ruscha was inspired by the Hollywood billboards and signage he saw on a daily basis. *Large Trademark with Eight Spotlights* (pp. 14–15) depicts the logo of the film studio 20th Century Fox, the red lettering receding in sharp perspective; the palette of primary colours and the diagonal composition are employed again in *Honk* (1962). *Actual Size* (1962), a flying can of meat painted beneath the Spam logo, may be a wry comment on absurd brand names.

Roy Lichtenstein (1923–1997), too, made words comic – or rather, used what appear to be enlarged comic-strip images as the basis of his paintings. Comic books employed the Ben Day technique, a means of introducing tone and shadow to line drawings by overlaying a screen of coloured dots during the printing process. Lichtenstein reproduced the dots at a much larger scale, combined with primary colours, black outlines and text in speech bubbles. Some critics accused Lichtenstein of plagiarizing the work of the original comic-book artists, but in transferring an image from strip to painting (and not only changing the scale, but also altering colours and removing details), he foregrounded the function of text in the visual arts. Works such as *Blam* (1962) and *Whaam!* (1963), both depicting the shooting-down of a plane, have the same

punch as those of Ruscha, Warhol and Indiana, and are celebrated as archetypal Pop paintings.

The dominance of Pop art led to a counter-reaction and from the late 1960s the development of what came to be known as conceptual art – art that takes the idea, or concept, as its starting point, existing separately from physical form. The finished work – if it exists at all – is a documentation of this idea. At the forefront of this movement were John Baldessari on the West Coast of the United States, Lawrence Weiner, Mel Bochner (see p. 19) and Joseph Kosuth in New York, the Art & Language group in the UK, the Japanese artist On Kawara and the Italians Alighiero Boetti and Maurizio Nannucci, all working in very different ways. Weiner (b. 1942) is perhaps the best known, and his site-specific texts were at first sight very disruptive to the gallery system. The texts were painted directly on to gallery walls and seemed completely at odds with the commercialism of Pop; yet, as time passed, these works have become monetized, as has much of the historic conceptual work. Weiner's art is poetic and often cryptic, and the visual arrangement of the words is as important as their legibility. They started out as simple black capitals, as in *TO SEE AND BE SEEN* (1972), and then became more playful, as in *PUSHED AS IF & LEFT AS IS* (2012), which incorporates colour and a visual interaction of the text with other graphics.

In the Communist bloc, many artists took up conceptualism as a means of protest against their limited freedoms. In Poland, Zdzisław Jurkiewicz (1931–2012) created minimalist works based on black-and-white text. *Białe, czyste, cienkie płótno* (1970) has the words 'White, clean, thin linen' printed on to a piece of fabric matching this description. It hangs on the wall, almost like a white flag of surrender, yet one that evokes freedom of thought. Stanisław Dróżdż (1939–2009) was a concrete poet who made works that took many physical forms. For example, for

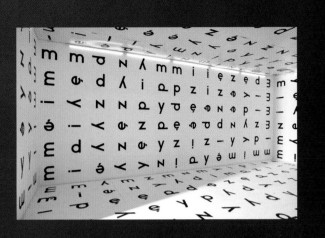

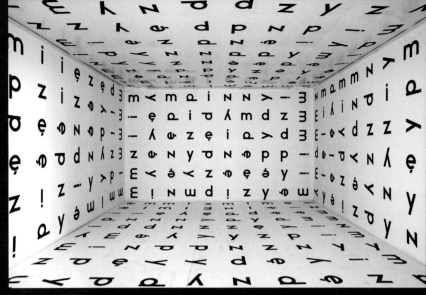

Stanisław Dróżdż · *Miedzy* (Between), 1977 · Installation: letters of the Polish word *miedzy* arranged systematically and painted on floor, ceiling and walls

Hassan Massoudy · *Tolerance*, 1982

Miedzy (Between; p. 17), the letters of the work's title were rearranged according to a detailed system and repeatedly painted in black across the white floor, ceiling and walls of a room, allowing the viewer to inhabit the poem physically.

The Belgian artist Marcel Broodthaers (1924–1976) is best known for his installations that investigate the very nature of what a museum is or should be. For *La Salle Blanche* (The White Room, 1975), he built a life-size replica of part of his home; he left it empty, but covered the walls in terms associated with museums and art-making, with the intention of questioning the way in which words influence our perception of the world and how museums affect the production of art. *Nous n'irons plus au bois...* is a diptych of two black-and-white plaques that depict the letter A (and next to it, an A crossed out), a pair of scissors (and a crossed-out pair) and, beneath, a text that translates as 'We won't go to the woods any more, the laurels are/aren't cut' – a reference to Louis XIV's ban on prostitutes in the royal grounds during the building of Versailles. This meant that the women moved into nearby brothels, which were identified by the placement of laurels in the windows. The phrase became part of a popular song of defiance. Broodthaers's work references the prostitutes' refusal to submit to the establishment and likewise his own.

In the early 1960s, Alighiero Boetti (1940–1994) was a leading artist of the Arte Povera movement, sculpting works from commonplace, non-traditional materials. He began to conceive ideas for works of art, but left their execution or production to others (a notion proposed by Duchamp decades earlier). In the early 1970s, Boetti and a business partner established the One Hotel in Kabul, Afghanistan, and he then had local women embroider a series of brightly coloured maps (*Mappa*) and word pieces (*Arazzi*) that have become his signature works. The *Arazzi* are embroidered texts of Boetti's own writings or selections from global poetry (see p. 13).

When the Russians invaded Afghanistan in 1979, many of the women fled to Pakistan, where the production of his art continued. However, local Muslim customs prevented Boetti from visiting the women directly, forcing him to work through middlemen and adding another layer of complexity to the interpretation of his directions for the making of his works.

The place of women in the world, and in the art world in particular, was at the core of a series of paintings by Louise Fishman (b. 1939) in the early 1970s. Her 'Angry Women' series (1973) spoke of the fury that many women felt towards a patriarchal art establishment that did its best to exclude them. At the time, only a small percentage of museum exhibitions were devoted to women artists (and even today the figure averages only 30% of such shows), and they were rarely represented by commercial galleries. Fishman's works featured the first names of noteworthy figures in the feminist movement, preceded by the adjective 'angry': for example, *ANGRY JILL* (p. 13), *ANGRY MARILYN, ANGRY DJUNA* and *ANGRY RADCLYFFE HALL*. The words, set against backgrounds of both vibrant and murky colours, and paired with energetic loops and slashes, resolve into exciting works of art, and the artist's rage is palpable.

Among the other women artists working with text, Liliane Lijn, Irma Blank, Sturtevant and Hanne Darboven all made a significant impact in the art world. The American artist Lijn (b. 1939) is best known for creating conical forms called Koans. *ABC Cone* (opposite), *Sky Never Stops* (1965) and *Homage to Charlie Parker* (1968), the last two using parts of poems by Leonard D. Marshall, are Koans set on a motorized turntable; as the turntable spins, the words painted on the surface of the Koan accelerate into a blur of movement and energy. Over the decades, Lijn has continued to expand her practice, making 'Poem Machines' of increased size and complexity, as in her new series of Poemdrums (using cylinders, rather

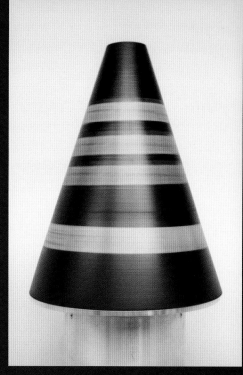

Liliane Lijn · *ABC Cone*, 1965
Letraset on painted truncated cork cone and motorized turntable
Height 40.7 × base diameter 24 cm (16 × 9½ in.)

Mel Bochner · *Working Drawings and Other Visible Things on Paper Not Necessarily Meant to be Viewed as Art*, 1966
4 identical loose-leaf notebooks, each with 100 Xerox copies of studio notes, working drawings and diagrams

than cones), and digital works (see pp. 132–33). The German artist Blank (b. 1934), who lives and works in Italy, developed a series of *Eigenschriften* (Self-Writings, *c.* 1965–72; opposite), works that appear to be densely packed lines of handwriting but, on close inspection, are markings in an unidentifiable script. In her more recent series, 'Global Writings' (since 2000), Blank writes using only eight consonants; the script is legible but incomprehensible. In stripping writing of its content, and in highlighting the similarities between writing and drawing, she aims to suggest new meanings.

In the late 1960s and the early '70s, neon increasingly came to be used as an artistic medium. Bruce Nauman (b. 1941), Maurizio Nannucci (b. 1939; see opposite), Mario Merz (1925–2003; see opposite) and Joseph Kosuth (b. 1945) were among the many artists who brought what had formerly been seen as a medium for signage into the visual arts by means of texts that were not advertisements. In the 1980s, Jenny Holzer (b. 1950) started using other types of light-emitting technology for her text works, including projection and LED signage. The use of light to focus the viewer's attention on an artistic text was a dramatic change from earlier depictions of words, and the introduction of moving words (in neon, LED and video, for example) added a time-based dimension, pushing many such works into the realm of real-time cinema. Light continues to be a powerful medium for many artists working with words (see pp. 88–121), and younger generations embrace new media as enthusiastically as the pioneers of decades past (see pp. 122–51).

In the United Kingdom, having found fame with *The Singing Sculpture* (first presented in 1969), Gilbert and George (Gilbert b. 1943; George b. 1942) began their 'Pictures' series. Initially they took images of their environment, working them into sophisticated contemporary comments as well as disruptive artworks, as in *Bent* and *Fucked*

Up (1977; opposite). They progressively took to creating their art in the studio, making them larger and more colourful. They often depicted themselves alongside skinheads and black and Asian youths from the East End of London, with the titles of the works printed almost as if they were captions: for example, *Bad God*, 1983; *Him*, 1985; *Spore*, 1986. Gilbert and George continue to make challenging work, and they have also assisted younger artists such as David Robilliard (1952–1988), whose word-and-image paintings from the 1980s they promoted. Robilliard died from HIV/AIDS-related complications, as did the film-maker Derek Jarman (1942–1994), who in his final years made a series of word-based paintings, including *Letter to the Minister* (1992), *Spread the Plague* (1992) and *Fuck Me Blind* (1993), that addressed his illness.

The 1980s were a time often associated with the growth of free-market capitalism and globalization, when greed was seen as good and Wall Street became a new arbiter of taste and style. But the decade also saw the emergence of a postmodern art world in which no single style or school of thought was dominant. This enabled artists with very diverse voices and from many cultures – for example, the Iraqi calligrapher Hassan Massoudy (see p. 17) – to come to the fore, each with a different vision of how text and art could coexist. Critiquing consumerism and female stereotypes, Barbara Kruger (b. 1945) produced such prints as *Untitled (I Shop Therefore I Am)* (1987) and *Untitled (Your Body is a Battleground)* (1989), comprising a found photograph overlaid with a caption in bold type against a red, black or white ground. The art activist group Gran Fury took art and words on to the street with its *Silence=Death* graphic, originally conceived in 1987 as a neon installation for the New Museum in New York. With the words of the work's title arranged beneath a pink triangle (the symbol used in Nazi concentration camps to identify homosexuals), the design appeared on a poster and T-shirts, highlighting

Mario Merz · *Igloo di Giap – Se il nemico si concentra perde terreno se si disperde perde forza* (Giap Igloo – If the Enemy Masses His Forces, He Loses Ground: If He Scatters, He Loses Strength), 1968/94
Metal tubes, wire mesh, neon tubes and dirt
Diameter 300 cm (118⅛ in.)

Maurizio Nannucci · *The Missing Poem is the Poem/1969*, 1969
Neon, installed here at MAXXI Roma, 2015
320 × 210 × 4 cm (126 × 82⅝ × 1⅝ in.)

Irma Blank · *Eigenschriften, Spazio A-28*
(Self-Writings, Space A-28), 1972
Pastel on paper · 70 × 49.5 cm (27½ × 19½ in.)

Gilbert & George · *Fucked Up*, 1977
Mixed media · 241 × 201 cm (94⅞ × 79⅛ in.)

the Reagan administration's lack of commitment to the sexual health of gay men as the AIDS crisis swept the world. Another work, *Read My Lips* (1988), featured a photograph of two sailors kissing, with the slogan placed across the image. Playfully employing the same words used by the presidential candidate George H. W. Bush when he promised no new taxes, it underscored the fact that HIV cannot be transmitted by kissing; furthermore, that kissing is just as much part of a gay relationship as sex. Many credit the work of groups such as Gran Fury, ACT UP and General Idea (based in Canada), and of artists such as Tom Fecht (see opposite), with bringing about changes to drug protocols and a greater acceptance of the LGBTQ+ community.

Words also started to appear in the works of painters who were at the forefront of a new wave of collecting. These included Jean-Michel Basquiat, Richard Prince, Simon Linke, Christopher Wool and Roni Horn (see opposite). Basquiat (1960–1988) combined text and street-based imagery, as in *Notary* (1983), while Prince (b. 1949) retold old quips in his 'Monochromatic Jokes' series (1987–90). In *Tell Me Everything* (1987), purple letters sit on a brown ground, reading, 'I went to see a psychiatrist. He said, "Tell me everything." I did, and now he's doing my act.' Since the mid-1980s, Linke (b. 1958) has been making thick impasto paintings based on advertisements in *Artforum* magazine for other artists' exhibitions (see opposite). Around the same time, Wool (b. 1955) began creating paintings of large black stencilled letters on white canvas (see pp. 240–41). Even though these artists had very different styles, the purely visual impact of text was a major feature of their work alongside its readability; the painted word was still very much a painting.

Many artists working with words in the 1980s and '90s, ranging from Raymond Pettibon to Shirin Neshat (both opposite), are still working today alongside a younger generation, exploring a wide variety of media, both traditional and new, in our digital, online age. The chapters that follow present works created (with a few exceptions) since the turn of the 21st century, proving that, while the way in which we write and use text in everyday life may be changing, the word still has a place in our art.

Raymond Pettibon · *Freud's Universe*,
cover, 1982 · Printed paper
21.6 × 14 cm (8½ × 5½ in.)

Simon Linke · *Remembering Marcel*, 1987-88
Oil on linen · 91.4 × 91.4 cm (36 × 36 in.)

Shirin Neshat · *I Am Its Secret*, 1993
Ink on RC print, photo by Plauto
125.7 × 85.7 cm (49½ × 33¾ in.)

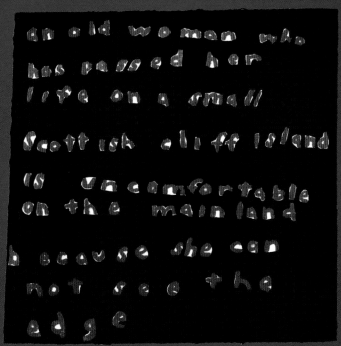

Roni Horn · *An old woman who has passed her life on a small Scottish cliff
island is uncomfortable on the mainland because she can not see the edge*, 1984
Gouache, transparent watercolour and gum arabic on paper
34.9 × 36.1 cm (13¾ × 14¼ in.)

Tom Fecht · *Homage – Names and Stones (Mémoire
nomade – documenta IX, Kassel)*, 1992 · 250 stones, names
0.5 × 27 m (19¾ in. × 88 ft 7 in.)

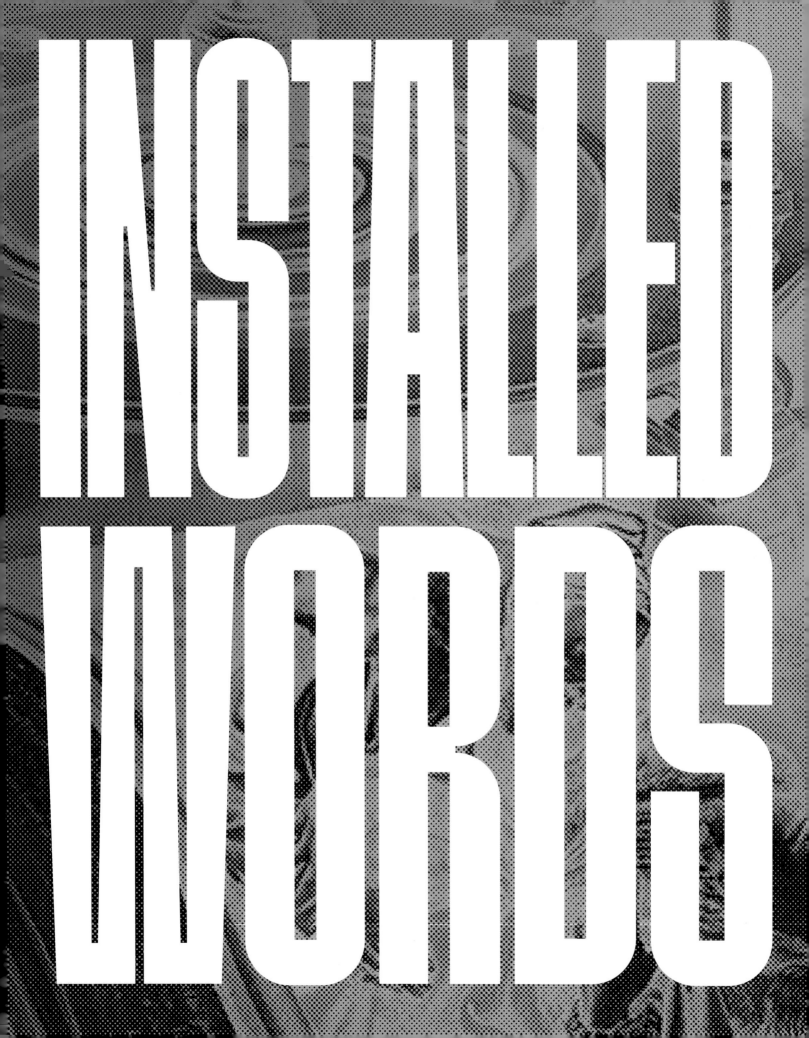

Text works installed directly on gallery walls or in complex social situations have become a staple of many high-impact exhibitions. Visitors are often confronted with words on a human scale or even larger, so that the individual letters turn into sculptural objects or the work as a whole becomes cinematic. Lawrence Weiner is the artistic godfather of this move to present text on walls as a form of visual poetry, an evolution of the concrete poetry of the 1960s. Artists may use the blank wall as their canvas, and in most cases such interventions are limited to the length of the exhibition. The market has, however, caught up with such conceptual practices as installation art, and these works are now also available for sale (a certificate of authenticity and directions for the reinstallation are usually provided at purchase).

Younger artists who have taken their cue from Weiner's signature works include Micah Lexier, who takes a strong conceptual stance in his immersive black-and-white wall pieces. Some of his works – and those of Mark Themann – are so large that they spread across two or three large gallery walls, and the viewer is in effect inside the pieces. The use of black text (often in vinyl or professionally painted by sign writers) on white walls has become a trope seen across the art world. By way of contrast, Beni Bischof adds colour and an element of humour to his graffitied wall interventions. Mark Titchner often presents large-scale texts in full technicolour to startling effect. Jukka Korkeila makes colourful wall works, on top of which he often places his paintings on canvas, adding another layer of visual complexity.

Not all textual wall works are two-dimensional: Annette Messager utilizes a variety of materials to make her pieces, including netting, while Anatol Knotek makes humorous use of cardboard letters that appear to have fallen off the wall. Beyond the gallery walls, Enrique Ježik creates sculptural letters of cardboard and steel. Anka Dabrowska employs satire in her well-placed graffiti-style signage in order to disrupt its austere surroundings. Kate Murdoch places three-dimensional letters into equally unusual contexts to create missing narratives.

What all these works have in common is the visual impulse of the words themselves. They may be profound, prosaic or poetic, but the viewer must assimilate them in one go, along with their surroundings, whether that is a gallery space or a more unconventional venue.

The Tunisian-French artist eL Seed's installation *Perception* (pp. 26–27) was painted across more than fifty buildings in Cairo without the consent of the Egyptian government, which has stopped street artists making work and censures artists across many media. The neighbourhood is called Manshiyat Naser and its inhabitants are Coptic Christians known as *zabaleen*, which means 'garbage people' (they do not use the term themselves). For decades they have collected and sorted through the city's rubbish, and made a living from selling the salvaged material, yet they are marginalized because their work is seen as dirty. The text, a saying from St Athanasius – a 4th-century bishop of Alexandria – translates as 'Anyone who wants to see the sunlight clearly first needs to wipe his eye.' The work took eL Seed and his team more than three weeks to install, and it can be viewed as a whole only from Mokattam Mountain.

The American Lawrence Weiner is one of the most influential artists using text. His early wall-based text pieces include *TO SEE AND BE SEEN* (1972), in which the words of the title were painted in black capitals directly on the gallery wall. The piece raises questions about what it is we see when we look at a conceptual artwork, and how we see it. Weiner's works have become more colourful, visual and compositionally complex over the years, and have also moved on to the floor and other surfaces. *PLACED ON THE TIP OF A WAVE* (above) presents the words in turquoise blue, with each letter outlined in black, and – similar to the layout of a concrete poem – the text slides up and down on a black curve, recalling the motion of a wave.

PAGES 26–27 · eL Seed · *Perception*, 2016
Anamorphic painting over 56 façades, Cairo · Width 90 × depth 300 m (295 ft 3¼ in. × 984 ft 3 in.)

ABOVE · Lawrence Weiner
PLACED ON THE TIP OF A WAVE, 2009
Language + the materials referred to, Regen Projects II, Los Angeles
Dimensions variable

ABOVE · Niels Shoe Meulman
Graffiti Are the Weeds of Art, 2016
Mural, New Delhi · Approx. 10 × 30 m
(32 ft 9¾ in. × 98 ft 5⅛ in.)

The Dutch artist Niels Meulman goes by the graffiti tag 'Shoe' for his urban interventions. He uses the term 'calligraffiti' (originally attributed to Brion Gysin) to describe his work, which merges calligraphy, graffiti and performance art. Meulman combines elements of Japanese and Arabic calligraphy with English to make works that are almost abstract, even though the words can be read as text. For *Graffiti Are the Weeds of Art* (2016), he covered the front of a New Delhi building in bright pink, yellow and blue, overpainted with black text, which reads, 'sans serifs no letters, and no words to read, sans words no signs, no names in the streets, just rows of buildings, and gardens sans weeds'.

The German conceptual artist Sebastian Bieniek works across many media, including performance, painting and installation. His 'Perfect Circle' series of text works features phrases painted in black on the back of stretched canvases, for example, *Close Your Eyes (To See This Painting)* (2013), *Die Kunst ist keine Kunst* (Art is Not Art, 2013) and *In the Future Everything'll Be the Same* (2015). For the *Please Ignore This* installation at the Millerntor Gallery, Hamburg, in 2016 (above), Bieniek scrawled the text directly on to the wall, leaving behind drips of paint. In his work he seeks to investigate how art and language function and how easily they are disrupted.

At the core of the British artist Mark Titchner's work is the use of words. He combines often elaborate typefaces and dense backgrounds to create works such as *I Want a Better World, I Want a Better Me* (2012). *Why is There Something Instead of Nothing?* (1999) has been translated into several languages for billboard-sized public installations. Titchner also makes works within a gallery or museum context, and in 2014 was commissioned for a project at Foyles bookshop in London (opposite). On one side the wall read 'AN IMAGE OF TRUTH' and on the other 'NOT ONE WORD LESS'. The mirrored vinyl background reflected the viewer, placing them in the frame of the piece, within the social frame of the store and in the broader frame of how words function in society. Titchner explains that his work is 'a dialogue about how you receive thought and ideas'.

ABOVE · Sebastian Bieniek (B1EN1EK)
Please Ignore This, 2016
Acrylic on wall, Millerntor Gallery,
Hamburg · 200 × 500 cm
(78¾ × 196⅞ in.)

OPPOSITE · Mark Titchner
An image of truth. Not one word less, 2014
Digital print on mirrored vinyl
240 × 961.2 × 80 cm
(94½ × 378⅜ × 31½ in.)

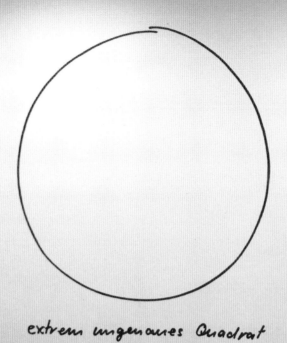

extrem ungenaues Quadrat

Existenzängste Champagner!

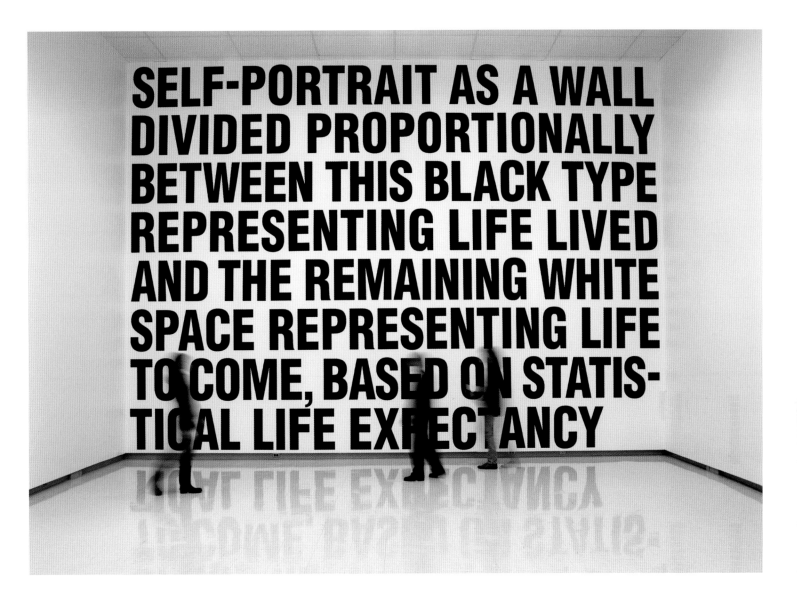

SELF-PORTRAIT AS A WALL DIVIDED PROPORTIONALLY BETWEEN THIS BLACK TYPE REPRESENTING LIFE LIVED AND THE REMAINING WHITE SPACE REPRESENTING LIFE TO COME, BASED ON STATIS-TICAL LIFE EXPECTANCY

The Swiss artist Beni Bischof uses minimal gestures and text to make complex word pieces. In *Existenzängste* (opposite, bottom), which comprises two colours of spray paint, it looks as if the blue graffiti has been tagged with red to cancel it out. The blue text means 'existential fear' or 'angst', while the red shouts 'champagne!' Bischof's prescription for overcoming ennui might not be for everyone, but it does highlight two very different ways of living in the modern world. A badly sprayed red circle on a gallery wall is captioned *Extrem ungenaues Quadrat*, meaning an 'extremely imprecise square' (opposite, top). Bischof references failure and our fear of it, while proposing that perhaps it is better just to jump in and make the best of any situation.

For his survey show in 2013 at the Power Plant in Toronto, the Canadian artist Micah Lexier remade a 1998 work called *Self-Portrait as a Wall*, which describes his conceptual approach to portrait-making. As the text explains, the black vinyl letters represent the portion of Lexier's life already lived and the white background reflects the years he has left, based on average life expectancy. The work has been installed in various galleries (above) – retypeset to fit the dimensions of the wall, but always in the same ratio until it was remade – and has been translated into French (1998) and German (2005). Lexier's immersive graphic investigations into what art is, how it functions, and how it is written about, allow viewers to experience text in a physical way.

OPPOSITE, TOP · Beni Bischof
Quadrat/Square, 2015
Acrylic on wall, Kunstmuseum
Liechtenstein, Vaduz
Diameter 380 cm (149⅝ in.)

OPPOSITE, BOTTOM · Beni Bischof
Existenzängste (Existential Fear), 2011–17
Spray paint on wall, installed here at
Galerie Rupert Pfab, Düsseldorf, 2013
250 × 450 cm (98⅜ × 177⅛ in.)

ABOVE · Micah Lexier
Self-Portrait as a Wall, 1998/2007
Vinyl on wall, Owens Art Gallery,
Sackville, New Brunswick
350 × 520 cm (137¾ × 204¾ in.)

Mark Themann is an Australian artist who works across various media, including projections, performance and wall-based installations. For the two-room installation *Sensorium – Go Into This Space* in Berlin in 2012, black text was applied directly on to the walls of Gallery A. Installed in Gallery B were other text-based works on video, paper and small brass plaques, the last featuring compositions beginning with the term 'glossolalia', which is used to describe 'speaking in tongues' or the utterance of language or supposed language, usually unknown to the speaker, particularly in religious worship.

ABOVE · Mark Themann
Sensorium – Go Into This Space, 2012
From a solo, two-room installation,
Künstlerhaus Bethanien, Berlin
Site-specific dimensions

ABOVE · Kay Rosen · *Hi*, 1997/2012
Acrylic on wall, Contemporary Art
Museum, Raleigh, North Carolina
Dimensions variable

In the 1970s, before she began making text-based works, the American artist Kay Rosen was an academic, lecturing in language and linguistics. Her works are often painted directly on to prepared walls and are frequently reinstalled in several locations. In *Blurred* (2004/15, Art Gallery of New South Wales, Sydney), 'BLU' is painted in blue on one wall and 'RED' in red on an adjacent wall. The first 'R' is painted in purple (a mix of the two colours) where the walls join. *Hi* (above) has been installed in a variety of media. In 1997 it was a window display (Galerie Michael Cosar, Düsseldorf), then several times a highway billboard (including MASS MoCA, 1999; The 606, Chicago, 2015); it has also been featured in exhibitions, such as the survey show 'Kay Rosen: Lifeli[k]e' (Geffen Contemporary at MOCA, Los Angeles, 1998–99) and at 'Girl Talk: Women and Text' (CAM Raleigh, 2012).

ORA PRO NOBIS · MATER SALVATORIS · ORA PRO NOBIS · SALUS INFIRMORUM · ORA PRO NOBIS · VAS HONORABILE · ORA PRO NOBIS

ORA PRO NOBIS · STELLA MATUTINA · ORA PRO NOBIS · MATER DIVINAE GRATIAE · ORA PRO NOBIS · REGINA SANCTORUM OMNIUM · ORA PRO NOBIS

ORA PRO NOBIS · CONSOLATRIX AFFLICTIONEM · ORA PRO NOBIS · REGINA CONFESSORUM · ORA PRO NOBIS · SEDES SAPIENTIAE · ORA PRO NOBIS

ODOTAN TULE

ABOVE · Jukka Korkeila
Mater et Magistra (Mother and Teacher),
2014 · Poster installation,
Helsinki Contemporary
337.5 × 934/886 × 97.3 cm
(132⅞ × 367¾/348⅞ × 38¼ in.)

Mater et Magistra (Mother and Teacher) was part of an exhibition in 2014 by the Finnish artist Jukka Korkeila that was dedicated to his partner, Mikko, who had recently taken his life. The installation considers the importance of the Virgin Mary in the Roman Catholic Church. Korkeila explains that the Catholic Church is almost non-existent in Finland, and that the Lutheran tradition (the largest church in the country) hardly mentions Mary. The work's title is a phrase used by Pope John XXIII in an encyclical of 1961. The Latin phrases on the work are titles given to the Virgin – for example, *Mater Salvatoris* – in the Litany of Loreto of 1587. The words are handwritten within black lozenges that recall both those found in Tuscan church architecture and cheap sales signs displayed in discount stores. The adjacent wall was painted blue, the colour associated with Mary, on which Korkeila added 'ODOTAN TULEVAN MAAILMAN ELÄMÄÄ' (I look for the life of the world to come).

TSANG Kin-Wah is a Chinese artist well known for his use of text in dizzying immersive video installations (see pp. 142–43) and in his 'wallpaper' works. From a distance, these works appear to be floral designs stencilled on to the wall, floor or ceiling, but on close inspection they reveal themselves to be words – mainly obscene ones. Many are in blue on white grounds, recalling traditional Chinese porcelain. Text pieces such as *Let Us Build and Launch a Blue Rocket to His Heaven* (right) could be described as concrete poems in three dimensions, as there is no correct way to 'read' them. The viewer is led on a textual journey through the swirling patterns.

For much of his career, the American artist Michael Petry has been interested in creation myths. Many of his works, including the 'Libation to Eros' series, reference Greek mythology (other works relate to Christian, Muslim, Jewish and Hindu mythologies). Petry stencils his texts in 24-carat gold leaf either directly on to a wall or on to large travertine marble tiles that can be installed in different locations. The lettering is deliberately rough to make the words appear as if they are graffiti (among the earliest known appearances of which is on Egyptian pyramids, scratched into their surface by ancient Greek travellers). For his show at the Mary Wilfred Moffett Gallery in Ruston, Louisiana, in 2014 (opposite), Petry also installed texts in the men's and women's restrooms as an offering to the gods for a successful academic year. The janitorial staff removed many of them before the opening, not having been informed of their status as artworks.

RIGHT · TSANG Kin-Wah
Let Us Build and Launch a Blue Rocket to His Heaven (detail at bottom), 2009
Silkscreen on lino paper and vinyl,
La Sucrière, 10th Biennale de Lyon
Dimensions variable

OPPOSITE · Michael Petry
Libation to Eros, 2014
24-ct gold leaf and Japan gold size on tile, Mary Wilfred Moffett Gallery, Louisiana Tech University, Ruston
Dimensions variable

The Polish artist Anka Dabrowska makes small sculptures, delicate drawings and stencilled installations. In 2013, as part of an exhibition at the headquarters of the law firm Clifford Chance to celebrate Pride in London, she placed throughout the executive floor (where the senior partners take lunch with their clients) a series of signs that were at odds with the genteel, business-like atmosphere. The works included *Don't Forget Me, You Will Never Sleep Again* and, between the men and the women's toilets, *TOSSER* (above), all spray paint on wood. Dabrowska explains: 'I love concrete and always make my work out of low-grade materials such as cardboard, wood, fabric, polystyrene, plaster – concrete things I find on the streets, materials that make our cities. I make work which finds beauty in what we overlook and throw away.'

In 2009 the British artist Nicky Hirst was commissioned to make an installation for Bracknell and Wokingham College in Berkshire. For *Wild Blue Yonder* (opposite), she started with a quote from the journalist Sydney J. Harris: 'The whole purpose of education is to turn mirrors into windows.' The work, comprising adhesive vinyl over glazed panels, covers the front of the building. Hirst used readymade systems to create the piece. The colours are from the RAL colour chart, typically used by architects; the names, however, are of Crayola crayons. Additionally, Hirst used Helvetica, a standard typeface for the college, thereby integrating her work into its existing visual language. Of mismatching the colours and names, she says: 'On the whole I chose the most poetic [names] that conjure up a picture.'

ABOVE · Anka Dabrowska
TOSSER (detail at left), 2013
Spray paint on wood, Clifford Chance headquarters, London
125 × 95 cm (49¼ × 37⅜ in.)

OPPOSITE · Nicky Hirst
Wild Blue Yonder, 2009
Printed adhesive vinyl and text, Bracknell and Wokingham College, Berkshire · 8 × 25 m
(26 ft 3 in. × 82 ft ¼ in.)

tumbleweed
purple heart
goldenrod
tropical rain forest
tickle me pink
dandelion
lavender
eggplant
cerulean
blue
grey
fern
gold
periwinkle
shadow
piggy pink
green
mango tango
laser lemon
manatee
salmon

The British artist Fiona Banner became widely known for her 1,000-page book work *The Nam* (1997), in which she describes in detail the plots of six Vietnam War films. She has continued to explore how books, words and punctuation can function as art. The sculptural performance *Buoys Boys* (above) featured black helium-filled inflatables in the shape of full stops in five typefaces. The works were sited on the south coast of England, facing France, and hinted at the unsaid in the relationship between the UK and mainland Europe. Banner comments: 'The black abstract forms are markers within language, but also markers within space and time; sometimes they seem absurd, comical or even surreal.'

In 2016 the Indian artist Vibha Galhotra was invited to make a site-specific work for the 4th Biennial of Land Art Mongolia 360°. In *Who Owns the Earth?* (opposite), the question was placed directly on the ground. The text was made of cow dung, a natural material in plentiful supply in the district of Dariganga. The work addresses the fragile ecosystem of Mongolia, the nomadic culture of its people and the threat that climate change poses to their way of life. Galhotra quotes Ban Ki-moon, the former Secretary-General of the United Nations: 'Already, hundreds of millions of people are facing increased hardships. Three-quarters of all disasters globally are now climate-related...'

ABOVE · Fiona Banner · *Buoys Boys*, 2016 Full-stop inflatables, from left to right: Courier, Didot, Capitalist, Bookman, Onyx; De La Warr Pavilion, Bexhill-on-Sea, East Sussex Courier: diameter 320 cm (126 in.), Didot: diameter 180 cm (70⅞ in.), Capitalist: 230 × 300 × 230 cm (90½ × 118⅛ × 90½ in.), Bookman: diameter 200 cm (78¾ in.), Onyx: 300 × 200 × 200 cm (118⅛ × 78¾ × 78¾ in.)

OPPOSITE · Vibha Galhotra *Who Owns the Earth?*, 2016 Mixed-media installation, 4th Biennial, Land Art Mongolia 360°, Dariganga Sum 3 × 30 m (9 ft 10⅛ in. × 98 ft 5⅛ in.)

Untitled (above), by the British artist Jack Cheetham, consisted of a white banner with red text installed across the façade of Charles Rennie Mackintosh's Glasgow School of Art. The work suggested that the school had been turned into a curry house, a reference to the fact that, across the UK, many older buildings, such as schools and churches, have been sold to developers for housing or indeed restaurants, while some supermarkets have become independent Christian churches or mosques. Cheetham explains that the banner 'invited the viewer to reflect on a range of issues, including multiculturalism, social class, architectural rhetoric, urban signage, and the effects of the recent economic downturn'. The building was badly damaged in 2014 when a fire began in the basement.

The Argentinian artist Enrique Ježik uses a variety of materials to create large sculptures that spell out phrases. *Déclaration formée par 49 sculptures* (Statement Formed by 49 Sculptures; opposite) was an installation of cardboard letters spelling out, in French, 'I cannot eat as much as I would like to puke.' This was the response of the German-Jewish artist Max Liebermann in 1933 to the rise to power of the Nazis. Ježik's work was installed in 2015 at Belfort Citadel in north-eastern France, where it was left outside during winter to be covered by snow. The individual letters seem to recall the suffering of victims of the Nazi regime, who were often worked to death in freezing conditions.

ABOVE · Jack Cheetham · *Untitled*, 2013 Printed vinyl banner, installed on the façade of the Mackintosh Building, Glasgow School of Art, for the Master of Fine Art interim show
1 × 11.1 m (39⅜ in. × 36 ft 7 in.)

OPPOSITE · Enrique Ježik
Déclaration formée par 49 sculptures (Statement Formed by 49 Sculptures), 2015 · Installation of 49 cardboard letters in steel frames, Belfort Citadel Approx. 0.7 × 12 × 45 m
(27½ in. × 39 ft 4½ in. × 147 ft 7⅝ in.)

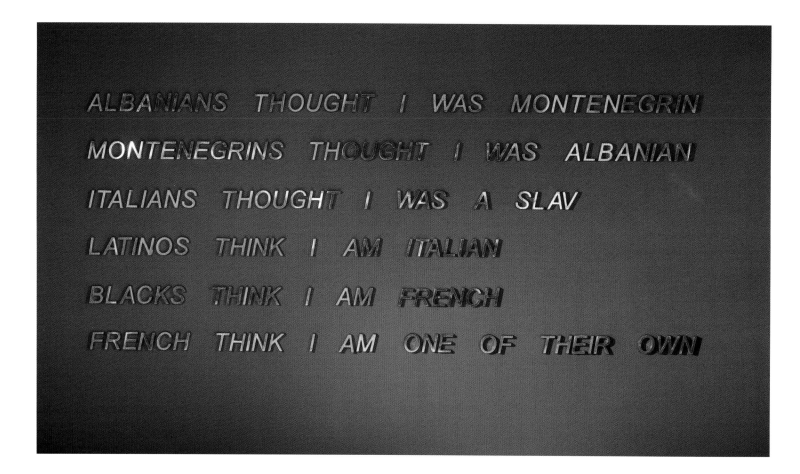

ALBANIANS THOUGHT I WAS MONTENEGRIN

MONTENEGRINS THOUGHT I WAS ALBANIAN

ITALIANS THOUGHT I WAS A SLAV

LATINOS THINK I AM ITALIAN

BLACKS THINK I AM FRENCH

FRENCH THINK I AM ONE OF THEIR OWN

Aleksandar Duravcevic was the official artist for the Pavilion of Montenegro at the 56th Venice Biennale in 2015. His exhibition, 'Ti ricordi, Sjećaš li se, You Remember', was based on cultural, personal, clan and religious memory, and consisted of objects, images and an installation. The exhibition title is in Italian, Montenegrin and English, and while the artist is part-Albanian, this particular mix of languages makes reference to the complexities of identity and memory associated with his place of birth. Duravcevic does not take a documentary approach to memory; instead, he aims to explore the possible ways in which it functions in a country that was at war in recent decades. *Identity* (above) is a visual and verbal joke made from bronze letters fixed on a blackened wall. The use of bronze hints at institutions and permanence, yet the work reminds the viewer of our continued insistence on difference.

The British artist Kate Murdoch may live in London, but she keeps her Celtic roots close to her heart. In 2009 the Scottish government initiated the 'Homecoming Scotland' project, a series of events encouraging those with Scottish ancestry to return there. Murdoch's series 'HAME' (Home; opposite) consists of four commercially made white wooden letters, which she placed in various locations throughout Scotland, from a farmyard in Muirkirk, where her father was born, to the wild, rocky hill of Arthur's Seat and the steps of the Scott Monument in Edinburgh, and alongside a huge stone marker delineating the England–Scotland border. Murdoch's work often considers the more permanent presence of physical objects in contrast to our brief, fragile lives. The artist resides in England and therefore did not have a vote in the independence referendum of 2014, which failed to make Scotland an independent country.

ABOVE · Aleksandar Duravcevic
Identity, 2015 · Bronze letters, Pavilion of Montenegro, 56th Venice Biennale
Dimensions variable

OPPOSITE · Kate Murdoch
HAME #3, 2015
Wooden letters, intervention in landscape · 20 × 85 cm (7⅞ × 33½ in.)

The French artist Annette Messager is interested in simple materials, including yarn, fabric and synthetic hair, which are often considered the domain of women. Numerous works feature dismembered children's toys, in reference to the fragility of life. The 'Chance' works – drawings as well as installations – remind the viewer that their life is subject to outside elements, over most of which they have no control. In the large wall work shown above, the word appears to have been washed ashore after some disaster. The colour black suggests tragedy, and the fronds of mesh that hang from the letters add a gothic touch, often seen in Messager's art. She says: 'For me, the fantastic is in daily life; real life is more extraordinary than all of the imagination.'

The work of the Austrian artist Anatol Knotek melds poetry and art. His word pieces may seem simple, but they are full of depth and meaning. In *Nothing Lasts Forever* (opposite), letters spelling out the word 'FOREVER' are mounted on a gallery wall; several letters, however, are arranged on the floor, as if they have become unstuck. 'FOREVER' turns to 'OVER', and the viewer is asked to reflect on their own mortality. Knotek succinctly demonstrates that time is fleeting. What could be a joke becomes an arresting moment of contemplation. The work was installed at the City Gallery, Melbourne Town Hall in 2014 and at xpon-art, Hamburg, in 2016, and also in 2016 was presented in Lego at the Jósa András Múzeum, Nyíregyháza, Hungary.

ABOVE · Annette Messager
Chance, 2011–12
Mesh and fabric
140 × 200 cm (55⅛ × 78¾ in.)

OPPOSITE · Anatol Knotek
Nothing Lasts Forever, 2009
Cardboard letters, installed here
at xpon-art, Hamburg, 2016
180 × 140 cm (70⅞ × 55⅛ in.)

The Israeli artist Miri Segal investigates the way in which consumers interact with the internet. *Don't be evil* (2011) was originally conceived as part of a larger body of work, *Future Perfect*, co-created with Or Even Tov. Large, brightly coloured aluminium letters recall the graphics of the search engine Google. The phrase was previously the motto of the company's code of conduct. Google has been accused of not living up to that ambition in its dealings with smaller online companies and in working with the Communist Party of China, which prevents online searches for the Tiananmen Square Massacre of 1989. In 2004 the firm's founders, Larry Page and Sergey Brin, sent a letter to potential shareholders stating that Google was 'a company that does good things for the world even if we forgo some short-term gains'. Google's new holding company, Alphabet, assumed overall control in 2015 and dropped the motto.

LEFT · Miri Segal
Don't be evil, 2011
Aluminium letters
100.1 × 730.5 cm (39⅜ × 287⅝ in.)
Edition of 3

Since the late 1970s the American Barbara Kruger has been one of the most influential artists working with text. Her well-known photomontages, such as *Untitled (I Shop Therefore I Am)* (1987), pair pre-existing black-and-white photographs with captions in bold type, and have become part of the greater cultural language. Kruger's works have appeared on posters, in magazines and also as large-scale installations. The *Belief+Doubt* installation (left) at the Hirshhorn Museum and Sculpture Garden in Washington, DC, completely covers the downstairs lobby, including the sides of the escalators. Among the phrases printed on the vinyl covering are 'PLENTY SHOULD BE ENOUGH' and 'YOU WANT IT. YOU BUY IT. YOU FORGET IT.' The immersive work questions both public and private spheres of behaviour.

LEFT · Barbara Kruger
Belief+Doubt, 2012
Installation, Hirshhorn Museum
and Sculpture Garden, Washington, DC
Dimensions variable

THREE DIMENSIONAL WORDS

One of the most diverse areas of text in the visual arts is that where words, letters and characters jump off the page, canvas, wall or screen and become objects in their own right. The fact that the words are composed of a variety of materials, such as wood, metal and stone, places the text in a direct bodily relationship with the viewer. When we read a text and it goes straight into our consciousness, we understand it on an intellectual level; but when words adopt a three-dimensional form, we may have a visceral reaction to them.

Ildikó Buckley and Jane Palmer have brought the word 'YES', in oversized form, into the lives of many viewers who have made use of the sculpture in non-artistic ways (for example, to ask for someone's hand in marriage). Monica Bonvicini's huge letters forming the word 'RUN', commissioned for the 2012 London Olympic Games, seem as much a command as a comment, and the viewer feels their towering presence in a way he or she would not were they painted on to the side of a building. Words may seem to be only abstract notions in our world, but billboards and electronic signage remind us that they have a different power the physically larger they become. Deborah Kass plays with the legibility of text as a sculptural object in a piece that reads as one word in one direction and another in reverse. All of these works are large, if not monumental, in size.

This chapter also features three-dimensional works that are much smaller in scale, such as Jake and Dinos Chapman's etched cigarette lighter and Rosana Ricalde's bracelet of silver and gold. A diverse range of materials is also in evidence, from marble (George Henry Longly; Colin Booth), wood (Fiona Shaw) and glass (Shan Shan Sheng) to brick clay (Rirkrit Tiravanija). Artists may choose to employ different media as a means of commenting on those materials or as a way in which to utilize their unique sculptural qualities, or to confound expectations about what sculpture and text might be.

Antonio Riello takes existing objects, such as bicycles and cars, and reworks them into new text works, whereas Darryl Lauster has white marble carved to look as if it were a fragment of an ancient text – a faux 'readymade', to borrow Duchamp's term. Once the texts have moved into the three-dimensional world of sculpture, many take on aspects of Dadaist humour, as the viewer is not always sure how to read such objects. Are they merely large texts, or does their autonomy turn them into a different kind of written object?

'Gapfill', an exhibition by the Irish artist Alan Magee in 2013, featured the large sculpture *SORRY*, made from MDF and wood, with each letter standing 240 cm (94½ in.) tall. The work formed a barrier in the pop-up exhibition space at the Highlanes Gallery, Drogheda, acting as an obstacle to viewing smaller works in a room behind the sculpture. The former Francisan church was a natural backdrop for Magee, whose work often focuses on power, politics and the mechanisms of control. *SORRY* controlled the visitors' access to the other works and functioned as much as a guard as an object worth guarding. Much of Magee's art has a relationship to his own body, and here the letters stand in for the (rather tall) artist, who is interested in continually questioning what it is we are looking at, how it comes to be displayed, and who has the power to speak or prevent speech. In 2014 the work was shown in an empty office block in London (left) as part of the 'Interchange Junctions' exhibition curated by HS Projects.

LEFT · Alan Magee
SORRY, 2013
MDF and wood
Each letter 240 × 120 cm
(94½ × 47¼ in.)

ABOVE · Santiago Sierra
NO, 2009 · Painted wood
264 × 470 × 225 cm (104 × 185 × 88⅝ in.),
installed on support frame

The Spanish artist Santiago Sierra is known for his activism, which often considers the pressures on, and the conditions of, workers and the unemployed. The 'NO, Global Tour' featured *NO*, a sculpture of large wooden letters in the Arial typeface, weighing half a ton. The work was first shown in 2009 in Lucca, Italy, then in Germany, Canada, the United States, Japan and numerous other locations. In 2011 Sierra made a film about the work's transportation around the world, which he refers to as a 'road movie'. The word 'no' was chosen because it can be understood in many different languages and contexts. Sierra's aim was that viewers would respond by shouting 'no' at those who maintain the current global power imbalance.

ABOVE · Ildikó Buckley and Jane Palmer
YES, ongoing since 2011
Paint, shimmer discs and fixings
on wood · 240 × 640 × 50 cm
(94½ × 272 × 19¾ in.)

In 2011 the British artist Ildikó Buckley and the designer Jane Palmer collaborated on the large mirrored sculpture *YES*. In 2013, as a highlight of the Thames Festival, it toured ten riverside locations, including Battersea Power Station and the Old Royal Naval College in Greenwich (above), and it is still exhibited extensively. The sculpture has inspired a large community, and, as Buckley explains, it seems to radiate optimism: 'It makes people shout out "YES" with joy, and has a powerful ability to instil in viewers an expanded understanding of art as energizing and accessible. Even in the present political and economic climate, the work continues to serve as a triumphant and invigorating tonic of positivity.'

The American artists Ryan Everson and Jason Garcia channel the extreme anxiety found in contemporary culture. The artists usually work solo, but collaborated to create *Fear Expanded* (above). The sculpture is made from mirror on wooden supports, and is set in a field in Last Chance, Colorado. Its location – seemingly in the middle of nowhere, or the middle of middle America – heightens the tension inherent in the work. Out in the open, what is there to fear? It could be argued that, since the 9/11 terrorist attacks, the US news media has cultivated a fear of others, a fear of nature (along with a denial of climate change) and, under the administration of President Trump, a heightened fear of Muslims. The work reflects its surroundings as well as any viewer bold enough to approach it.

In 2000, the Italian-born, Berlin-based artist Monica Bonvicini created the work *RUN*, comprising twenty-four sheets, each displaying the title of a song from the 1960s and '70s that features the word 'run'. On the occasion of the London Olympic Games in 2012, she developed this idea in order to make a permanent work for the Queen Elizabeth Olympic Park in Stratford. *RUN* (opposite) is a large, free-standing piece that glows at night by means of high-performance LED lights. The lights are sequenced as if they are disappearing into the centre of each letter, increasing the sense of movement implicit in the word itself. As in the case of the earlier work of the same name, Bonvicini's intention is to bring to mind such songs as 'Run Run Run' by the Velvet Underground and 'Running Dry' by Neil Young.

ABOVE · Ryan Everson and Jason Garcia
Fear Expanded, 2013
Mirror on wooden supports
127 × 279.4 × 25.4 cm (50 × 110 × 10 in.)

OPPOSITE · Monica Bonvicini
RUN, 2012 · Glass panels, Dibond mirror, stainless steel and high-performance LEDs
Each letter 900 × 500 × 120 cm (354⅜ × 196⅞ × 47¼ in.),
9 × 21.5 × 18.6 m (29 ft 6⅜ in. × 70 ft 6½ in. × 61 ft ¼ in.) overall

A very public sculpture by the American artist Deborah Kass, *OY/YO* (above) is bright canary yellow and large enough to command its site in Brooklyn, between the Manhattan and Brooklyn bridges. Seen from Brooklyn, the Yiddish word 'OY' shouts out a salute to the bustling crowds of Manhattan, where many wealthy Jewish people live and work. Viewed from Manhattan, the work reads 'YO', as if the cool hipsters who live in Brooklyn have communally bellowed a greeting (perhaps to the chagrin of the borough's former, overwhelmingly working-class residents). Kass's sculpture echoes Robert Indiana's *LOVE* (1965) in its graphic quality and its accessibility, and it has been similarly well received.

The Lebanese artist Zena el Khalil's *A'Salam Aleykum: Peace Be upon You* (opposite) features the word 'Allah' (god) in Arabic script. The sculpture is covered in mirror tiles fixed on to a Styrofoam structure that the artist had carved by a family of traditional furniture-makers. 'Allah' gently rotates as if it were a huge disco ball in a nightclub. The work is always accompanied by live music or a DJ, to encourage viewers to dance. El Khalil's piece references the ongoing conflict in the Middle East, and she asks viewers to dance 'to remember the bonds between them'. The sculpture was originally commissioned for the 'Meteorite in Giardino' exhibition at the Fondazione Merz in Turin, Italy, and has since been exhibited in Germany, Belgium and England.

ABOVE · Deborah Kass · *OY/YO*, 2015
Fabricated 3-mm (⅛-in.) aluminium
with aluminium interior framework
painted Kass-Yellow with Matthews
Acrylic Polymer exterior paint
243.8 × 495.3 × 138.4 cm
(96 × 195 × 54½ in.)

OPPOSITE · Zena el Khalil
A'Salam Aleykum: Peace Be upon You, 2009
Mirror tiles on carved Styrofoam,
metal and engine
400 × 400 cm
(157½ × 157½ in.)

The Egyptian artist Ghada Amer has earned a reputation for her embroidered canvases (see pp. 232–33), but she has also created a series of outdoor gardens that feature text. *HAPPILY EVER AFTER* (right) at the Queens Museum of Art, New York, takes the form of the closing words from many fairy tales, planted in a protective circle of greenery (climbing roses and jasmine inside metal structures) around a circular bench. For *S'IL PLEUVAIT DES LARMES* (If It Rained Tears; below), Amer frescoed the words of a poem by the French writer Boris Vian around the edges of an abandoned garden in a monastery in Padula, Italy. The poem laments that 'If it rained tears when a love dies', and on the occasion of other sad events, 'on the whole earth there would be nothing left'.

While the American artist Jack Pierson may be best known for his photographs documenting masculinity, his word-based sculptures, which he has been making since the early 1990s, have been equally influential. *Desire, Despair* (1996), *In Sunshine or in Shadow* (2003), *Pornography* (2004), *Listen, Darling* (2007) and *You Don't Own Me* (opposite) all allude to different stories. In the same way as his photographs, they depict another side, a queer side, to the American dream. The pieces are made from found advertising signage, hence the different sizes, typefaces and colours of the letters. It is Pierson's skill and his merging of the disparate elements into a whole that make them art, offering multiple readings.

RIGHT, ABOVE · Ghada Amer
HAPPILY EVER AFTER, 2005
Wood, metal and foliage
Dimensions variable

RIGHT · Ghada Amer
S'IL PLEUVAIT DES LARMES
(If It Rained Tears), 2003
Frescoed installation
Dimensions variable

OPPOSITE · Jack Pierson
You Don't Own Me, 2014
Acrylic, steel, enamel, metal
and aluminium
368.3 × 297.2 × 30.5 cm
(145 × 117 × 12 in.)

YOU DON'T OWN ME

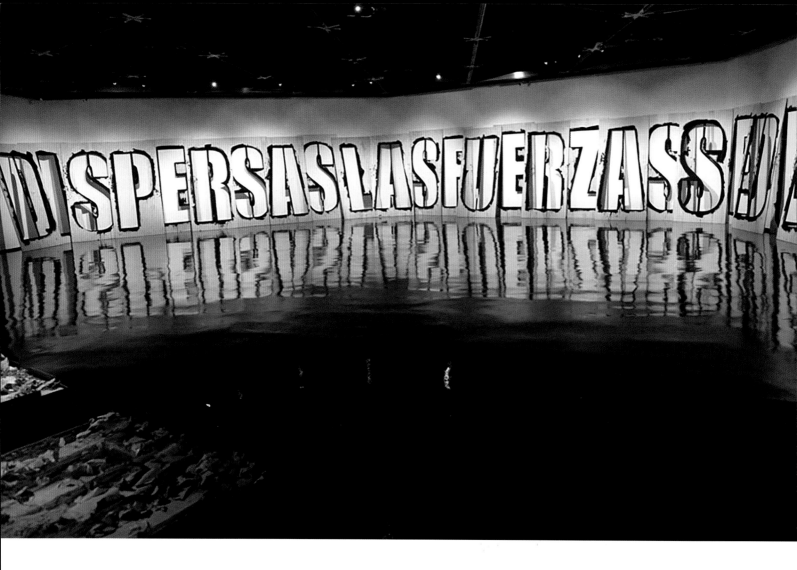

For his work *Dispersas las fuerzas se debilitan* (Scattered, the Forces Weaken, 2016), Enrique Ježik placed in a gallery space large letters that look like individual stencils, complete with black paint around the outline of each letter – as if the stencil had just been used. The text is from a speech made in the 1920s by the Argentinian political activist Alicia Moreau de Justo, who called for equal rights for women. The words are doubled-up, clearly reflected in the dark, polished floor, yet – perhaps like the alternative world into which Alice steps in *Through the Looking-Glass* – equal rights are often only a chimera shimmering in the distance.

ABOVE · Vibha Galhotra
Asuvidha ke liye khed hai (Sorry
for the Inconvenience), 2008
Automotive paint on mild steel
33 × 221 × 15.2 cm
(13 × 87 × 6 in.)

Asuvidha ke liye khed hai (2008) is Vibha
Galhotra's satirical response to the
ubiquitous presence in public settings
of this Hindi phrase, which translates
as 'Sorry for the inconvenience'. As
viewers or inhabitants of these settings,
we frequently encounter this phrase
in the form of impersonal printed
notices or recorded phone messages.
The words offer a constant reminder of
our helplessness and alienation from
the utopian city structure. In many
cases, we are the cause of much of the
inconvenience we face each day, and
we may therefore find ourselves making
continual apologies.

In 2012 the Chinese-American artist Shan Shan Sheng was commissioned by the San Francisco Arts Commission to make the cascade-suspension sculpture *Active Memory*, which explores the Chinese-American experience through calligraphy. The work comprises eight strands of Chinese characters made from red Venetian glass at the Berengo Studio on Murano. The characters include fragments of ancient verse by famous poets dating from the Tang (618–907 CE) and Song (960–1279) dynasties. Strand 3 quotes Li Bai (701–762 CE): 'Under the blue sky, your lonely sail turns into a silhouette, only the long river rolls on its way to heaven.' Strand 4

quotes Su Shi (1036–1101): 'With a cup of wine in hand, I look at the sky and wonder when the moon first appeared.' Strand 6 is inspired by the historical experiences of immigrants and by the California landscape; it incorporates fragments of poetry written by Chinese immigrants in the early 20th century and discovered on Angel Island in the San Francisco Bay. Strand 8 displays key words and phrases – such as 'gold rush', 'railroad track' and 'computer' – used in online searches concerning the history of the Chinese immigrant community in the United States. Together, the glass characters relate to more than 2,500 years of Chinese history.

ABOVE · Shan Shan Sheng
Active Memory (detail), 2012
Handmade red Venetian glass and stainless steel, installed at the Betty Ann Ong Chinese Recreation Center, San Francisco · 487.7 × 243.8 × 121.9 cm (192 × 96 × 48 in.)

ABOVE · Doug Aitken
EXIT (LARGE), 2014
Red glass, mirror and
powder-coated steel
172.7 × 236.2 × 40.6 cm
(68 × 93 × 16 in.)
Edition of 4

The American artist Doug Aitken has made 'text sculptures' in a variety of media. The sculpted words often seem at odds with the material from which they are made, as in the case of *SEX* (2010), where each of the large plastic letters that spell out the word is filled with moss and other living plants. Aitken comments: 'One of the things I believe in is friction, and how to generate friction within an artwork.' Several of his text sculptures utilize mirror, as in *EXIT (LARGE)* (above). The work has been shown at several art fairs and is the subject of a painting of the same year by Eric Fischl, who depicts several bored fair-goers standing with their backs to it, thereby creating a type of metafiction. Aitken explains his love of text: 'My mother was a writer and my parents really valued long-form language. Maybe a word, or a letter, or a number, speaks to who I am...'

The collective FORT was founded in Berlin in 2008 by Anna Jandt, Jenny Kropp and Alberta Niemann; Jandt left the group in 2014. FORT works in the liminal space between art and architecture, often re-creating found structures or making works that appear to be real objects. For example, *Center* (left) seems at first to be the entrance sign to the gallery as the viewer looks down the stairs. On closer inspection, the viewer sees that the letter C at the start of the word has been snapped off, turning a sculptural work into what appears to be functional signage. *One in a Million* (below), from a series of found and imagined windows, is a replica of an empty shopfront. The letters 'DIES' can be seen alongside closed blinds, discarded plastic cups and a 'For Sale' notice. The window is abject in itself, but is made even more so when one realizes, from the gaps left by the missing letters, that the shop was called 'PARADIES', the German for 'paradise'.

LEFT, ABOVE AND CENTRE · FORT
Center, 2015 · Mixed media
48 × 230 × 51.5 cm
(18⅞ × 90½ × 20¼ in.)

LEFT, BELOW · FORT
One in a Million, 2015
Mixed media
220 × 240 × 30 cm
(86⅝ × 94½ × 11¾ in.)

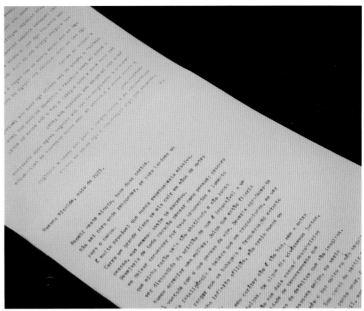

ABOVE · Rosana Ricalde
Cartas sobre o amor (Letters about Love),
2013 · Roll of paper and 2 typewriters
Dimensions variable

ABOVE, RIGHT · Rosana Ricalde
A palavra é prata, o silêncio é ouro (The
Word is Silver, Silence is Golden), 2012
Bracelet in silver and gold, produced by
Atelier Schiper · Diameter 9 cm (3½ in.)

A palavra é prata, o silêncio é ouro (The Word is Silver, Silence is Golden; above, right), by the Brazilian artist Rosana Ricalde, takes the form of a bracelet made of gold and silver with the words 'PALAVRA' and 'SILÊNCIO' embossed on the circumference. The work can be worn or displayed as a discrete object. The title refers to a traditional proverb that teaches that speaking up, especially in times of difficulty or oppression, is admirable, but that sometimes it is better to wait, listen and above all retain self-control. Ricalde's work addresses issues of power, and her bracelet highlights the fact that many of those whom she seeks to engage would never be able to afford such metals, much less artworks. *Cartas sobre o amor* (Letters about Love; above, left) takes the form of one long piece of text produced between two typewriters. The words are taken from a series of poems in Ovid's *Letters of Heroines*, in which he writes as if he were women from Greek or Roman myth whose lovers have neglected or abandoned them.

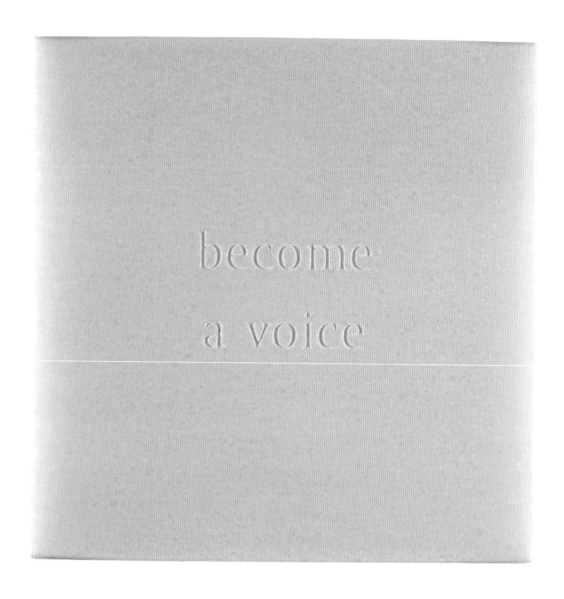

The 2016 exhibition 'If Not Winter' by the British artist Colin Booth featured wall-mounted marble squares etched with fragments of verse by the ancient Greek poet Sappho (*c.* 610–*c.* 570 BCE). Much of her lyrical poetry has been lost, yet she is considered an equal of Homer. She lived on the island of Lesbos, from which the word 'lesbian' derives, and was herself a same-sex lover. Booth, who is not homosexual, emphasizes that he does not aim to appropriate Sappho's voice, but rather to highlight the universality of poetry. The marble works included *If not winter*, *Everywhere glory* and *Become a voice* (above). Etching Sappho's words into marble might seem to fix what is fluid, but Booth does as in classical times, securing great words for future readers.

The American artist Darryl Lauster has created a series of works called 'Trace', each carved into white marble. Every piece looks as if it might be a broken fragment of a historic or ancient monument. The wording on the marble combines short phrases from the Old Testament, the Founding documents of the United States and manifestos of right-wing militias, scrambled and taken out of context. The words appear to be part of a greater whole yet cannot be made to make sense. The viewer can make out such phrases as 'DECREES IT', 'FROM THE BEGINNING...DAYS WE HAVE STRUGGLED...WE ARE CHOSEN...BLESSED' and 'KINGDOMS OF...MIGHT...TYRANNY'; they hint at Lauster's opinion of the direction that his nation is taking.

ABOVE · Colin Booth
Become a voice, 2016
Marble · 30 × 30 cm (11¾ × 11¾ in.)

OPPOSITE · Darryl J. Lauster
Fragment #6, from the series 'Trace', 2016
Carrara Bianca marble
33 × 17.8 × 16.5 cm (13 × 7 × 6½ in.)

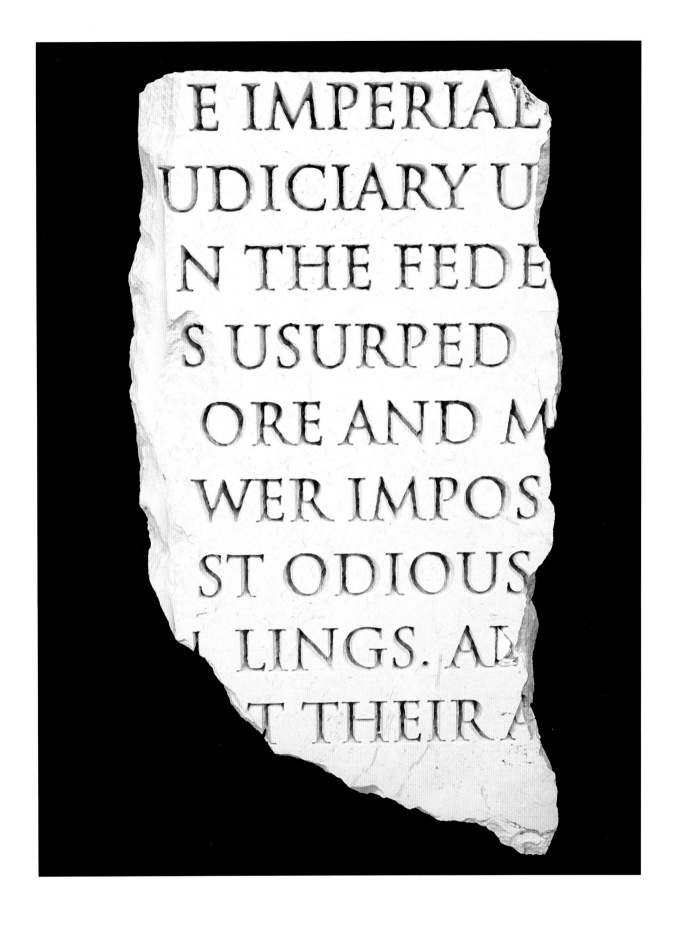

During the 56th Venice Biennale of 2015, Rirkrit Tiravanija – an Argentinian artist of Thai parentage who is known for his socially engaged performance works – had several Chinese makers hand-producing bricks, which were allowed to dry naturally (left). Each brick was then imprinted with a serial number (from 1 to 14,086) and the characters 別干了 ('Never work'). First used by Guy Debord in 1953, this was the slogan of the Situationists, who argued that all labour should be equal. The work had originally been presented in Beijing in 2010, and for that version the bricks had been fired. The number of bricks refers to the average number used in building a modest family home in China. Viewers could make a donation in return for a brick, and thus the work was dispersed among a larger community. The money raised was given to ISCOS, a non-profit organization that promotes Chinese workers' rights.

The Korean artist Chun Kwang Young has made 'Aggregation' works (opposite) since 1995. Each work is composed of thousands of pieces of Styrofoam individually wrapped in printed mulberry paper known as *hanji*. The small pieces are tied with string before being assembled into the whole. Mulberry paper is made from the bark of the *dak* tree and has a special place in Korean culture. The paper is printed with Korean and Chinese characters that often express wishes for good health and fortune, and thus Chun merges the man-made with the natural. Many of the works look like crystalline structures, and their colours amplify this effect. Chun was inspired by parcels of medicinal herbs, which are traditionally wrapped in paper, and describes the individual pieces as 'the minimal unit of information'.

LEFT · Rirkrit Tiravanija
untitled 2015 (14,086 unfired)
(detail at bottom), 2015
Brick workshop, bricks, wooden
stamps, tools and people
Dimensions variable

OPPOSITE · Chun Kwang Young
Aggregation 16-SE080, 2016
Mixed media with Korean
mulberry paper
195 × 132 cm (76¾ × 52 in.)

The British brothers Jake and Dinos Chapman are well known for making sculptures that have outraged conservative viewers, from multi-bodied children (*Zygotic Acceleration, Biogenetic, De-sublimated Libidinal Model (Enlarged × 1000)*, 1995) to a representation of the slaughter of Nazis, arranged in the shape of a swastika (*Hell*, 1999–2000). On a much lighter note, their *Skull Etched Zippo Lighter* (above) is inscribed with the words 'fucking hell'. The work was a proposed Christmas edition for the company Momart, which provides an art storage, transport and handling service. The idea was rejected, and the brothers produced the lighter as a limited edition themselves.

Ghiora Aharoni, a New York artist, has presented a continuing series of work on the possibility of coexistence between Jews and Muslims. *GER/ The Stranger* (opposite) was made for the 'Divided Waters' exhibition in Venice in 2016. It features two glass spheres engraved with texts in Hebrabic/Arabrew©, a combination of Hebrew and Arabic created by the artist. Aharoni says that while the people these languages represent have grown apart over the millennia, 'their two languages have a common origin', and that the sculpture examines the perception of otherness, advocating compassion and humility as the reconciler of coexistence. The work was inspired by the founding of the Jewish Ghetto in Venice in 1516, and the spheres – representing the segregation of the Jews – are connected by antique Torah finials. The placement of the work in a historic building, the Palazzo Fontana, echoed the otherness that Shakespeare sought to impose in *The Merchant of Venice*.

ABOVE · Jake and Dinos Chapman
Skull Etched Zippo Lighter, 2015
Etched Zippo lighter
5.5 × 3.5 × 1.2 cm (2⅛ × 1⅜ × ½ in.)

OPPOSITE · Ghiora Aharoni
GER/ The Stranger, 2016
Assemblage sculpture with antique Yemeni Torah finials and Torah crown; antique silver processional angel with bells; antique silver collar clasp; metal clamps and base; tubular light filaments; glass beakers engraved with two phrases in Hebrabic/Arabrew© (a combination of Hebrew and Arabic created by the artist): 'The stranger shall not lodge in the street: I will open my doors to the traveller'; 'Love the stranger, for you were strangers in the land of Egypt' · 117 × 60 × 70 cm (46 × 23⅝ × 27½ in.)

The Berlin-based Catalan artist Josep Maynou has collaborated with women rug-weavers in Tazroute, Morocco, to produce works that reflect his love of storytelling, as 'carpets traditionally pass from generation to generation, so it is a way to keep the stories alive, flowing and changing'. He has lived in the village and says of the women: 'We spend so much time together because there is a communication/language divide, and it can be challenging, but... there is something beautiful about what misunderstandings and mistranslations can create.' For *True Girl* (above), shown at the exhibition 'A Lover's Discord', curated by Alana Lake at the Museum of Contemporary Art (MOCA), London, Maynou was inspired by a story in which someone continually bets on a horse called True Girl; it never wins, but the devotion proves that love might be just around the corner.

Antonio Riello is fascinated by the politics of his homeland, Italy, where the phrase *né capo né coda* (neither heads nor tails) can be used in various contexts. He has made a series of sculptures in which he has bifurcated then recomposed modes of transport. A Ferrari-red bicycle (opposite, top), shown in 2016 at the 'Creativity and Vehicles' exhibition at the Museo dell'Automobile Bonfanti-Vimar, looks as if it could go very fast, but is stilled. Riello also remade two Autobianchi A112 cars into two fronts and two rears, and has done the same with scooters and domestic objects. For *Not Made in Italy* (opposite, bottom), he had a Vicenza weaver make a roll of deluxe fabric in grey and black wool that, up close, reads 'NOT MADE IN ITALY', but from afar 'MADE IN ITALY'; it highlights the fact that much clothing labelled 'Made in Italy' is designed there but fabricated in China or Bangladesh.

ABOVE · Josep Maynou
True Girl, 2016 · Wool and cotton
200 × 190 cm (78¾ × 74¾ in.)

OPPOSITE, TOP · Antonio Riello
Né Capo Né Coda (Bicycle) (Neither Heads Nor Tails [Bicycle]), 2016
2 modified bicycles
Each approx. 180 × 40 × 60 cm
(70⅞ × 15¾ × 23⅝ in.)

OPPOSITE, BOTTOM · Antonio Riello
Not Made in Italy (detail), 2011
Woven wool · 200 × 100 cm
(78¾ × 39⅜ in.)

OPPOSITE · Roni Horn · *White Dickinson*
I GIVE YOU A PEAR THAT WAS GIVEN ME – WOULD THAT IT WERE A PAIR, BUT NATURE IS PENURIOUS, 2006–7
Aluminium and solid cast white plastic
428.3 × 5.1 × 5.1 cm (168⅝ × 2 × 2 in.)

ABOVE · Fiona Shaw · *Collide*, 2014
Timber, OSB, enamel and steel
215 × 130 × 80 cm (84⅝ × 51⅛ × 31½ in.)

The American artist Roni Horn has been using words in her sculptures since the 1980s. She has taken lines from the poems and – in the case of the 'White Dickinson' series (opposite) – the published letters and diaries of Emily Dickinson, cast them in plastic and embedded them in aluminium bars. Each bar is propped against the wall so that the letters are visible from the front and back, but from the sides appear as white or black lines. In *Thicket No. 1* (1989–90), text is embedded around the edges of an aluminium slab that rests on the floor. The viewer is encouraged to see the work in the round, to read the text and to view the piece as an object. Seeing text in three-dimensional form changes the way viewers experience and comprehend it.

A series of wooden sign sculptures by the British artist Fiona Shaw look as if they have been hastily made by an angry lover. In *This* (2011), black letters hang on a frame, spelling out 'I KNOW YOU CARE BUT IT DOESN'T BREAK MY HEART'. Shaw's works interact with the surrounding architecture and the site; *Collide* (above) is perhaps the most symbiotic with its installation. Sited in the offices of Clifford Chance at Canary Wharf in London, as part of the law firm's annual Pride exhibition, it overlooked the River Thames. The rickety-looking structure proclaimed 'BUT I SAW THE TWO COLLIDE'. A crushed piece of steel at its base made viewers imagine boats or planes crashing into the building or one another.

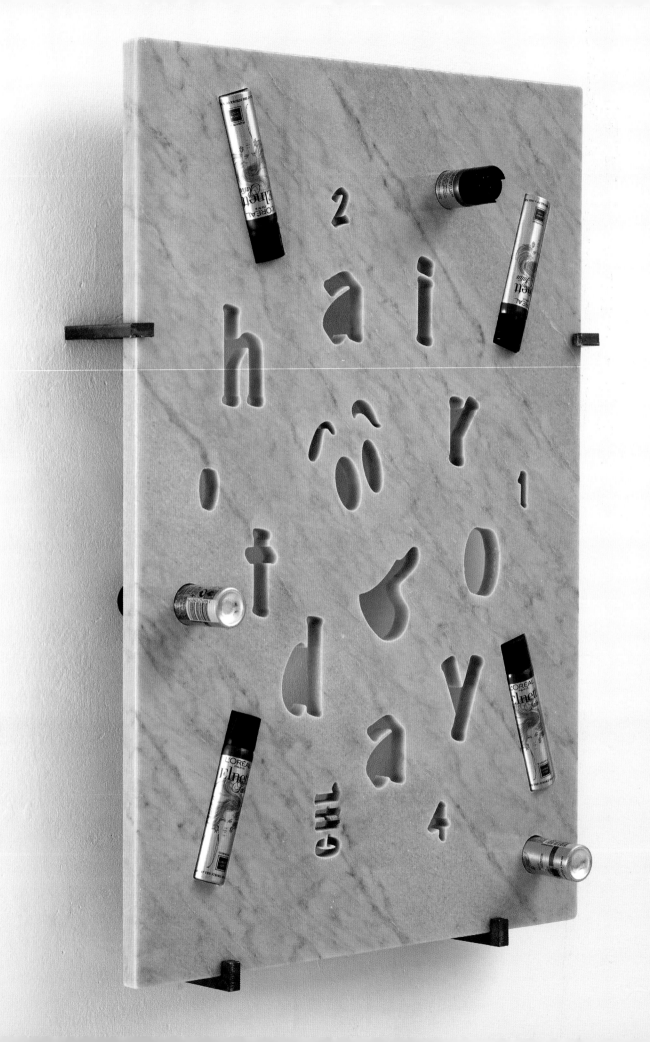

OPPOSITE · George Henry Longly
Hair Today (Supreme Hold), 2014
Waterjet-cut marble, Elnett
Supreme Hold hairspray and
laser-cut steel brackets
81 × 57 × 12 cm (31⅞ × 22½ × 4¾ in.)

ABOVE · James Balmforth
*THE_____DOES NOT GO
UNNOTICED*, 2016
Stamped lettering on
anodized aluminium
18 × 25 cm (7⅛ × 9⅞ in.)

Among the luxe materials employed by the British artist George Henry Longly are marble, polished and powder-coated metals, gold and even live snakes (in the trailer for a performance at the Serpentine Gallery, London, in 2013). There is a sensuous if not erotic pull to many of his pieces – such as *Lady Death Strike* and *Projecteur* (both 2016) – that makes the viewer want to touch them. A series of wall-mounted marble sculptures, known as 'posters', feature hair and beauty products. The cans of hairspray in *Hair Today (Supreme Hold)* (opposite) are set into the surface of the slab. Longly explains that the work 'is a nod to the notion of a timeline of histories (art, sociopolitical, geopolitical, design, fashion, etc.) and how things come in and out of relevance', and attempts to flatten hierarchies. Longly is also a DJ and, with Eddie Peake and Prem Sahib, runs the Anal House Meltdown club night.

The British artist James Balmforth works with words in a variety of media, including metal and in digital form. *THE_____DOES NOT GO UNNOTICED* (above) consists of an anodized aluminium plate stamped with the title. Balmforth then used an electronic grinder to violently erase what could be the most important word in the sentence. The viewer can conceptually insert any word they like into the blank space. The roughness of the word's removal implies censorship and the use of power to prevent knowledge or information being passed on.

The British artist Nicole Polonsky co-opts found signage to make comic, surrealistic and confounding works. Each box set of different coloured laminate plaques re-presents original texts that in their intended environments make sense, but, freed from their context, become works of art (left). Polonsky's minimal interventions speak of loss, allusion and public concerns. While some are tragicomic, the artist does not make fun of these concerns; rather, she highlights the ambiguity between words and meaning.

The ceramic books made by the British artist William Cobbing are only cover-deep. Each cover is unique in terms of glaze colouration, and the series includes a wide variety of titles, among them Hans Ulrich Obrist's *Gilbert & George* (published in 2007), Lucy R. Lippard's *Undermining* (2014), Kenneth Goldsmith's *Wasting Time on the Internet* (2016) and Chris Kraus's cult novel of 1997, *I Love Dick* (opposite). Cobbing explains that his works consider the book as a fetish object, getting only 'skin deep, as if the contents have become petrified'. His books, he says, echo tablet computers and 'Bronze Age clay tablets imprinted with Cuneiform characters, exploring the tactile interplay between image and text'.

LEFT, ABOVE · Nicole Polonsky
Untitled (Zoo), 1999
3 limited-edition engraved laminate panels (verso: initialled and numbered in pencil on vinyl stickers; printed vinyl stickers bearing artist's name); cardboard box with debossed lid (verso: printed type; initialled and numbered in pencil on vinyl sticker; printed vinyl sticker bearing artist's name); stainless steel screws and resealable bag
Each panel 10.7 × 15.7 × 0.3 cm
(4¼ × 6⅛ × ⅛ in.),
box 12 × 18 × 3 cm (4¾ × 7⅛ × 1⅛ in.)

LEFT · Nicole Polonsky
Engraved laminate panel
from *Untitled (Abbey)*, 1999
10.7 × 15.7 × 0.3 cm
(4¼ × 6⅛ × ⅛ in.)

OPPOSITE · William Cobbing
Cover Version 2, 2017
Glazed ceramic
20 × 13.5 × 1 cm
(7⅞ × 5¼ × ⅜ in.)

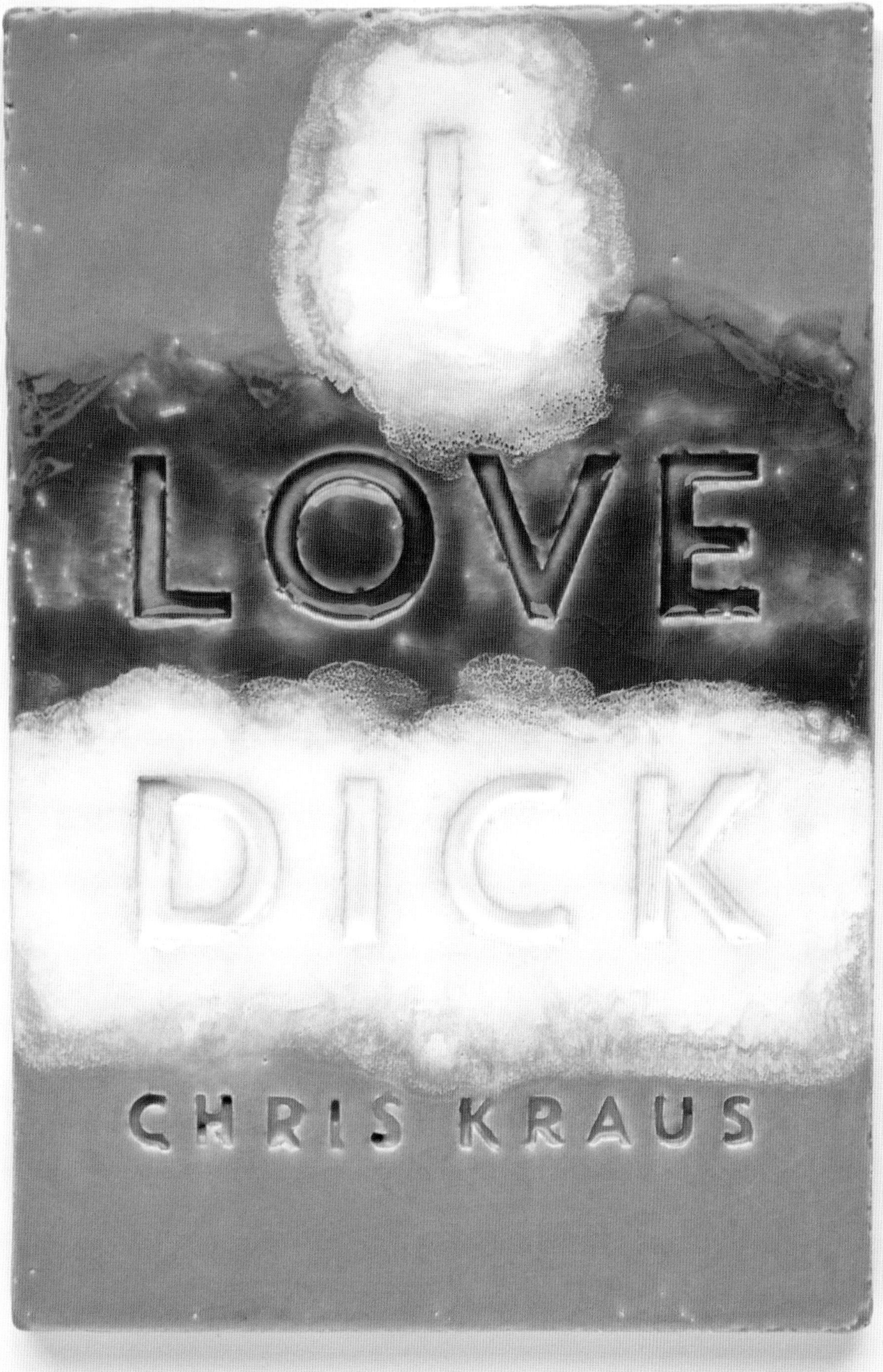
I
LOVE
DICK
CHRIS KRAUS

The Belgian artist Fred Eerdekens works with light as much as he does with text, for without the correct directional illumination his interventions cease to fully exist. He is best known for his hand-manipulated pieces of thin copper, which to the viewer's eye, without the proper light, would appear as abstract sculpture. Yet with lighting, the sentence 'Could suggest something vague and unclear or say something that is not true' comes into focus. Eerdekens grabs the viewer's attention with the physical artistry of the works and through the poetry of his texts. The shadow is a thing itself and yet is also nothing; it is both there and not there, and – like most art – is illusive and nearly impossible to hold completely in the mind.

ABOVE · Fred Eerdekens
Could suggest something vague and unclear,
1999 · Copper and light source
14 × 220 × 18 cm (5½ × 86⅝ × 7⅛ in.)

ABOVE · Mark Dutcher
IWantYourFistInsideMe, 2007
Oil, wax, cardboard and string
17.8 × 304.8 cm (7 × 120 in.)

The American artist Mark Dutcher is best known as a painter (see pp. 236–37), but he also makes sculptural objects and installations. At first glance, *IWantYour FistInsideMe* (2007) appears to be a banner for a child's birthday party. It is painted in bright colours, and the letters are a bit wonky, as if they have been made by a child, but the content is decidedly adult. The banner hangs oddly, even queerly, in a brightly lit space that seems at odds with sexual intimacy. All of this adds to the tension for the visitor viewing and reading it.

Light is a bearer of information; it carries that knowledge from its source to our eyes as it reflects off the object we are looking at. In the pitch dark, we may be looking at the same object, but without a light source the object will be unknown to us. We might reach out and feel it and have some notion of its shape and texture, but other information about it, such as its colour, will be lacking. That information is carried in the light, so it is no surprise that many visual artists use light sources to create their works. This type of work has a distinguished, decades-long history (for example, pieces by Jenny Holzer, Bruce Nauman and Joseph Kosuth), and many of its pioneering practitioners are still making challenging and exciting art.

Neon signs have been used for advertising since the early 20th century, and over the years neon has been adopted as an artistic medium (with many artists freely acknowledging commercial signage as their source material). The urban environment is full of neon signage, and when artists mimic or evoke these signs, they likewise enfold the notion of the commercial world into their art practice. Such works may also have a look of reproducibility or multiplicity, and again many artists play with this quality, as in Michael Shaowanasai's humorous large neon pink signage. Other works deliver a sharp political message: for example, Hubert Czerepok's neon that alludes to racism in Polish society. Darryl Lauster uses neon in his work to hint at the past – a past that, in the glow of nostalgia, may seem easier than it was in reality for the American population, and one that Sheldon Scott tackles directly in his red, white and blue neon works.

Light bulbs, which are also often found in commercial signage, may be employed for the presentation of bright, almost overly optimistic text, as in the work of Tim Noble and Sue Webster. Monica Bonvicini uses bulbs that evoke the glamour of 1940s Hollywood to introduce very stark, dark messages. By way of contrast, Robert Montgomery and Nathan Coley place light texts in the environment (both urban and natural) to create poetic disruptions to the viewer's normal daily encounters.

Julien Breton takes the creation of work with light to its logical end, as he writes text directly in the air using a variety of small hand-held light sources. His Arabic calligraphy shines out in long-exposure photographs, which meld his text with their distinctive backgrounds, including sand dunes and Islamic courtyards.

Light as a medium is likely to be used by a financially better-off minority of artists (as are such expensive materials as bronze and marble). Benjamin Carrick reflects on the way in which light has become almost a cliché in contemporary art-making simply by referencing its lack.

ECHOES OF VOICES IN THE HIGH
TOWERS ALL WOUNDS EXPLAINED
HERE ALL KNIVES BANDAGED
ALL EMPIRES ARRESTED ALL CASTLES
UNBUILT ALL HEARTS UNBROKEN

Robert Montgomery, from Scotland, employs a variety of light sources for his poetic text sculptures. *Whenever You See the Sun* (2010) is made of LEDs and white letters on a wooden structure, spelling out 'WHENEVER YOU SEE THE SUN REFLECTED IN THE WINDOW OF A BUILDING IT IS AN ANGEL'. The work was installed on a cliff edge, with only the sea behind it, so there were no buildings in sight. Another 'light poem', *All Palaces* (2012), was positioned at the bottom of an empty swimming pool in Berlin, stating 'ALL PALACES ARE TEMPORARY PALACES'. In the same year, Montgomery installed two further illuminated poems in the German capital, at the disused Tempelhof Airport. Both parts of *Tempelhof Poem* (one is above) allude to the temporary nature of our lives and the built environment. One line read 'FOREST HERE ONCE FOREST HERE AGAIN'.

The American artist Jenny Holzer started using words in her work in the late 1970s, when she produced her 'Truism' series of black texts on white paper, which she fly-posted across New York. She has reproduced these aphorisms and slogans and other texts in a wide variety of media, including carved into stone benches, etched on to glass, cast in bronze and printed on T-shirts. Perhaps best known, however, and most in tune with the public imagination, are her works using LEDs and other light sources. Holzer is interested in reaching the widest audience, and public art is one of her major preoccupations. In addition to being displayed in museums and galleries, her art has been projected on to buildings across the world. Holzer's phrases 'Protect Me from What I Want' and 'Abuse of Power Comes as No Surprise' have entered the public consciousness to an extent that is unrivalled by the work of few other artists.

ABOVE · Robert Montgomery
Tempelhof Poem (North Side), 2012
Recycled PVC letters, wood, LED lights and solar panels attached to existing structure of US Army softball field at the old Tempelhof Airport, Berlin
480 × 750 cm (189 × 295¼ in.)

OPPOSITE · Jenny Holzer
New Corner (detail), 2011
7 LED signs with amber, blue, green and red diodes, installed at the Kukje Gallery, Seoul; text: *Survival*, 1983–85
Each 15.2 × 244.2 × 9.2 cm
(6 × 96⅛ × 3⅝ in.)

The work of the Scottish artist Nathan Coley investigates how notions of public and private space collide. He works in a variety of media, but is best known for his illuminated signs that display a variety of phrases. While the signs are installed in an art-world context, the viewer could almost mistake them for advertising billboards. *There Will Be No Miracles Here* (above; shown at Mount Stuart on the Isle of Bute and in galleries) and *Heaven is a Place Where Nothing Ever Happens* (opposite; commissioned by the Folkestone Triennial) comment on the way in which religion is both a private and a public function that occupies building space (churches) and the space inside the viewer or believer. *You Imagine What You Desire* was an installation at the St Nicholas of Myra Church in Brighton, East Sussex, in 2015. In such a religious environment, Coley asks the viewer to consider their belief systems, including art as a construct.

ABOVE · Nathan Coley
There Will Be No Miracles Here, 2006
Illuminated text on scaffolding
500 × 500 × 250 cm
(196⅞ × 196⅞ × 98⅜ in.)

OPPOSITE · Nathan Coley
Heaven is a Place Where Nothing Ever Happens, 2008
Illuminated text on scaffolding
600 × 600 × 400 cm
(236¼ × 236¼ × 157½ in.)

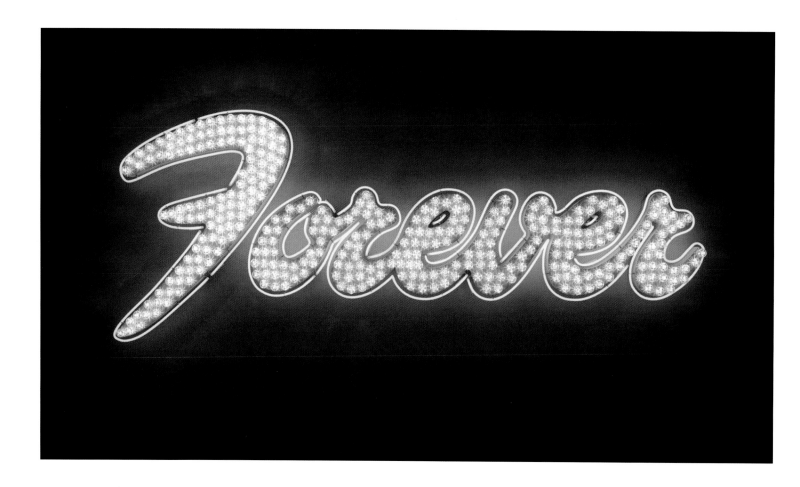

The British duo Tim Noble and Sue Webster have a large body of work that uses light to cast intricate shadows on a wall once a beam is directed at what first appears to be a pile of rubbish (*Real Life is Rubbish*, 2002; *HE/SHE*, 2004; *Metal Fucking Rats*, 2006). They have also made a series of Las Vegas-style illuminated signs called *Forever*. The first, made in 1996 with a shimmer effect, led to such word pieces as *YE$* (2001), *Forever* (2001), with added neon, and *Bloody Forever* (2011), with dangling red lights that look like drips of blood. In the most recent version, *Forever (yellow)* (above), the word is rimmed by yellow neon; there is also a pink version. It was shown at the Summer Exhibition of the Royal Academy of Arts, London, in 2016. Noble and Webster's work with shadows and light plays against notions of Britishness, punk and the divide between high and low culture. The contrast between the Hollywood-style works and the shadow pieces challenges the viewer to decide what is good taste.

Monica Bonvicini is interested in the way in which art, architecture and power come together to inform social, economic and gender relations. Light has always been an important material in her videos and installations. Works such as *NOT FOR YOU* (opposite), *Built for Crime* (2006) and *Light Me Black* (2009) comprise primarily fluorescent lights or light bulbs. Bonvicini often composes the rhythm with which the lights turn off and on as if it were a piece of music. She is sensitive to the use of architecture as a medium to 'connect politics with culture…in order to build history', and her engagement with light, whether used as signs and billboards or in outside installations, continually questions both the awareness of the institutions in which these works are exhibited and that of the viewers.

ABOVE · Tim Noble and Sue Webster
Forever (yellow), 2015
Matte white stoved enamelled aluminium shaped boxes, 13-mm (½-in.) diameter yellow neon around the outside of the piece, 7 off 3025 neotran transformers for the neon, 330 off white lens, 330 off EIO LED lamps, warm white, 24v, 4 off 3-channel DMX decoders, 3 off 100W 24V PSU, 1 off DMX blue box and power supply
124.6 × 325.5 cm (49 × 128⅛ in.)

OPPOSITE · Monica Bonvicini
NOT FOR YOU, 2006
Alucore Dibond, aluminium frame, bulbs, dimmer packs, LanBox and cables
2.3 × 14 m (7 ft 6½ in. × 45 ft 11⅛ in.)

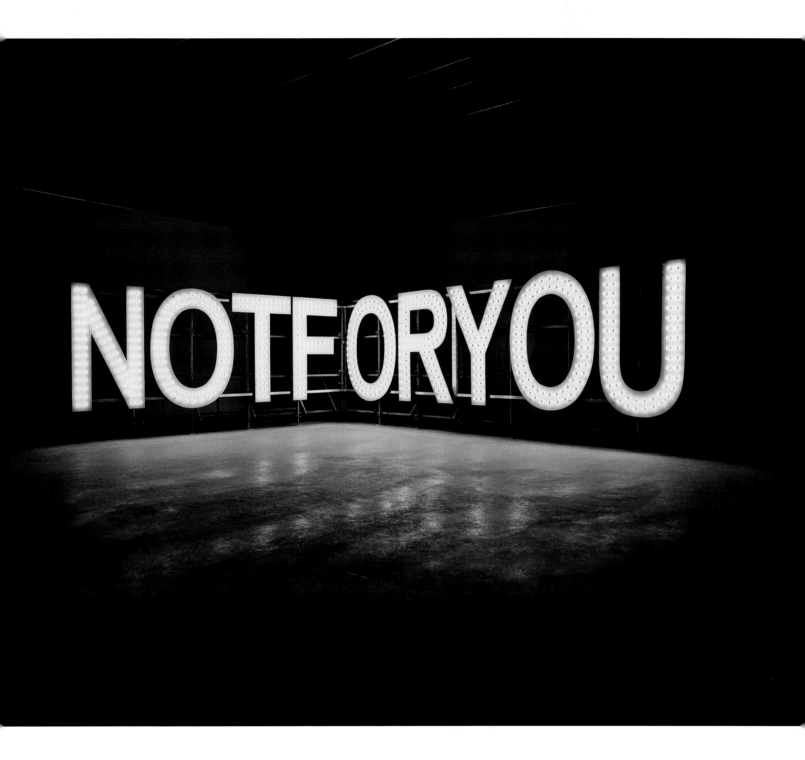

Also known as Kaalam, the French artist Julien Breton is a calligrapher of light, employing a fusion of performance art (often accompanied by music and dance) and the camera lens. Working with the photographers David Gallard and Cisco, he uses long exposures – and no digital manipulation – to record his mark-making. Breton writes in the air with hand-held illumination, frequently using more than one colour. The camera captures only the strongest light sources, so the artist's body disappears from the final composition. Breton is thus a ghost in his own art. The texts are always significant to the locations he chooses. *La beauté* (Beauty, 2015) was created in a traditional Islamic tiled courtyard in Morocco. Breton works with both Arabic calligraphy and a Latin-based alphabet, aiming to find a universal language of, and in, light.

LEFT · Julien Breton, aka Kaalam
La beauté (Beauty), 2015
Long-exposure photography by Cisco,
no digital manipulation, Arabic calligraphy
by Julien Breton, Tétouan, Morocco

Commissioned for the exhibition 'Tate Triennial 2006: New British Art', the neon sculpture *In Girum Imus Nocte et Consumimur Igni* (above), by the Welsh artist Cerith Wyn Evans, is based on a Latin palindrome, meaning that the words read the same backwards as forwards. The phrase, which is sometimes referred to as 'the devil's verse', may be translated as 'We go round and round in the night and are consumed by fire'. This particular translation works well with the shape of Wyn Evans's work – the viewer must walk around the sculpture in order to read the text in full – but it also refers to his 'Firework' series, in which texts composed of firecrackers mounted on wooden supports are set alight: for example, *Firework Text (Pasolini)*, 1998.

The American artist Glenn Ligon has long sought to investigate American history, literature and society. His paintings feature stencilled black text that repeats over and over, often until the image is totally blacked out. Ligon has used texts by Gertrude Stein, James Baldwin and the comedian Richard Pryor. The works ask how race, sexuality and social status function in the modern world, and why people of colour suffer inordinate discrimination. Ligon's *Double America* (opposite) features partially blacked-out neon that emits white light only from behind the letters, suggesting that, for some Americans, the promise of liberty and justice for all is harder to achieve than it is for others.

ABOVE · Cerith Wyn Evans
In Girum Imus Nocte et Consumimur Igni,
2006 · Neon
Height 20.3 × diameter 175 cm
(8 × 68⅞ in.)

OPPOSITE · Glenn Ligon
Double America, 2012
Neon and paint
91.4 × 304.8 cm (36 × 120 in.)
Edition of 3 and 2 artist's proofs

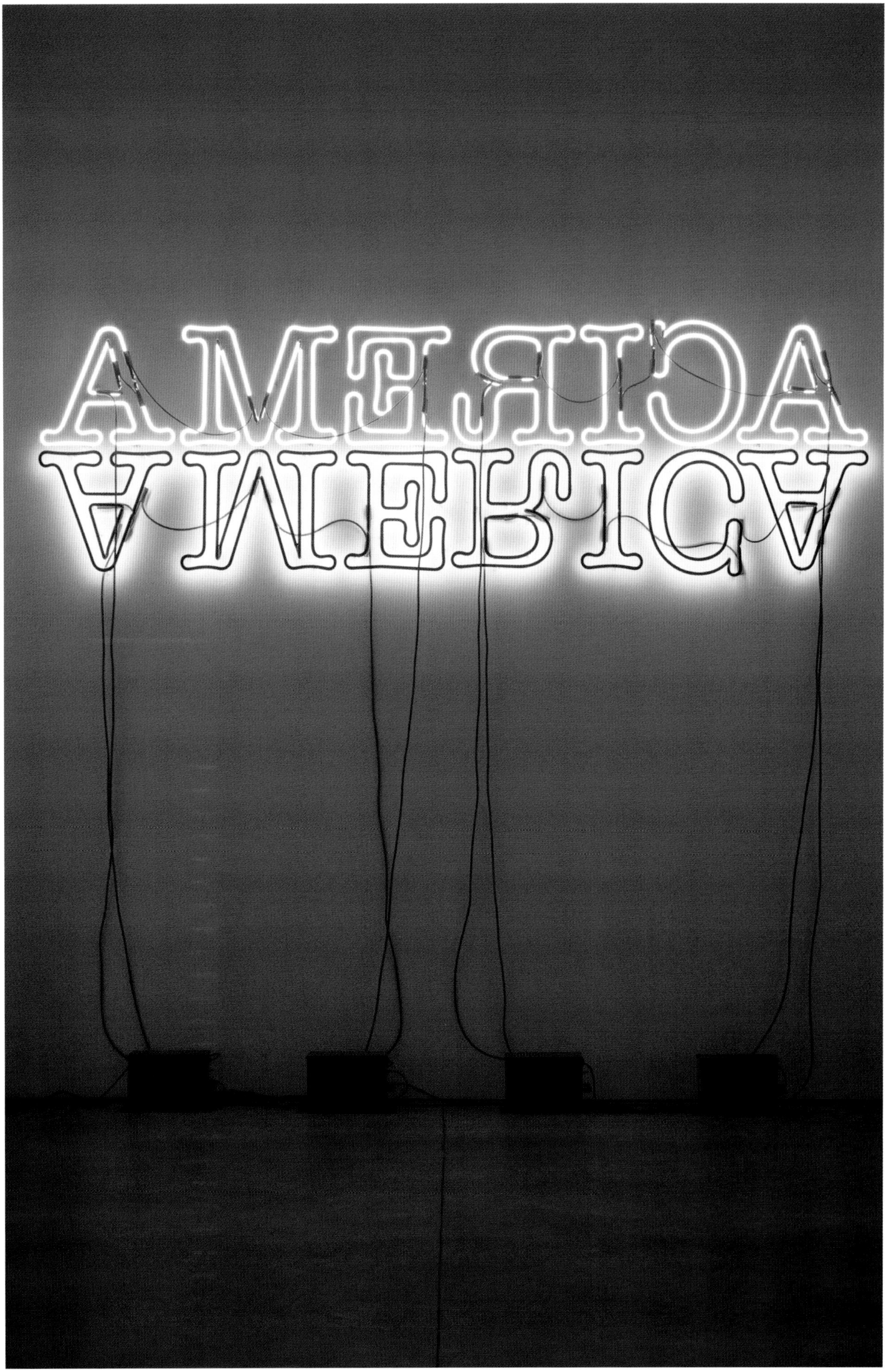
AMERICA

The German artist Nasan Tur explores different economic and political systems in many of his works. For *Variationen von Kapital* (Variations of Capital, 2013), he painted, in Indian ink on handmade Tibetan paper, 800 variant spellings of the word *Kapital*, randomly generated by computer from more than 40,000 possible spellings. It was almost as if human and machine were having a dialogue about mass production. In *Komunismus Soziallismus Kapietalismus* (2008), Tur presented misspellings of the three major economic systems in advertising-type illuminated letters. For an English-language version, shown

at the Museum of Art, Architecture and Technology in Lisbon (above), he used neon as a means to highlight the way in which human mistakes so often undermine utopian ideals.

ABOVE · Nasan Tur · *Comunism Capihtalism Sociallism*, 2016 · Neon 'Comunism': length 236 cm (92⅞ in.), 'Capihtalism': length 300 cm (118⅛ in.), 'Sociallism': length 236 cm (92⅞ in.)

ABOVE · Tao Hongjing 陶弘景
(Alexandre Ouairy)
To Get Rich is Glorious (先富起来), 2006
Neon light mounted on enamel-painted
aluminium board
150 × 250 cm (59 × 98⅜ in.)
Unique edition, collection of Brian
Wallace, Red Gate Gallery, Beijing

In 2005 Alexandre Ouairy, a French artist, was living in China and, frustrated at the lack of opportunity to exhibit his work, decided to adopt a Chinese alter ego; thus Tao Hongjing began making art. The neon work *To Get Rich is Glorious* (2006) was shown in 2008 at the 1918 ArtSpace in Shanghai alongside a series of prints entitled 'Places I Have Never Been To', featuring famous views of China. The exhibition received acclaim, and Tao's work became widely sought after. In 2015 Ouairy revealed his identity, and said that the ruse had been a 'conceptual art project'. The title of the neon piece is an adaptation of a quote by Deng Xiaoping, a former leader of China, and reflects the great increase in the number of Chinese collectors of contemporary art since the turn of the 21st century, many of whom were initially interested in supporting only native-born artists.

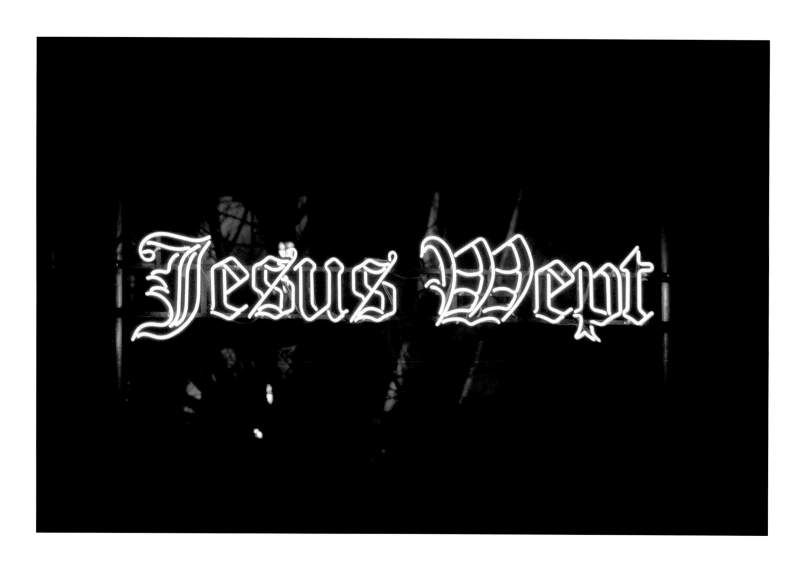

Colin Booth's neon work *Jesus Wept* (above) was commissioned for a derelict space next to Warrior Square railway station in St Leonards-on-Sea, East Sussex, where it was installed on scaffolding. The phrase is the shortest verse in the King James Version of the Bible (John 11:35), to describe Jesus' emotions at the death of Lazarus, and can be interpreted as signifying the compassion that Jesus felt for humankind. It is also commonly used as a mild expletive to express indifference to a predicament or to convey incredulity. The work was exhibited in All Saints Church in Folkestone, Kent, in 2014, and at the Observer Building, Hastings, in 2016.

The British artist Alexander Hidalgo's white neon work *Who's Hot Now?* (opposite) refers to Marcel Duchamp's iconic 'rectified readymade' of 1919 (see p. 11). Duchamp took a commercial print of the *Mona Lisa*, drew a moustache and goatee on to her face and added the letters 'L.H.O.O.Q.' beneath as a caption. Duchamp loved word games, and when the letters are spoken aloud in French, they sound like *Elle a chaud au cul* (She has a hot arse). Hidalgo's work removes the image of the *Mona Lisa*, but it stays in the mind's eye for those familiar with the original. The neon letters become hot as the work glows, yet its whiteness seems glacially cold. Hidalgo brings a new paradox to Leonardo's masterpiece.

ABOVE · Colin Booth
Jesus Wept, 2012
Neon and stainless steel
40 × 186 × 15 cm (15¾ × 73¼ × 5⅞ in.)

OPPOSITE · Alexander Hidalgo
Who's Hot Now?, 2004
Neon and mirror
Dimensions variable

The American artist Joseph Kosuth is one of the founders of the conceptual art movement, making such text-based works as the 'First Investigations' series of dictionary definitions: *'Titled (Art as Idea as Idea)' [Water]* (1966) is a photostat of the definition of water mounted on board. Kosuth has also made neon works installed in galleries and museums. *'The Wake (An arrangement of references with all the appearance of autonomy)'* (above) features white neon on grey walls. The work references James Joyce's *Finnegans Wake* (1939), a modern classic renowned for its experimental style. Kosuth selected phrases from the book based on their location on the printed page. The novel has not been translated into Turkish, but he used both English and Turkish translations for the installation at the KUAD Gallery, Istanbul.

The British artist Tim Etchells – who is artistic director of the influential performance-art group Forced Entertainment – has worked across many media. The neon work *Conscientious Objectors* (opposite) displays the words of Alfred Evans, a First World War 'conchy' who, after being imprisoned in 1916 and sent against his will to France with fifty other men, refused to participate in military drills. The piece was exhibited during the 'After a War' programme at the Battersea Arts Centre, London, as part of the city's biennial LIFT festival. Etchells explains that he is attracted to 'the speed, clarity and vividness with which [language] communicates narrative, image and ideas', yet simultaneously creates 'uncertainty and ambiguity'.

ABOVE · Joseph Kosuth
'The Wake (An arrangement of references with all the appearance of autonomy)', 2012
Warm white neon mounted directly on wall · Dimensions variable

OPPOSITE · Tim Etchells
Conscientious Objectors, 2014
Neon · Approx. 246 × 100 cm
(96⅞ × 39⅜ in.)

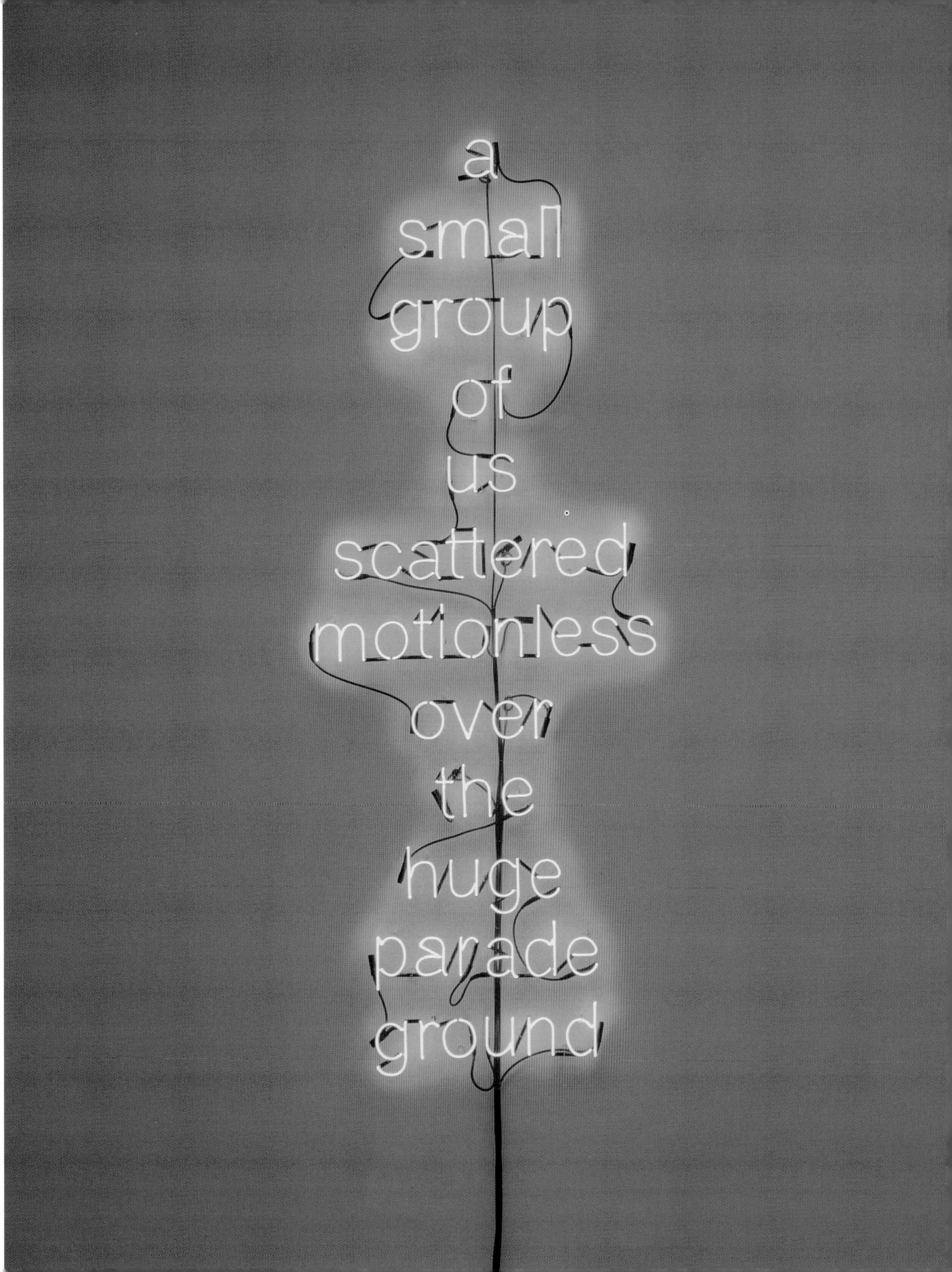

a
small
group
of
us
scattered
motionless
over
the
huge
parade
ground

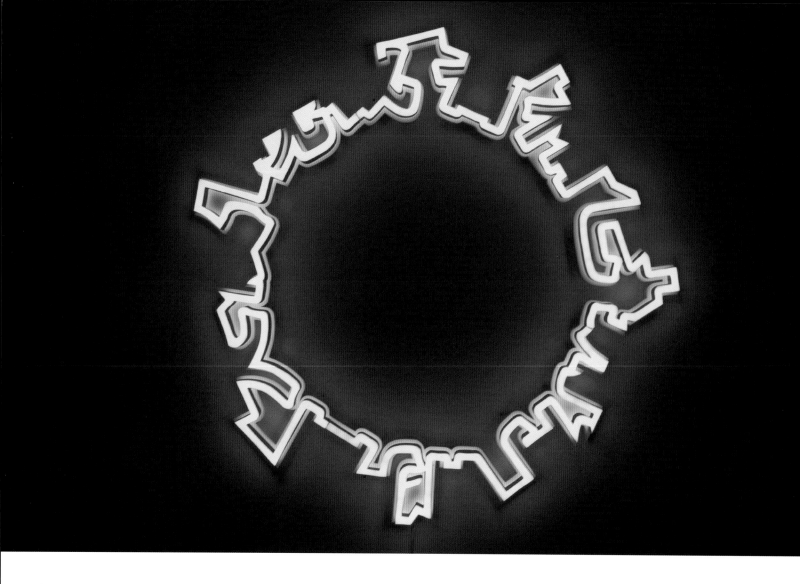

To create *Night or With Its Daytime* (2015),
the Chinese artist He An used acrylic
and LED lights on a metal base. The nine
different Chinese characters that make
up the sentence merge into a never-
ending circle of text, as night always
follows day. The blue light recalls both
twilight and dawn, as if the intensity of
the sky has been captured in the text.
The artist explains: 'It all began in 2000,
when I went out drinking one night in
Shenzhen. That's when I first noticed
the neon lights; the quality of the light
was full of the emotions of the city...I
feel that the lights from various cities are
actually different. The neon lights I saw
in Shenzhen were clearly not the kind of
lights used by domestic families.' He An
aims to capture the poetry of light and
text, as they blend into a whole.

ABOVE · He An
Night or With Its Daytime, 2015
Acrylic and LED lights and metal
Diameter 150 × depth 13 cm
(59 × 5⅛ in.)

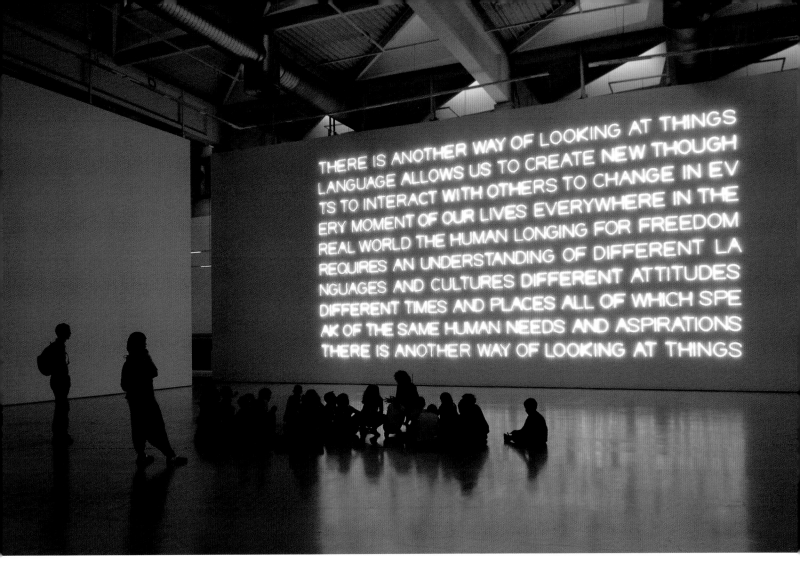

THERE IS ANOTHER WAY OF LOOKING AT THINGS
LANGUAGE ALLOWS US TO CREATE NEW THOUGH
TS TO INTERACT WITH OTHERS TO CHANGE IN EV
ERY MOMENT OF OUR LIVES EVERYWHERE IN THE
REAL WORLD THE HUMAN LONGING FOR FREEDOM
REQUIRES AN UNDERSTANDING OF DIFFERENT LA
NGUAGES AND CULTURES DIFFERENT ATTITUDES
DIFFERENT TIMES AND PLACES ALL OF WHICH SPE
AK OF THE SAME HUMAN NEEDS AND ASPIRATIONS
THERE IS ANOTHER WAY OF LOOKING AT THINGS

ABOVE · Maurizio Nannucci
There is another way of looking at things,
2012 · Neon · 12 × 6 × 0.05 m
(39 ft 4½ in. × 19 ft 8¼ in. × 2 in.)

OVERLEAF · Fiona Banner
Every Word Unmade, 2007
26 neon parts bent by the artist,
paper templates, clamps, wire
and transformers
Each 70 × 100 cm
(27½ × 39⅜ in.)

The Italian artist Maurizio Nannucci is one of the pioneers who introduced the medium of neon into a fine-art context. Since the 1960s he has been making striking works that have been exhibited in museums and also installed in outdoor settings, as in the case of *Von so weit her bis hier hin/Von hier aus noch viel weiter* (2008) in Magdeburg, Germany. The words 'From afar to here' appear in blue neon on one side of an old railway bridge and 'From here to much further away' in red on the other, reflecting and blurring together on the surface of the River Elbe below. *There is another way of looking at things* (above), at the Musée d'Art Moderne, Saint-Etienne, France, features a text in white neon that reflects on the gallery floor, where visitors may interact with it in addition to reading the contemplative words.

Fiona Banner's *Every Word Unmade* (overleaf) is a neon work comprising the twenty-six letters that make up the Latin alphabet, installed in the corner of the Power Plant gallery in Toronto. Banner formed the white neon herself, which is highly unusual for artists working with the material. The technically demanding (and usually highly skilled) manipulation of the glass tubes over a hot flame was itself part of the work. She had to blow continuously into the tubes to keep them round and, thus, in a way, spoke each letter into being. She has said that the 'Z' was hardly any better made than the 'A', and that the wonkiness of the letters was almost a 'stutter'. All the letters can conceptually combine into all possible words in the English language. Banner refers to the work as the 'ultimate piece of concrete poetry', with 'all of the potential, but none of the content'.

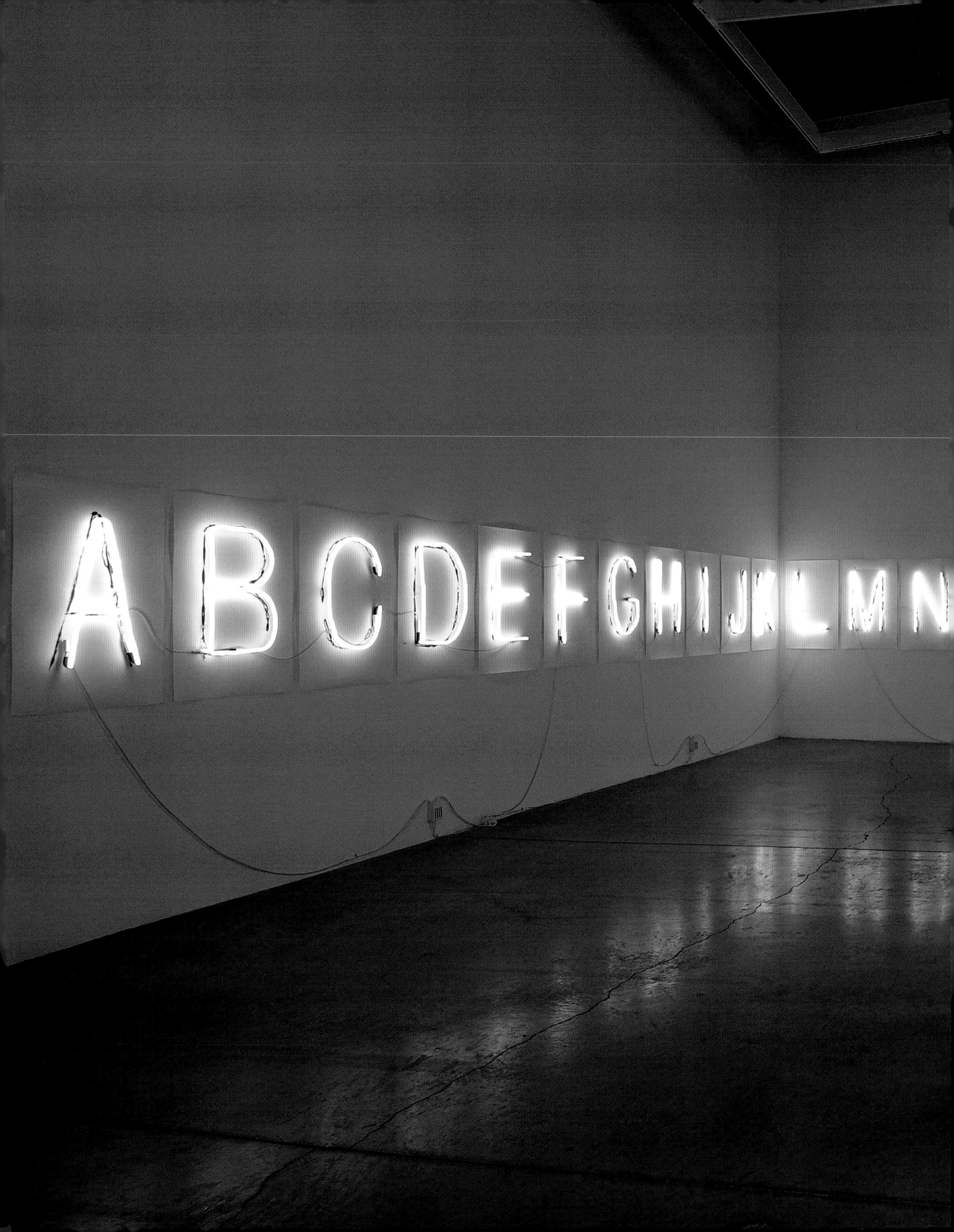
ABCDEFGHIJKLMN

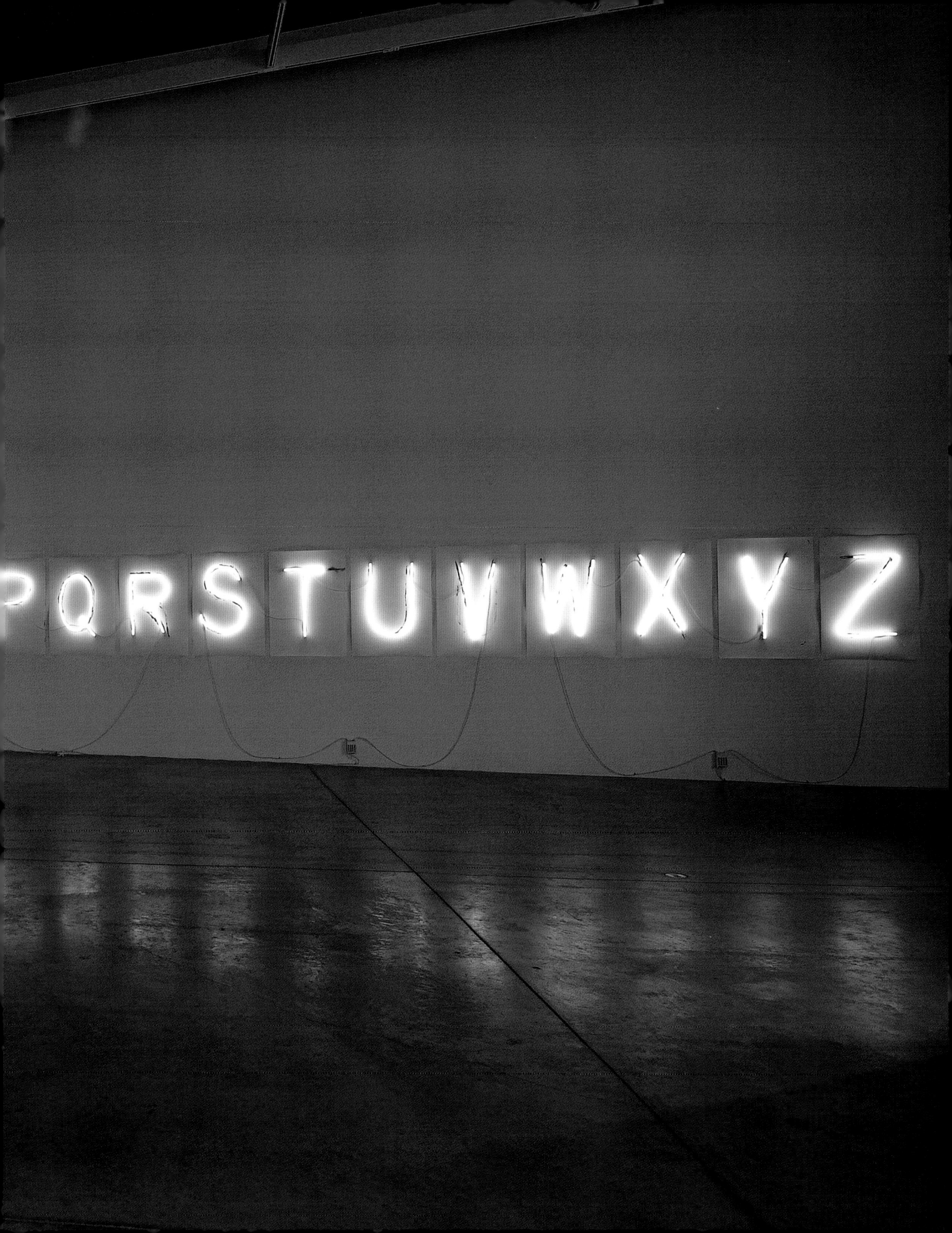
PQRSTUVWXYZ

The British artist Martin Creed is known for his conceptual works, all of which are numbered. *Work No. 1092, MOTHERS* (above) features the word in white neon and steel, standing at 5 metres (over 16 ft) high. It slowly rotates, and the viewer is invited to stand beneath it; the idea of the mother is literally placed on a pedestal. Originally shown in London, the piece has since been exhibited several times, including at the Museum of Contemporary Art in Chicago in 2012. Creed explains: 'I think the most powerful and difficult relationship in the whole world is between a mother and a child. That is the one where the baby is literally part of the mother and is not separate, and then you have to come out and be separate...I think to actually be a mother is very difficult and to have a mother is difficult.' The work is highly personal yet speaks to a global audience.

Kendell Geers, a South African artist, uses a wide variety of media in his text-based works, from paint for wall-based installations to neon. *S:LAUGHTER* (opposite) is a play on words and the ways in which meaning can quickly change. The large neon 'S' turns on and off, so that the viewer reads either 'SLAUGHTER' or 'LAUGHTER' – words that are emotionally worlds apart. Discomfort and disruption of meaning are at the core of the piece, as Geers asks the viewer to try to merge the words into one work. It has been shown in various locations, including outside the Nobel Peace Center, Oslo, and the Contemporary Art Museum St Louis, Missouri.

ABOVE · Martin Creed
Work No. 1092, MOTHERS, 2011
White neon and steel
5 × 12.5 × 0.2 m
(16 ft 4⅞ in. × 41 ft ⅛ in. × 7⅞ in.)

OPPOSITE · Kendell Geers
S:LAUGHTER, 2003
Neon · 10 × 2 m (32 ft 9¾ × 78¾ in.)

OPPOSITE, TOP · Claire Fontaine
Foreigners Everywhere (German), 2011
Neon · 12 × 132.5 × 4.5 cm
(4¾ × 52⅛ × 1¾ in.)

OPPOSITE, BOTTOM · Claire Fontaine
Foreigners Everywhere (Tibetan), 2010
Neon · 48 × 325.5 × 4.5 cm
(18⅞ × 128⅛ × 1¾ in.)

ABOVE · Shi Yong
A Bunch of Happy Fantasy, 2009
Neon lights, acrylic stands
500 × 500 × 1 cm
(196⅞ × 196⅞ × ⅜ in.)

Claire Fontaine is a collective artist, founded in Paris in 2004 and now based in Palermo; her name is taken from a brand of French school notebooks. As a 'readymade artist', she references Marcel Duchamp, applying his theory to subjects rather than to objects. Her work includes performance, neon, painting, sculpture and video, and it questions notions of both authorship and appropriation. Artworks include the large outdoor neon *Capitalism Kills Love* (2007); the 'Foreigners Everywhere' series (opposite), which presents the phrase in more than twenty languages, among them Chinese (2008), Romany and Tibetan (both 2010) and Cherokee and German (both 2011); and, in 2016, *Untitled (I am your voice)*, made of wall-mounted LED letters.

The Chinese artist Shi Yong presents *A Bunch of Happy Fantasy* (above) on a gentle slope, so that the viewer's eye travels up the many distinct Chinese characters in bright red neon. The 5-metre-squared (16.4-ft-squared) work depicts the poem 'A Rose Made from Water', which was written by one of the artist's friends while taking opium. Shi explains: 'I imagined the words upside down, their reflections rippling in the water.' The resultant work indeed shimmers as if it were a reflecting pond where viewers can dream of happiness just out of reach. The title of the piece suggests that modern China may also be chasing an illusion.

Sheldon Scott was born in South Carolina, one of the US southern states where, in some areas of life, people of colour continue to be disproportionately disadvantaged. In 2015 the young white supremacist Dylann Roof entered a church in Charleston with a firearm and murdered nine African-Americans at prayer. The Confederate flag that flew over the state Capitol was finally taken down as a result of the shooting. This type of open racism is at the heart of Scotts' work *Eeny Meeny Miney Mo* (above), in which the words are written in red, white and blue neon above piles of Brazil nuts. The original version of the children's rhyme includes the line 'Catch a nigger by the toe', and in the US South, Brazil nuts are sometimes called 'nigger toes'. Scott forces the viewer to confront such repugnant, yet at one time seemingly inoffensive language, highlighting how views on race are formed from an early age.

Jamaican-born Nari Ward repurposes many found objects from his urban New York neighbourhood. For *Palace LiquorsouL* (opposite), Ward took a discarded liquor store (off-licence) sign and, by turning round several letters and illuminating others, presented the viewer with the word 'SOUL'. The work is adorned with artificial flowers and shoelaces, linking it further with its original siting: alcoholism and drug addiction are major killers among the American underclass, and prejudicial stereotypes of people of colour suggest that these social problems are a greater issue for them (although, according to federal government figures, 'African-Americans and whites report similar levels of frequent heavy drinking').

ABOVE · Sheldon Scott
Eeny Meeny Miney Mo, 2014
Neon and Brazil nuts
Dimensions variable

OPPOSITE · Nari Ward
Palace LiquorsouL, 2010
Metal and neon sign, wood with artificial flowers, shoelaces and shoe tips · 472.4 × 78.7 × 53.3 cm (186 × 31 × 21 in.)

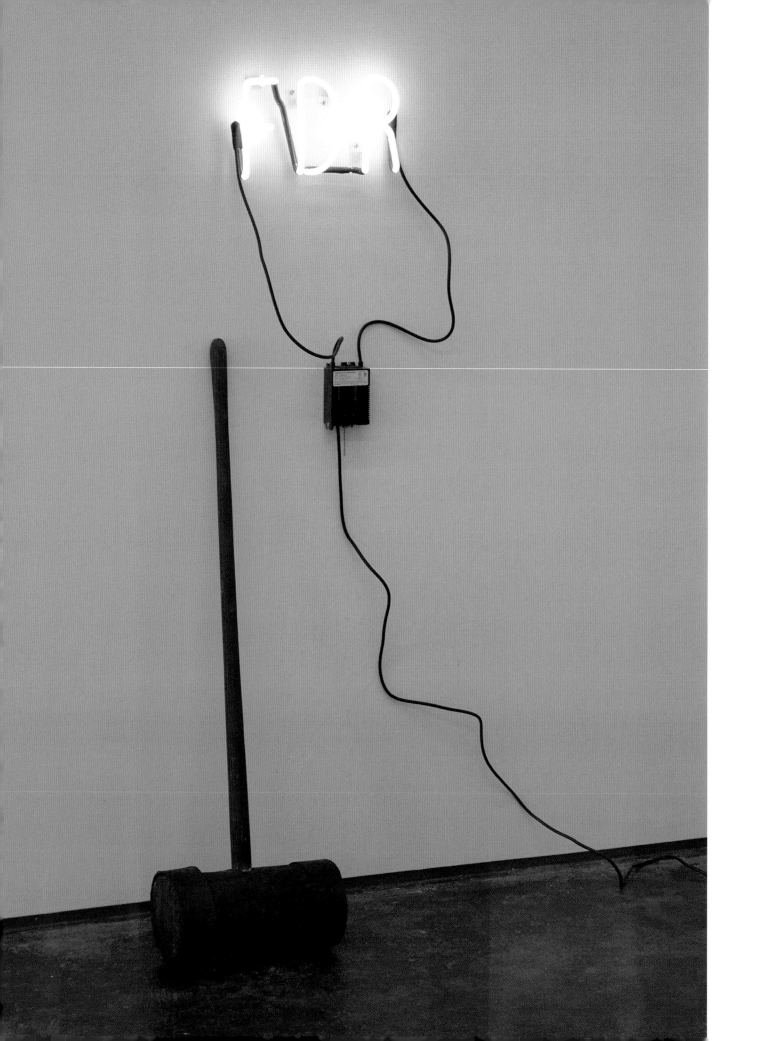

OPPOSITE · Darryl J. Lauster
In Case of Fire, 2010
Neon and wood
Dimensions variable

ABOVE · Terence Koh
Felt, 2016 · White neon
7.6 × 20.3 cm (3 × 8 in.)

Darryl Lauster is interested in American history and its repercussions for contemporary society. *In Case of Fire* (opposite), shown at the Devin Borden Gallery in Houston, Texas, in 2014, considers Franklin D. Roosevelt's New Deal, which in the 1930s introduced a series of programmes, including social security – now under threat. The reforms were a response to the Great Depression and were thought to be sacrosanct in US politics. Lauster highlights both the fragility of attempts by enlightened Americans to help the less fortunate, and how easily reforms can be overturned. He describes how the neon 'blinks in a similar way to old diner signs, drawing the viewer in with a hint of nostalgia'.

Many of the works of the Canadian artist Terence Koh feature light, and often they are monochrome, either black or white. His 2007 untitled installation for the Whitney Museum of American Art, New York, featured an incredibly bright light in a white room. He has made a number of white neon *Felt* works, and the version depicted above has been installed on the ceiling of a dental surgery. In order to view it, visitors must sit in the dentist's chair and look up.

Hubert Czerepok's neon *Nigdy nie będziesz Polakiem!* (You Never Be a Pole!, 2009) is a reference to the racist attitudes of football fans in the Polish cities of Białystok and Wodzisław Śląski, where they hung banners at matches when Roger Guerreiro was on the field. The Brazilian was one of the first players of colour in the country, and many were angry that he was speedily granted citizenship in order to play for the national team; they shouted, 'Roger, you will never be a Pole!' A concerted campaign of intimidation against the player was led by far-right nationalists, who displayed a Celtic cross (sometimes used by white supremacists as a symbol of heritage) and a Second World War resistance symbol, the *kotwica*, known as the 'red anchor of fighting Poland'. In Czerepok's work, the *kotwica* can be

seen in the letter 'P'; it also resembles an erection. The Polish national colours are white and red. Czerepok has used red neon in many works as a comment on the rightwards drift in Polish, European and American politics, and the open hatred and violence shown to 'others'.

ABOVE · Hubert Czerepok
Nigdy nie będziesz Polakiem! (You Never Be a Pole!), 2009 · Neon
40 × 190 × 10 cm (15¾ × 74¾ × 4 in.)

ABOVE · Michael Shaowanasai
อยาก? (Horny?), 2015 · Neon
Each letter approx. 200 × 120 cm
(78¾ × 47¼ in.)

The Thai artist Michael Shaowanasai has long explored the boundaries of the sex industry in Bangkok, from selling pre-packed *Thai Boy Cum* in sachets to his alternate persona, Iron Pussy, a drag superhero who has starred in her own full-length action musical movie. Shaowanasai's solo show at the Adler Subhashok Gallery, Bangkok, in 2015 – called 'Michael Shaowanasai Presents...' – featured a large pink neon work called *อยาก?* (above). The meaning of the Thai word is elusive and fluid, rather like Shaowanasai himself. He explains that it can be translated as 'WANT, NEED, CRAVE, HUNGRY, all the way to HORNY....[It] also indicates the intention/class of the speaker.... [It] can be very common, very normal, very naughty and very coarse (vulgar) to some.' The addition of the question mark turns it into a query: 'Horny?' Thai is a very tonal language (it has more than twenty different tones), and the tone of a word can change its meaning. This tonal variety also parallels the gender fluidity of Shaowanasai's personas and work.

Fred Eerdekens works with many different materials that cast shadows to spell out words. These include metal (see p. 86), clothes, food packaging, artificial trees and, in *Neo Deo* (above), clouds of synthetic material. The miniature floating clouds spell out the title by blocking the spotlight directed towards them. Eerdekens says that his work 'is all about looking, reading and allowing the unexpected'.

The British artist Benjamin Carrick makes minimal conceptual works that question the act of making art and the context for its distribution. *Untitled or: Confessions of a Post-Post-Modernist* (2013) features simple black text on white paper, proclaiming 'I USED TO MAKE CONCEPTUAL ART, NOW I JUST SAY I DO.' At first glance, the work appears to be a poster slogan, but the bold typeface and the unusual layout of the words lead the viewer to look again and see that it is itself a conceptual work. *I Couldn't Afford Neon* (opposite) presents the titular phrase printed in black and pink ink on paper, and alludes to the plethora of neon work in the contemporary art world (as this chapter attests). The work makes a strong graphic statement, and the pink glows as if it actually were neon, but its self-proclaimed failure tugs at the viewer as much as it makes them smile knowingly.

ABOVE · Fred Eerdekens
Neo Deo, 2002
Synthetic material and light projector
4 × 14 m (13 ft 1½ in. × 45 ft 11⅛ in.)

OPPOSITE · Benjamin D. Carrick
I Couldn't Afford Neon, 2011
Acrylic on paper
59.4 × 42 cm (23⅜ × 16½ in.)

I COULDN'T AFFORD NEON

The works in this chapter generally match most people's idea of what constitutes new media – that is, digital (on- and offline) and video works, and those that incorporate computers or new technologies. But new media is a difficult term, as what a few years ago was considered to be cutting edge has now become outdated. It is not my intention to argue for the newest forms of media, since they will soon also be outmoded, but to offer a brief record of works produced over the past decade or so that fit within these non-traditional forms. It is important to consider the impact of new digital media on the art world and on society as a whole.

Many of us write electronically every day. Whether we are using email, Facebook, Twitter or WhatsApp (all of which are one day likely to be replaced by newer technologies), we use the typed word, along with the occasional emoji, to connect with family, friends and colleagues. Digital media may be employed to make political statements, express anger or concern, or – as this chapter shows – to create artworks.

This chapter also includes two QR codes, which are codes that store information and can be read by the camera on a smartphone. With some phones, you can simply open the camera and scan the code; on others, you will first need to open a QR reader app. Scan the codes to see the works – by Joseph Imhauser and Anatol Knotek – in animated GIF format. They can also be viewed as stills (as on the printed page) or video loops, but they are truest to their form as short, computer-animated sequences. Animated-GIF artworks may eventually become standard, as in the case of video projections, but at the moment they have a high-tech frisson for many viewers or readers.

Several artists featured in this chapter have projected their art either on to buildings (Bill Claps; Pablo Gimenez-Zapiola) or inside them (Pilvi Takala). The content may be social comment or abstract and predominantly visual, but these artists embrace a technology not long ago seen as new, and they all endeavour to push the boundaries of how projections can deliver textual information.

Other artists are working with and designing their own computers and computer-controlled machines that produce their artworks for them (for example, So Kanno and Takahiro Yamaguchi). Liliane Lijn (a former artist-in-residence at NASA) works with real-time computer simulations that show text projected on to the moon, while Jason Salavon uses real-time data from the internet to create his work. It is this notion of making art in the now, the exact moment of seeing, that perhaps represents the newest of the new.

The American artist Joseph Imhauser uses language in a way that would not have been possible in decades past: he creates online mini-animations of text. *Genesis* (2015) is a 22-second GIF in which the words 'another time on top of time appears' shimmer across the screen, their fluttering creating a digital space parallel to our physical one. The name brings a metaphysical dimension to the work. *Genesis* is also the title of a 1982 book by the philosopher Michel Serres; Imhauser explains that this cross-disciplinary exploration of chaos, order and 'the sound and the fury' of life has greatly influenced him. The artist releases solo sound works under the pseudonym Marcel Proust and sings in the New York-based music project Gemtactics. He is also the co-founder of Lyeberry, a series of publications and events that focus on preserving the social and informal origin of the library.

BELOW · Joseph Imhauser
QR Code #1 (Genesis), 2017
Dye sublimation on Dibond aluminium
30 × 30 cm (11¾ × 11¾ in.)
Edition of 3

BOTTOM, LEFT AND RIGHT ·
Joseph Imhauser · *Genesis*, 2015
Animated GIF

Anatol Knotek's native language is German, but he uses English in his word pieces. *Just in Time* (2011) is an animated GIF in which the second arm of the letter 'm' rotates as if it were the second hand of a watch. The GIF comprises sixty individual images, making it a true sweep of the clock as it endlessly marks the passage of time. The subject of time interests Knotek, and many of his works address the topic, including *Time is Running Out* (2011), in which an outline of the word 'time' is painted on a canvas and black ink trickles down from each letter on to the floor, as if the contents were dripping out of the word. *Signs of Our Times* (2008) features the words of the title and, beneath, the symbols those letters make on a smartphone when the keypad is changed to numeric. *Our Days Are Numbered* (2015) is a text piece originally published in Knotek's book *Anachronism*. The words of the title are repeated on several lines, but with each line some of the letters become numbers. When Knotek published the work online, some people liked it so much that they had it tattooed on to themselves; the artist has posted photographs of the tattoos on his website.

time

time

time

time

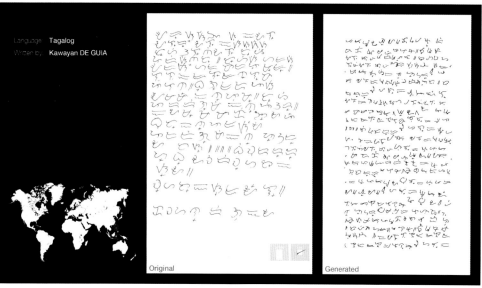

Language: Tagalog
Written by: Kawayan DE GUIA

Original

Generated

The Japanese artists So Kanno and Takahiro Yamaguchi have made a series of 'Senseless Drawing Bots' that write graffiti tags on gallery walls in what appear to be entirely random patterns. The first robot (opposite) appeared at the 'Utopia no Oshirase' exhibition in Tokyo in 2011, moving independently across the floor while spraying multiple colours of paint. The machine creates its own language by using a pendulum arm attached to a fulcrum to generate naturalistic handwritten marks. The artists have explored text and graffiti in numerous other projects, including *Asemic Languages* (above) at the Aichi Triennale in 2016. Ten international artists were first invited to provide handwritten statements. Using an artificial intelligence program, Kanno and Yamaguchi's plotter machine learned the shapes and patterns of each written language, and also the traits of each writer, and then generated lines that looked like real words, but in fact had no meaning. Only when the viewer examines the texts in detail do they realize that they are reading a new babel.

ABOVE · So Kanno and Takahiro Yamaguchi · *Asemic Languages* (Tagalog language at bottom), 2016
XY plotter, paper, pen, computer and handwritings
Machine learning program: Hironori Sakamoto
15 × 310 × 135 cm (5⅞ × 122 × 53⅛ in.)

OPPOSITE · So Kanno and Takahiro Yamaguchi · *Senseless Drawing Bot*, 2011
Motorized skateboard, spray paint, double pendulum and electronics
Metal works supported by Hitto Asai
146 × 120 × 60 cm (57½ × 47¼ × 23⅝ in.)

Pilvi

> What about pregnancies?

> Am I supposed to play the father?

Jesse

> I saw one where the girl just blurted out that she was pregnant.

> It was clear she didn't know the fake boyfriend well enough for it to be him.

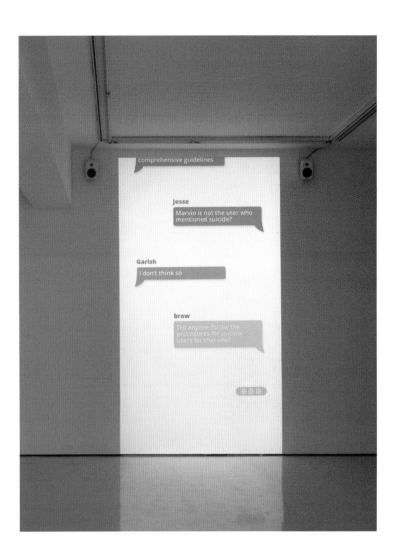

OPPOSITE · Pilvi Takala
Invisible Friend, 2015
Text-messaging service and poster
Dimensions variable

ABOVE · Pilvi Takala
Workers' Forum (installation view
at right), 2015 · HD animation
Duration: 6 minutes, 23 seconds
Dimensions variable
Edition of 5 and 2 artist's proofs

For the project *Invisible Friend* (opposite), the Finnish artist Pilvi Takala put up posters and handed out cards that invited people to use a free text-message service. The texters were promised 'a personal but anonymous conversation with someone who will always reply'. Seven writers answered texts and engaged in discussion. Takala explains: 'The main thing is mirroring the user's language, accepting the concerns that the user brings to the conversation, and building on them. Everything that the user has to say is interesting and worthy of attention. As a general rule,

you don't argue with the user. Of course, you respond to sexters by changing the subject.' The work addresses the notion of texting as a means of connection, especially as used by young people, who have grown up engaging with social media. Takala also created *Workers' Forum* (above), a video based on conversations that took place on a discussion forum among workers at a service in the United States where users pay to have a pretend boyfriend or girlfriend text them. Takala drew on her own experience of working for the US service.

The American artist Jason Salavon's work *Rainbow Aggregator* (above) uses Twitter and Google as raw material. In real time, computer software – designed by Salavon – scans the internet for 'trending topics' and translates them into visual language and colour. The leading names and events that are being discussed online continuously appear on the computer screen, and are updated every few minutes. The colours are generated from the data received by the computer. The work examines the global nature of all online conversations, whether public or private, and presents the viewer with a depiction of what otherwise might be regarded as pure digital noise. Salavon's use of the rainbow motif is a positive interpretation of something that many people consider to be a dystopia, and the piece questions what it is that we want from the digital world.

The British duo Jon Thomson and Alison Craighead are interested in how live networks affect those who view or participate in them. Many of their projects include an online element. *Hello World* (2014) is an LED sign that displays the current global population in real time, and *Decorative Newsfeeds* (opposite, bottom) uses live information from the web. Headlines of current events are projected on to the gallery wall in playfully curved forms, and thus news becomes drawing in digital space, a type of automatic writing, or concrete poetry. The found nature of the texts allows them to function as readymades for the 21st century. *Temporary Index* (opposite, top) depicts the time in seconds (up to one million years) that remains before various sites for the storage of nuclear waste around the world are considered safe for human habitation. The work includes a booklet that describes each site and the waste stored there.

ABOVE · Jason Salavon
Rainbow Aggregator, 2013
Real-time software, internet connection, computer and large display
Dimensions variable
Edition of 3 and 2 artist's proofs

OPPOSITE, TOP · Thomson & Craighead
Temporary Index, 2016
Digital projection from online sources, office table and chair, anglepoise lamp and folder · Dimensions variable

OPPOSITE, BOTTOM · Thomson & Craighead · *Decorative Newsfeeds*, 2004
Digital projection from online sources
Dimensions variable

Liliane Lijn has worked with text since she created her seminal 'Poem Machines' in the 1960s (see pp. 18–20). The ongoing project *moonmeme* takes her exploration of words into the digital world. The piece consists of a computer program working in real time to project the word 'SHE' on to an image of the lunar surface. The image updates every 26 hours and 13 minutes, as the program tracks the real moon's phase, and is accompanied by a soundtrack of Lijn chanting variations of 'she' and ancient lunar texts, in reference to cross-cultural beliefs that the moon is feminine. Over the course of a lunar month, as the moon moves through its different phases, the word 'SHE' becomes 'HE' and then re-emerges. Lijn has worked with NASA and plans to extend *moonmeme* to a laser projection on to the moon's actual surface when technology permits. As she explains: 'Currently *moonmeme* is presented on a monitor and the viewer is invited to type in their name and birthdate. On doing this, they see the lunar image with "SHE" or "HE" projected upon its surface, as it was at the time of their birth. Within 20 seconds, the lunar cycles of the first six months of the viewer's life appear on screen. After a brief interval, their data will be placed chronologically within all the birth data *moonmeme* has received to date. From seeing oneself as a unique cosmic phenomenon, the self is viewed as a small part of a much larger pattern.'

ABOVE AND OPPOSITE · Liliane Lijn
moonmeme, ongoing since 1992
Interactive digital real-time program
for Mac Mini and monitor, 'HESHE'
voice chant and 'Lunar Tales'
Programming: Andi Studer
Digital imaging: Richard Wilding
Lunar phases source material:
António Cidadão
Astronomical calculations and
programming: Tom Ruen
Voice: Liliane Lijn

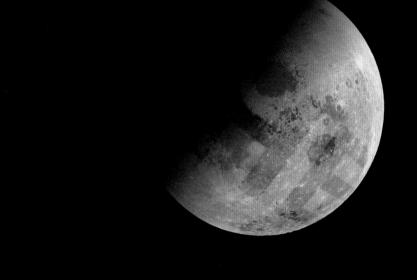

Luca Rossi, from Italy, was one of nine artists selected to exhibit at the 2017 SMACH Biennale of the Dolomites in San Martin de Tor. *If You Don't Understand Something Search for It on YouTube* (overleaf) consisted of large wooden letters and numbers – spelling out 'IMG 3733' – constructed in front of a local castle. The sign leads the viewer to think that they are looking at a digital image file on screen (IMG 3733 is also the YouTube file name given to video clips that are untitled), yet the setting is almost chocolate-box perfect in terms of its natural beauty. Thus Rossi conflates the real and the digital worlds, and asks us to re-examine our relationships with social and digital media.

OPPOSITE · Kurtis Lesick and Travis
Kirton · *Possibilities Exceed Nine*, 2011/17
Poetic performance reading for
artist and computer, performed here
at the Fountain Studio, Calgary, 2017

ABOVE · Aida Wilde
HASHTAG Save Vittoria Wharf, 2016
Screenprinted poster
118.9 × 84.1 cm (46¾ × 33⅛ in.)

The Canadian artist Kurtis Lesick created a live performance in which he and his lover interacted in front of a live audience (opposite). The fact that the lover was a computer that generated text in real time in response to Lesick's comments added a chilling patina to the work. *Possibilities Exceed Nine* was devised in 2011 for the Poetic Performance Lab at the John Dutton Theatre, Calgary, in collaboration with the programming artist Travis Kirton, who designed custom-generative scripts for the project. Lesick says that the performance is 'a dialogue between a man and his lover negotiating the traps of co-dependence and control they are both seeking'. The work considers the modern condition many find themselves in, where we depend on technology, yet are resentful of its control over our lives.

Aida Wilde uses the internet to campaign for many different issues. The Iranian-born, UK-based artist's use of hashtags is not limited to the online world, however, as she has also made a variety of pink, white and black posters that she pastes into the urban environment. Works such as *HASHTAG Save Everything!!!* (2014), *HASHTAG Save Hackney Wick's Artists* (2016) and *HASHTAG Save Vittoria Wharf* (above) are commentaries on both gentrification and the ways in which we interact with social media. Wilde also adds similarly coloured posts to existing billboards, as in her guerrilla action in 2017 that affixed the words 'PAY' or 'EQUALITY' above the Gap logo on the retailer's adverts. She is aware that online actions might have little effect on real-world outcomes, as *A HASHTAG Won't Save the World But... Women Might* (2014) makes clear.

The Russian artist Aristarkh Chernyshev uses LED displays to create such objects as *Urgently!* (2007) and *Big Knode* (above), which he calls 'Info-Sculptures'. Other pieces are wall-based, including *Big Lyric Economy* (2006), which he describes as being about our 'modern rationalized, globalized world', where 'no space [is] left for lyricism. [The p]oetry of today is stock exchange rates, oil and gold prices, celebrity news and ad slogans.' In *Loading. Connecting. Transferring.* (2008), the words of the title loop endlessly, representing the frustration of any computer user who has lost their network connection. Chernyshev's work highlights our exasperation with the digital world.

In James Balmforth's *WE MUST TAKE INTEREST IN THE ABILITY OF OTHERS* (opposite), the words of the title scroll continuously around an LED display set in a steel casing. The rust-coloured steel contrasts starkly with the LED lights, each representing very different methods of art-making. Steel might be considered a haptic work material and is therefore at odds with digital technologies; Balmforth utilizes this discomfort – both visual and related to touch – to emphasize the content of his text. This work demonstrates that different materials and different ways of making and seeing are all valid.

ABOVE · Aristarkh Chernyshev *Big Knode*, 2012 · Custom LED display connected to internet newsfeed 150 × 150 × 200 cm (59 × 59 × 78¾ in.)

OPPOSITE · James Balmforth *WE MUST TAKE INTEREST IN THE ABILITY OF OTHERS*, 2011 LED display with scrolling text in steel casing · Diameter 115 × depth 10 cm (45¼ × 4 in.)

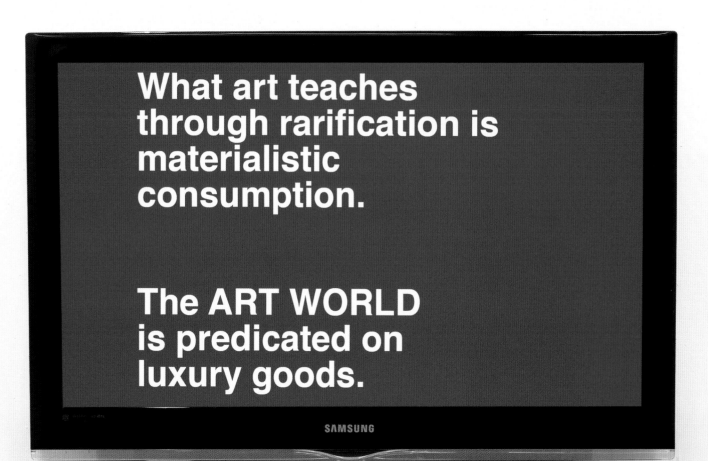

What art teaches
through rarification is
materialistic
consumption.

The ART WORLD
is predicated on
luxury goods.

SAMSUNG

The American artist Jonathan Horowitz employs various media, including video and sculpture (see pp. 192–93), to examine material and artistic culture. For his exhibition 'Minimalist Works from the Holocaust Museum' at Dundee Contemporary Arts in 2010–11, he aimed to highlight the way in which a minimalist aesthetic may become devoid of meaning and content when applied to such real-world situations as the Holocaust. Horowitz critiqued the minimalist Richard Serra by revisiting the video *Television Delivers People*, made in 1973 by Serra and Carlota Fay Schoolman. The original video denounced corporate mass media as a means of social control. Horowitz's

Art Delivers People (2010), set to organ music by Philip Glass, suggests that, in its fetishism of and reliance on governmental, institutional support, the contemporary art world likewise delivers a population to the capitalist market.

ABOVE · Jonathan Horowitz
Art Delivers People, 2010
Single-channel video and 50-in. monitor
Duration: 7 minutes

In 2013 the French artist Olivier Castel presented a solo exhibition, 'The Back of an Image', at the Rowing gallery in London under the pseudonym Louise Weiss. Visitors were greeted by a poster for the show – a photograph of a collage by Hans Arp, overlaid with text (below) – pasted on to the wall of the building opposite. The gallery space itself was darkened, and a rotating headlight, programmed to replicate the artist's handwriting, projected its beam on to the gallery walls. These walls had been painted with phosphorescent pigment, so that the words continued to glow after the light had passed over them. The gallery is located near a large, 1930s-built cinema, the Odeon Holloway, and Castel used this proximity as the starting point for his exploration of text and image. The handwritten projections were notes, quotes and doodles about the cinematic experience, including propositions for a film without images, reduced to light and movement only. Speakers in the courtyard played two overlapping soundtracks, one of them unused music from Stanley Kubrick's *2001: A Space Odyssey*. Castel asks the visitor to be the main character in his film, a participant as opposed to a voyeur, and the totality of the work – the visit to the gallery, the fictional film-maker, the images, the sound, the internal and external elements – creates a filmic experience that is completely different for each viewer.

RIGHT, ABOVE · Olivier Castel
The Back of an Image, 2013
Moving headlight, computer, phosphorescent paint, steel pipe of 45-cm (17¾-in.) diameter, at Rowing, London
Duration: 40 minutes, looped, silent

RIGHT · Olivier Castel
The Back of an Image, 2013
Digital print on blueback billboard paper with adhesive
540 × 385 cm (212⅝ × 151⅛ in.)

The German artist Mischa Kuball works across many media, including installation and sound works. *Musik in Tüten* (Music in Bags; right) was a sound performance with projected visuals in the famous Kling Klang Studio in Düsseldorf. The studio, now called Elektro Müller, is the former home of the innovative pop group Kraftwerk, and provided a unique social context for the work. Speakers were placed inside small green plastic bags and then positioned outside. Projections of letters and numbers bounced off the ceiling, and special soundproofing in the studio broke up the acoustics.

For the 56th Venice Biennale in 2015, TSANG Kin-Wah created a multi-channel video and sound installation called *The Infinite Nothing* (opposite). The piece was a digital manifestation of his vinyl text works, in which words flow along the walls of a space like a stream or the roots of a plant (see p. 38). The title references Friedrich Nietzsche's declaration of the death of God in *The Gay Science* (1882), where the philosopher posits: 'Are we not straying as through an infinite nothing?' TSANG explores through a variety of belief systems the relationship between humans and their deities, including Hindu and Buddhist ideas about karma. In one section, visitors stepped into an ever-changing digital river, a reflection on Heraclitus' famous saying that no one ever steps in the same river twice; and, in another, they were swamped by a surge of swirling, digitally projected text.

RIGHT · Mischa Kuball
Musik in Tüten (Music in Bags), 2016
Performance at Elektro Müller,
Düsseldorf, with music performance by
Axel Manrico Heilhecker, Thomas Klein
and Rosa Roedelius

OPPOSITE · TSANG Kin-Wah · *The Infinite Nothing: 0* (detail at bottom), 2015
Multi-channel video projection with
sound, Hong Kong Pavilion, 56th Venice
Biennale, commissioned by M+
Duration: 6 minutes, 19 seconds

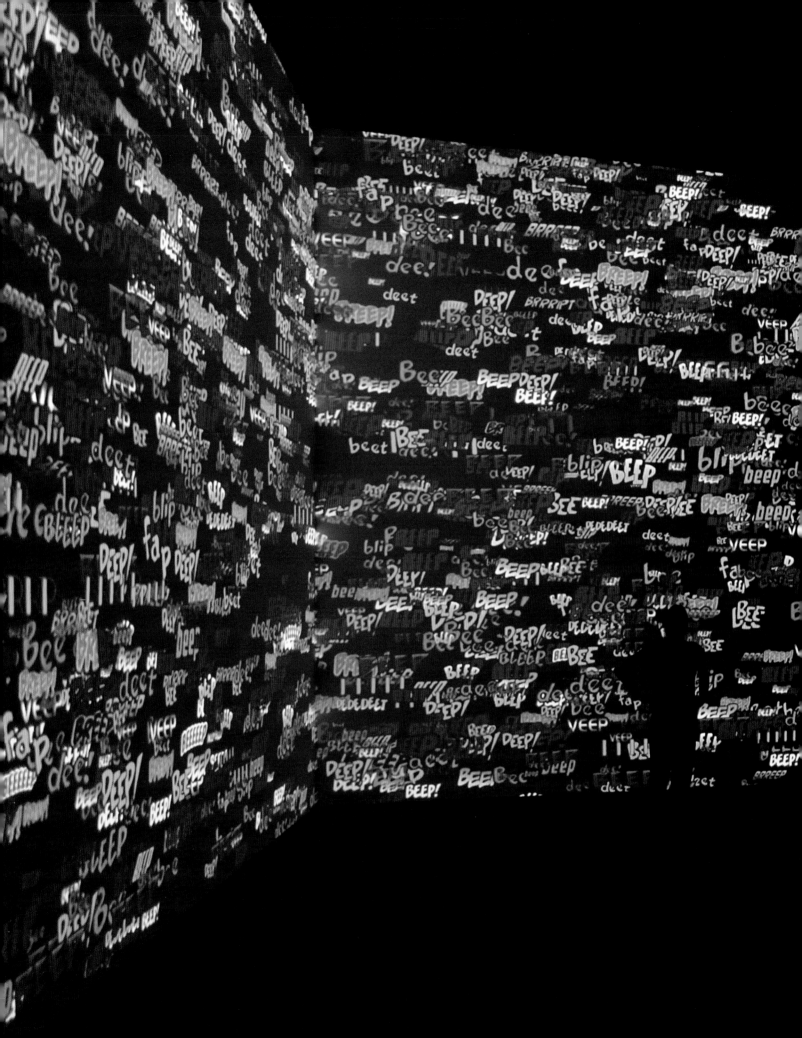

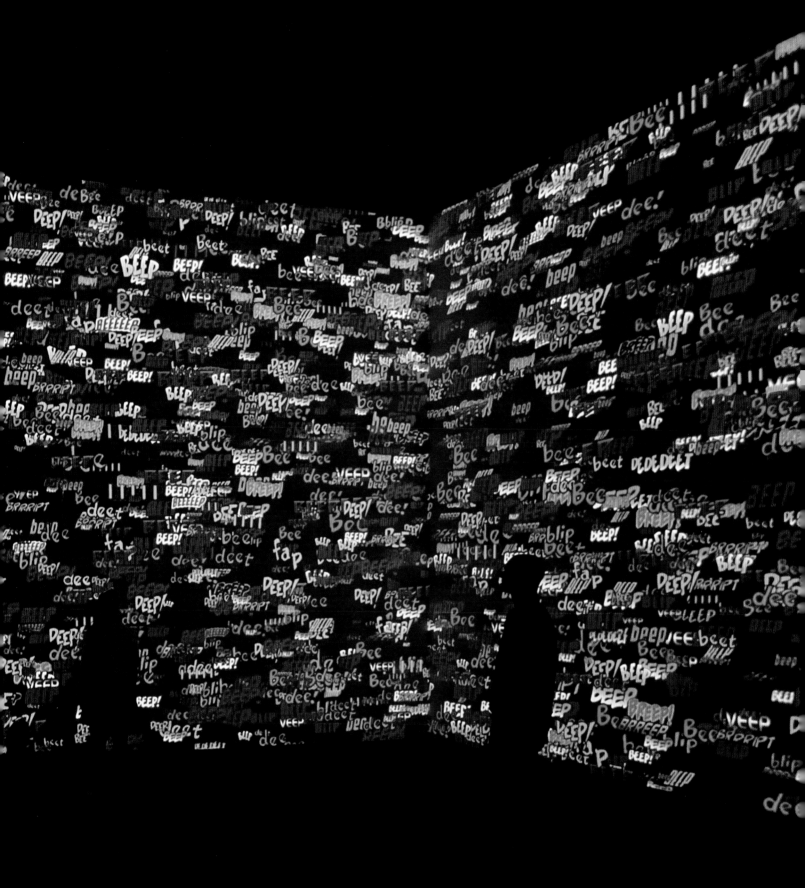

Surround Sounds (pp. 144–45), by the American-Swiss artist Christian Marclay, was a synchronized video installation of animated onomatopoeic words – that is, words that sound like the noise they describe. Using comic books as his source material, the artist made 'whizz' and 'zoom' race across the walls of the darkened gallery; 'beep' constantly appeared and disappeared. The work was completely silent, yet totally immersive: the viewer in essence heard each word as they read it. Marclay explains: 'I find silence is much more powerful because...in silence we can think about sound. Silence is the negative space that defines sound.'

Mark Themann's *Go Into This Space* (above) takes its title from a dual-channel work created for the Künstlerhaus Bethanien in Berlin (see p. 34). Reconfigured and expanded into a six-channel installation, it was subsequently shown at the MADA Gallery at Monash University, Melbourne. Six projectors on the floor cast animated texts – called 'event-scores' by the artist – against the gallery walls, each text beginning with the words 'Go into this space...'.

PAGES 144–45 · Christian Marclay
Surround Sounds, 2014–15
4 silent synchronized projected
animations; installation view at Paula
Cooper Gallery, New York, 2015
Duration: each 13 minutes,
40 seconds, looped

ABOVE · Mark Themann
Go Into This Space, 2012
6-channel silent video, MADA Gallery,
Monash University, Melbourne
Duration: 10 minutes
Site-specific dimensions

ABOVE · Shimon Attie
I've been wandering so long, constantly changing places as one would change clothes. I'm leaving now, but I remember my past as closely as tightly-sewn stitches, from the project 'Between Dreams and History', 1998 · Lasers writing out Chinese senior's favourite song from youth, on-location laser-projection installation and C-type print · Installation: 1:1 architectural scale; print: 76.2 × 96.5 cm (30 × 38 in.)

The American artist Shimon Attie has long worked with communities to develop projects that reflect local history and the memories and identities of residents. In 1998, for the 'Between Dreams and History' project, based on the New York immigrant experience, he interviewed seventy-five long-term residents of the city's Lower East Side, who then wrote down their favourite childhood rhymes, songs and poems and their hopes, prayers and reminiscences, all in their mother tongue, whether English, Spanish, Chinese or Yiddish. Attie developed an animated laser-projection technique that, in blue light, appeared to handwrite excerpts from these texts in real time across the façades of buildings in the

neighbourhood. One song recalled by an elderly Chinese resident included the poignant lyric: 'I've been wandering so long, constantly changing places as one would change clothes. I'm leaving now, but I remember my past as closely as tightly-sewn stitches.'

The American artist Bill Claps uses a variety of signs and symbols to introduce code into his language-based works. Many incorporate Morse code, while for his *Alphabet Project* (2015) he created his own verbal and visual language, the characters of which are combinations of elements of Arabic, Hebrew and Chinese. He employs this invented alphabet to transcribe art criticism. Claps took the notion of art being a coded language further in his *Artspeak Incinerator* project, which was commissioned for THE(un)SCENE Art Show in New York in 2015. He gathered 'artspeak' found on Twitter, translated these sound-bite clichés into Morse code, then projected the code on to the façades of art institutions across the city. Claps explains that the 'artspeak' was 'digitally incinerated' so that it could be released 'into the atmosphere in a purified state'. Participating institutions included the Museum of Modern Art, the Guggenheim Museum (above), the Whitney Museum of American Art and commercial galleries. Claps's sharp dissection of a certain way of speaking about art, used by both the art-world establishment and the market (which aims to present an authoritative voice), is often humorous, crushing and visually arresting.

ABOVE · Bill Claps
Artspeak Incinerator, 2015
Projection for THE(un)SCENE Art Show on the façade of the Solomon R. Guggenheim Museum, New York
Dimensions variable

ABOVE · Kay Rosen
AIDS, On Going, Going On, 2015
Projection for Visual AIDS on the
façade of the Metropolitan Museum
of Art, New York
Dimensions variable

Kay Rosen's guerrilla projection *AIDS, On Going, Going On* was commissioned by the arts organization Visual AIDS for World AIDS Day, 1 December 2015. The work was projected on to three New York buildings: the Guggenhcim Museum, the Metropolitan Museum of Art (above) and the former St Vincent's Hospital, which once had the largest AIDS ward on the East Coast. In 1990 Rosen made a poster for the public art exhibition 'Art Against AIDS on the Road', which was seen on the back of fifty Chicago buses. The black text on a pink ground comprised a list of synonyms for the word 'aid', including 'assist', 'help' and 'care'.

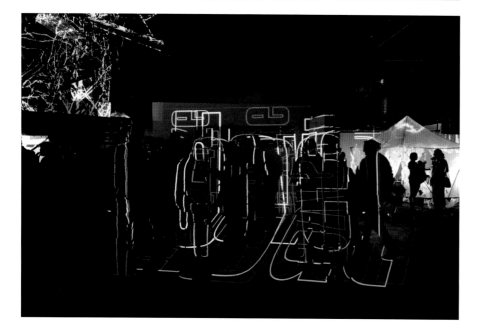

The US-based Argentinian artist Pablo Gimenez-Zapiola uses long-exposure photography to record projection performances. The works are presented as limited-edition photographs and videos, but the essence of them is in the live projection. For *De los cuerpos del amor* (From the Bodies of Love; left, above), Gimenez-Zapiola projected an excerpt from a poem by Javier Galarza on to the side of a moving train. The train passengers may or may not be in love or be loved, but the ghost of the notion of love seems to be caught in the image. Even more arresting is *Me plaga el abandono* (Abandonment Plagues Me; left, centre), for which the artist projected the poem by Felipe Gimenez-Zapiola on to a tree. A line from the poem may be translated as 'I look for my shadow, in a darkened room', and it is certainly true that Gimenez-Zapiola works with shadow as much as with projected light. For *Textuals* (left, below), visitors to his projection performance at El Rincón Social in Houston, Texas, became part of his canvas. Four digital light projectors shone an ever-changing series of words across the dark bodies of the viewers.

LEFT, ABOVE · Pablo Gimenez-Zapiola
De los cuerpos del amor (From the Bodies of Love), 2012 · Large-scale projections over moving trains; poem by
Javier Galarza · 61 × 91.4 cm (24 × 36 in.)

LEFT, CENTRE · Pablo Gimenez-Zapiola
Me plaga el abandono (Abandonment Plagues Me), 2016 · Large-scale projections over trees; poem by
Felipe Gimenez-Zapiola
61 × 91.4 cm (24 × 36 in.)

LEFT, BELOW · Pablo Gimenez-Zapiola
Textuals, 2015 · Large-scale projections
Dimensions variable

The work of the Asian-Scottish artist Maya Chowdhry often combines poetry, video and new media, including phone apps to augment reality. For the 'Ripple' series (2015; in collaboration with Sarah Hymas), viewers scanned an AR code on each 'poetic sculpture'; then, looking at the sculpture through their smartphone, they saw a digital superimposition, such as a butterfly orchid or a glacier, in real time. Chowdhry also employs other non-traditional, non-digital media, as in the case of *Eye on a Word* (2011). For the Manchester Mega Mela, an annual celebration of South Asian culture, she created an installation inspired by the Bengali poet Tagore in which she wrote in cress on blotting paper. The English translation of Chowdhry's haiku, which grew throughout the Mela, is: 'Eye on a word / nature's force / teaches us poetry.' Chowdhry also encouraged visitors to grow their own word (right), having provided them with a full kit.

RIGHT · Maya Chowdhry
Eye on a Word, 2011
Cress seeds and blotting paper
Each sheet 21 × 29.7 cm (8¼ × 11¾ in.)

THE CONCEPTUAL WORD

This chapter explores the ways in which artists use text in performance, where they create a work during a variety of live actions, or where the viewer works with the artist to make the artwork conceptually in their own mind. A perfect example is Ceal Floyer's *Monochrome Till Receipt (White)*, which initially appears to be simply a framed supermarket receipt. Many viewers probably will not investigate the work intellectually; they will not examine the list of goods, which are all white. Only on reading the list does the viewer understand that this is a total conceptual text work. Laure Prouvost also creates something in the viewer's mind through her presentation of a glass of water. The partially filled glass is an autonomous object in itself (and refers to another conceptual artwork by Michael Craig-Martin), but it becomes much more when the viewer reads the text above it. Carey Young's text on a gallery wall makes sense only when a spotlight hits it, illuminating the viewer as to its conceptual simplicity and purity.

Many text-based works are generated during performance, as in the case of William Mackrell's work. Mackrell uses his body and its abilities in much of his art, making his works in real time and often writing as he performs. The end product might be a sculpture or a painting, but it is the act of making that encapsulates the ideas behind his art; the live act is what is significant about such works. The remnant or relic of a performance may or may not enter the marketplace – the art market has become adept at selling such artefacts – but the experience the viewer receives while watching live is priceless. Live art has its roots in ancient shamanistic activities that sought to connect with ancestors, and shamans often presented participants with talismans from the performance to keep as a kind of aide-memoire, to help them relive or re-create it in their minds, in their own time.

Many artists perform in the confines of a gallery or museum, and there they have a somewhat receptive audience (although very few people want to participate in a live event, nor appreciate being roped into one). The situation is different for those who perform in the public realm. Mathieu Tremblin not only performs publicly, but he does so in a continual visual–textual dialogue with others who are not usually seen as artists, namely graffiti taggers. He scouts urban sites where the public often pass by and where taggers leave their territorial markers. He repaints the tags in typefaces that are much easier to read. Neither he nor the original text-makers have permission to do their work, and they are all at risk of arrest. The public nature of this writing aims to disrupt the norm. Words perform all the time: in advertising, they sell; in politics, they persuade; and for those who are given the privilege of voice, they contain and control power. Artists seek to speak without permission.

The Mexican artist Stefan Brüggemann works with language in a variety of media: neon, vinyl, spray paint and sculpture. What makes his conceptual practice stand out is his attention to detail and his ability to make words function as art. The neon *This Work Should be Turned Off When I Die* (2011) is humorous, as the work is turned off at night and at the end of the exhibition. *I Can't Explain and I Won't Even Try* (above, right) alludes to the fact that many people still find conceptual art difficult to understand. Black vinyl lettering fixed directly on the wall, as in *(This is Not Supposed to Be Here)* (2001) and *(No Content)* (2004), push the viewer's experience of art further. For the exhibition 'To Be Political It Has to Look Nice', at the Centro Galego de Arte Contemporánea, Santiago de Compostela, in 2016, many of Brüggemann's works were re-contextualized. In one room, graffiti sprayed on the walls – including phrases such as 'I LOVE YOU' and 'YOU WON'T FORGET ME' – was reflected in the sculpture *Trash Mirror Boxes* (2015). The handmade quality of the graffiti was directly at odds with the artist's more graphic texts, and the viewer had to construct meaning from these diverse forms of language.

ABOVE, LEFT · Stefan Brüggemann *Looks Conceptual*, 1999 · Black vinyl on wall, Kunsthalle Bern · Each letter 20 cm (7⅞ in.) high; font: Arial black

ABOVE, RIGHT · Stefan Brüggemann *I Can't Explain and I Won't Even Try*, 2003 Black vinyl on wall, Kunsthalle Bern Each letter 20 cm (7⅞ in.) high; font: Arial black

RIGHT · Stefan Brüggemann *Headlines and Last Line in the Movies (Wall)*, 2016 · Orange, silver and black spray paint on wall, Hauser & Wirth, New York · Dimensions variable

ABOVE, ON WALLS · Liam Gillick
The thought style fells... (at left) and
The thought style fails..., 2015
Vinyl text on grey wall · Dimensions
variable (as large as possible)

ABOVE, ON FLOOR · Liam Gillick
*A Broadcast from 1887 on the Subject
of Our Time,* 1996 · Short-wave radio
transmitter and receiver, Northern
Atlantic island, post-utopian
community, lighting, text and
instructions · Dimensions variable

In 2015 the British artist Liam Gillick's
exhibition at the Maureen Paley gallery
in London, 'The Thought Style Meets
the Thought Collective', occupied three
rooms, each one titled with the name
of the show followed by A, B or C. The
exhibition examined the processes of
collective production versus individual
production, and referenced texts by
the Polish physician and sociologist
Ludwik Fleck. In *Genesis and Development
of a Scientific Fact* (1935), Fleck proposed
that 'A truly isolated investigator is
impossible' and 'What we do think
and how we do see depends on the
thought-collective to which we belong.'
In room A of Gillick's show, there was
a sound installation of a broadcast to a
utopian community and two wall pieces
in which a single word changed the
entire meaning of the texts.

1,404,000 MILES PER HOUR

The British-American artist Carey Young works within a conceptual framework that many would consider minimalist, but which packs maximum visual punch. *Terminal Velocity* (above) appears to be a simple vinyl text on the gallery wall. But were it not for the spotlight directed on the text, the viewer could not read it, and this is where the work comes into focus. The light that enables legibility moves across the universe at about 186,000 miles per second and is denoted as c, a physical constant. Using this measure, Dr Malcolm Fairbairn of King's College London calculated that the Earth, the gallery, Young and all viewers are moving at a rate of 1,404,000 miles per hour relative to the Big Bang. The light is not only part of the installation; it enables the work to exist and sets the artistic context.

The Irish artist David Cunningham has created a work that presents 10,000 unique permutations of the Latin alphabet. *Alphabet* (opposite) is a series in which he uses all twenty-six letters in all possible combinations, so long as no two letters in the standard alphabet appear in consecutive order (for example, 'mn', 'st'). The work is a form of complexity theory in action in that, given only a few rules, a complex system arises. Cunningham is known for his music and sound installations, having been a founding member of The Flying Lizards, whose song 'Money' was an international hit in 1979. He continues to perform, and his visual and aural works are linked by a conceptual investigation into the legibility of art practice.

ABOVE · Carey Young
Terminal Velocity, 2010
Vinyl on wall with spotlight
8.3 × 141.6 cm (3¼ × 55¾ in.)

OPPOSITE · David Cunningham
Alphabet, 2007 · Giclée print on
archival matt A4 paper
29.7 × 21 cm (11¾ × 8¼ in.)

umbqhlgoisjvfxwdtanpecrzyk

At her exhibition 'For Forgetting' at the New Museum in New York in 2014, the French artist Laure Prouvost included a series of films and the objects seen in them. She refers to the stand-alone objects as 'reliques'. *Reliques This is the Shoe* (2013) features the text 'This is the shoe found being carried by hundreds of butterflies from Italy to central London on the day of Saint Buitono'. *At Night This Water Turns Black* (above) references a key work of conceptual art, *An Oak Tree* (1973) by Michael Craig-Martin. His work consists of a glass of water on a glass shelf with a text stating that the viewer is actually looking at an oak tree. Prouvost's work suggests another conceptual pathway through the dark, for, without a light source, all images are black to our eyes.

ABOVE · Laure Prouvost
At Night This Water Turns Black, 2014
Oil, collage and varnish on wooden board, and glass of water
26.5 × 31 × 22 cm (10⅜ × 12¼ × 8⅝ in.)

ABOVE · Rosana Ricalde
Fio de Ariadne (Ariadne's String), 2012
Ball of string made with excerpts from
the book *The Thousand and One Nights*
Diameter 60 cm (23⅝ in.)

Rosana Ricalde's *Fio de Ariadne* (Ariadne's String, 2012) is made up of sentences cut from a Spanish translation of *The Thousand and One Nights* (or *Arabian Nights*). Ricalde's work conflates two stories of female endangerment. The Arabian folktales relate the story of a Persian king who sleeps with a virgin each night, only to have her killed the next morning lest she dishonour him. Scheherazade outwits the king by telling him tales that continue over consecutive nights, thus saving her life. In Greek mythology, Ariadne is the daughter of the king of Crete. She falls in love with the Athenian hero Theseus and, by giving him a ball of thread, helps him to escape the Labyrinth, the home of the Minotaur, after he kills the monster. Ariadne elopes with Theseus, but he abandons her and, in some versions of the myth, she takes her own life. Ricalde's ball of string is a sphere of words winding across one another, forming a feminist Euclidean solid.

LEFT · Ceal Floyer
Monochrome Till Receipt (White), 1999
Ink on paper · 24 × 6 cm (9½ × 2⅜ in.)

Ceal Floyer is a British artist whose conceptual works take many forms, ranging from photography to performance. For *Monochrome Till Receipt (White)* (left), Floyer went to a local supermarket in London and bought a series of products that are all white in colour – for example, flour, milk, sea salt and mozzarella cheese. The till receipt not only documents Floyer's performative act, but also serves as a physical representation. Floyer's *Welcome* (2011) is a readymade floor mat that is always presented inside a venue. In 2016–17 it formed part of her solo exhibition at the Aspen Art Museum in Colorado, welcoming the viewer out of the establishment, rather than offering the usual polite entreaty to come inside.

The Mexican artist Jorge Méndez Blake looks for the poetry of language in both architecture and works of the global literary canon. In a series of monochrome paintings he conflates text and image into a new type of visual poetry. *All of Dickinson's Hyphens (Poems 351–711)* (opposite) is just that: a re-creation of all the hyphens found in the poetry of Emily Dickinson. The 19th-century poet often used hyphens or dashes to punctuate her verse, sometimes to link sections of poetry, other times to indicate a pause. There are six paintings in Méndez Blake's series, each relating to a volume of Dickinson's oeuvre.

OPPOSITE · Jorge Méndez Blake
All of Dickinson's Hyphens (Poems 351–711), 2016
Acrylic on linen
320 × 240 × 4.8 cm (126 × 94½ × 1⅞ in.)

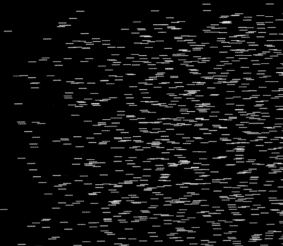
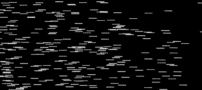

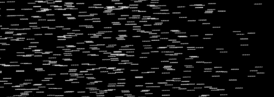
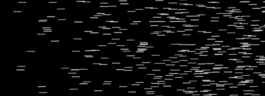

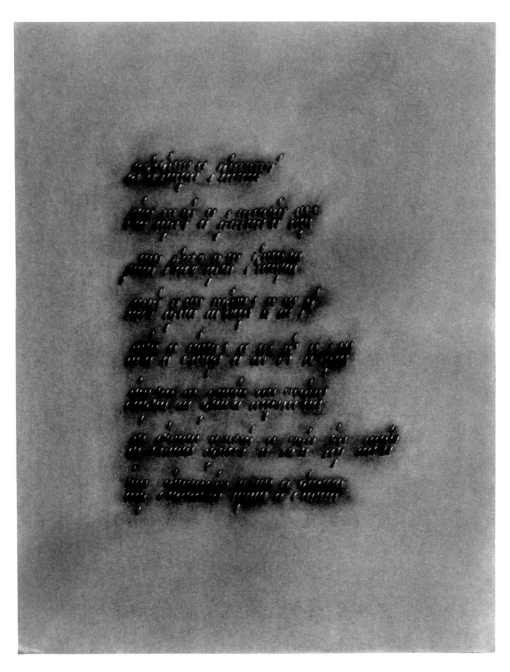

The Swedish artist Anne Thulin takes texts and turns them into shapes that recall their origin but are able to be read in outline form only. She has made a series of works based on poems by Katarina Frostenson, one of Sweden's most respected writers. Thulin says her works are 'a homage to the powerful physical expression in [Frostenson's] poems...how the words follow after one another, and attach themselves to the page to create a visual language'. Pieces such as *Ord ur Orden mot* (On the Poem 'Orden Mot', left), which resembles braille, manage to be evocative and mysterious, their original meaning known to the artist alone.

The overlooked elements of language – the punctuation marks that make text legible – interest the British artist Alex Dipple. For *A Continuous Line of Dashes and Hyphens* (opposite, left), she cut thousands of these marks out of newspapers and applied them in a line at eye height on the walls of the iO Gallery in Brighton, East Sussex (curator: Tom Trevatt). Above and below the dashes are cut-out spaces found around the punctuation, creating an imaginary textual landscape. The 'Dots and Full Stops' series (opposite, right) are framed works and installations comprising thousands of these punctuation marks, again cut carefully from newspapers. Dipple's pieces are as much performative as they are visual, and while they can no longer be read as text, the missing words are ever-present.

LEFT · Anne Thulin
Ord ur Orden mot (On the Poem 'Orden mot' by Katarina Frostenson), 2013
Pigment and staples on paper
35 × 28 cm (13¾ × 11 in.)

OPPOSITE, LEFT · Alex Dipple
A Continuous Line of Dashes and Hyphens
(installation view at top, details below), 2006 · Newspaper cuttings on wall, iO Gallery, Brighton
Dimensions variable

OPPOSITE, RIGHT · Alex Dipple
Dots and Full Stops 1 (details), 2007
Newsprint on board
40 × 40 cm (15¾ × 15¾ in.)

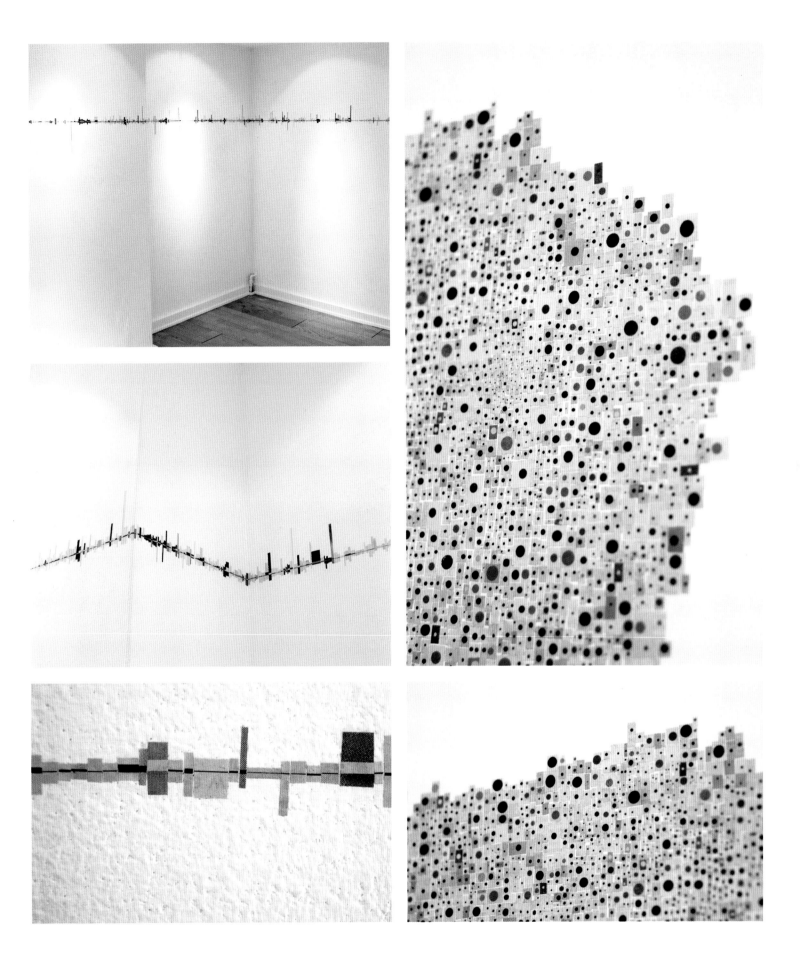

The pink sky was veined in lightning.
**My mouth was a pink channel that
ran the whole length of the mass.**
Across the park ran a path to the
wood gate, a fine ribbon of pink.
**She stood in the little front garden,
looking at the dewy flowers, the grey
bed of pinks in bud already.**
Up close, the roses are silver pink.
**And this tiny scene itself contains
another superimposition: the sky
behind the trees has been replaced
by an abstracted close-up: a blurry
mass of pink and green slammed up
behind this almost Biblical
landscape. Pull out a handful of
these supposed weeds and there are
sages and irises, pinks and lavenders
under the docks and ragwort.**
Her confident bearing, her supple
waist, her pink flared nostrils, her
large eyes faintly ringed with blue, all
pointed to one of those passionate
natures which give out a bouquet of
sensuality, just as flasks from the
Orient, however tightly sealed they
might be, allow the fragrance of the
fluids they contain to escape.
**Smoke streams out of Rosa's pink
nose. Venetian pink.**
In her pink fleshings, her breastbone
stuck out like the prow of a ship; the
Iron Maiden cantilevered her bosom
whilst paring down her waist to
almost nothing, so she looked as if
she might snap in two at any careless
movement. **I was surprised she saw
that tiny scrap of pink after months
and years of hardly recognizing
anything and picked it up for her.
True it was pink; it was gilt; and it
was from the King's table; but it was
tallow, and she gnawed it. Across the
crucifix, and half concealing it, lay a
small sprig of box, hanging from a
pink ribbon and fastened to one arm
of the cross.** And below, a procession
of chocolate figures, cats, dogs,
rabbits, some with raisin eyes, pink
marzipan ears, tails made of
liquorice whips with sugar flowers
between their teeth.....And mice. It

emerged, rowing its pink hands, and waving its blind gimlet of a face, with the tiny pink nose-tip uplifted. Its foot wore a down-at-heel pink velvet slipper trimmed with grubby swansdown.

The great chestnut trees, whose branches swept the ground, were red and half stripped already of their leaves; some of the bushes glowed through the rain with a crimson fire; beside them the grass took on a more vivid green; a few autumn crocuses showed on the garden lawns, and lower down, in the little valley, a field was pink with them - one could see it from the quarry, where, when the rain stopped, I used to go out and sit sometimes, on the same stone where I had sat with Casimir the first day - where perhaps Mademoiselle de Saint-Auréol herself had once sat and dreamed......and I imagined myself sitting beside her.

He fastened fluffy young oak-sprays round her head, and honeysuckle

withes round her breasts, sticking in tufts of bluebells and campion: and in her navel he poised a pink campion flower, and in her maidenhair were forget-me-nots and wood-ruff. Above his head there's a pink and white plaster angel, some photos of famous sportsmen and two or three pin-ups. Before we left, I found some remnants of a silk scarf, faded pink, which I placed in the centre.

A single page of typescript, photocopied onto pink paper then folded into two.

The chair waited at the top of the pink path. Yellow clouds stretch out across a blue-pink mackerel sky.

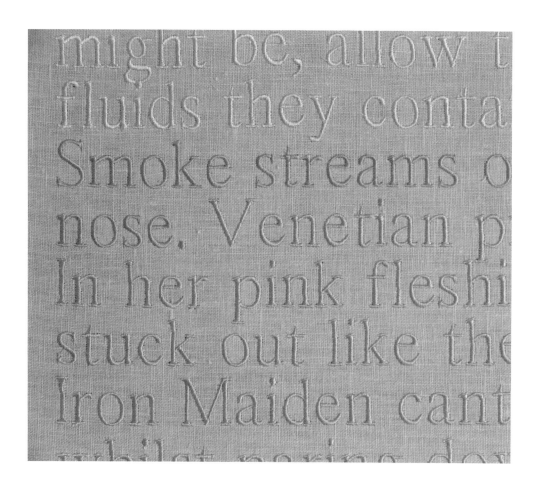

The Pink Investigator is the pseudonym of the British artist Lisa Z. Morgan, and the colour pink is central to most of her works. For *Be the Pink Panther and Your Loves Will be Like the Wasp and the Orchid, the Cat and the Baboon* (pp. 164–65 and above), she took twenty-five lines from a variety of books in which the word 'pink' appears, and merged them to create a new story. The text was then digitally embroidered on to panels in shades of pink. The lines came from sources as diverse as D. H. Lawrence's *Lady Chatterley's Lover* (1928), Gilles Deleuze and Félix Guattari's *A Thousand Plateaus: Capitalism and Schizophrenia* (1980) and Chris Kraus's *I Love Dick* (1997). Through her exploration of pink (in which she sees red as female and white as male), Morgan addresses the emotional and intellectual nature of desire.

The British artist Gavin Turk has made a variety of conceptual projects in which he inhabits the work of other artists. These works are usually fabricated by specialists, whether in wax, bronze or paint. He has authored works in the guise of Andy Warhol, Joseph Beuys and Elvis Presley, and also made pieces based on the *Arazzi* embroideries that Alighiero Boetti had sewn in Afghanistan (see pp. 13 and 18). Boetti commissioned works featuring his name spelled in bright colours. Turk has followed suit in *Day & Night* (opposite), in which his first name is spelled in one direction and his surname in the other. This is one of a series of embroideries featuring different permutations of the artist's name. Turk had the works sewn by prisoners through a rehabilitation programme called Fine Cell Work.

PAGES 164–65 AND ABOVE · Lisa Z. Morgan
Be the Pink Panther and Your Loves Will be Like the Wasp and the Orchid, the Cat and the Baboon (detail above), 2016
4 panels of embroidery on linen
Each 91.4 × 61 cm (36 × 24 in.),
91.4 × 243.8 cm (36 × 96 in.) overall

OPPOSITE · Gavin Turk
Day & Night, 2012 · Embroidery on cloth
13.5 × 13.5 × 2.3 cm (5¼ × 5¼ × ⅞ in.)

that JoeOvelman,
he gonna be
making them
gay yellow postits
for the rest
of his carreer.

He said he'd
be here in five
minutes. It's been
a half hour.
I'm taking this
wig off.

The American artist Joe Ovelman uses a queer sensibility to disrupt everyday possibilities of communication. He is best known for his 'Post-It Notes' series of works (above), which consist of either yellow or blue squares on to which he handwrites cryptic or satirical texts. The 'When I Grow Up' series of Post-Its (2005) includes *When I grow up I want to be a doctor so the other boys won't laugh when I want to touch their balls*. A series created for the NADA Art Fair in Miami in 2006 includes *He only came to my studio cuz I let him suck my dick* and *She sleeps with all her artists*. His most contentious series, 'For Whites Only' (2007), features notes that most people would find offensive – but that is the point. Ovelman asks why issues of race and desire are still so difficult for many Americans to face.

For her series of posters 'A Spectacle and Nothing Strange', begun in 2011, the American artist Eve Fowler used texts from Gertrude Stein's book of verse *Tender Buttons* (1914). Stein also authored *The Autobiography of Alice B. Toklas* (1933), the story of Toklas's life seen through the eyes of her long-term female lover. Stein advised that her texts should be read aloud, as the sounds of the words affect their comprehension, and their meanings change the faster or slower they are read. Fowler made twenty-one posters for the series and hung them around Los Angeles. *Rub Her Coke* (opposite) is one of Stein's more erotically charged lines. Fowler says: 'I see this language as queer – in both senses of the word – but I think it is open-ended and could be interpreted in various ways.' Fowler is interested in seeing art in non-institutional settings and addressing the public with as little mediation as possible.

ABOVE, LEFT · Joe Ovelman
that Joe Ovelman, he gonna be making them gay yellow post its for the rest of his carreer, from the series 'Post-It Notes', 2004
Sharpie on paper · 7.6 × 7.6 cm (3 × 3 in.)

ABOVE, RIGHT · Joe Ovelman
He said he'd be here in five minutes. It's been a half hour. I'm taking this wig off, from the series 'Post-It Notes', 2004
Sharpie on paper · 7.6 × 7.6 cm (3 × 3 in.)

OPPOSITE · Eve Fowler
Rub Her Coke, 2012
Letterpress silkscreen poster
71.1 × 55.9 cm (28 × 22 in.)
Edition of 100

RUB

HER

COKE

Kendell Geers's *The Treason of Images (WTC2)* (above) is a contemporary take on Magritte's *The Treachery of Images* (see p. 11), asking us to assess what is an image. Images are not the things depicted (a pipe or the World Trade Center), but a sign or signifier of meaning, often contested. Some people believe the terrorist attacks of 9/11 were not what they seemed, but rather a CIA conspiracy. Geers explains: 'What made the reactions to 11 September so interesting for me was that, for the first time in New York, people were suddenly confronted with the reality of death. The image of the collapsing towers became the contemporary version of the skull in 17th-century painting, a memento mori.'

Christian Marclay's *Rriippp* (opposite) is an example of onomatopoeia (the word depicted sounds like the noise associated with it), and is a graphic exploration of how image and sound function. It is reminiscent of the artist's *Surround Sounds* installation (pp. 144–46), in which similar words were animated and projected on the gallery walls. *Rriippp* looks as if it has been ripped from a comic book, so that its visual presence is matched by an aural one that is constructed by the viewer when they read the text. The print has itself been ripped, further compounding expectations about the sound. Marclay asks: can we hear the sound of the action?

ABOVE · Kendell Geers
The Treason of Images (WTC2), 2001
Inkjet on canvas
96 × 116 cm (37¾ × 45⅝ in.)

OPPOSITE · Christian Marclay
Rriippp, 2015
4-colour print on Hahnemühle Etching White paper
Original paper size: 78 × 53.5 cm (30¾ × 21 in.); height dimension of each edition is variable, as each is hand-torn by the artist
Varied edition; edition of 60 and 20 artist's prints

Nicky Hirst's *Lorem Ipsum* (above) presents the jumbled Latin that is often employed in the publishing industry as dummy or filler text, in order to give the impression of the finished book or magazine. Hirst's letters were designed with extravagantly intertwined foliage, printed and cut out of paper, and then pinned, overlapping, on to the gallery wall, as if they were exotic butterflies. The work requires the viewer to read the nearly illegible words as an art object, rather than as a decipherable text. In keeping meaning at bay, Hirst generates a desire to fulfil the function of reading – that is, to understand.

In collaboration with the National Institute of Legal Medicine and Forensic Sciences in Coimbra, the Portuguese photographer Edgar Martins made a series of images under the title 'Siloquies and Soliloquies on Death, Life and Other Interludes'. The images relate to death and how it may be possible to depict it. A number of photographs show a suicide note, seen from the side against a dark ground (opposite). The letters are barely visible in the images, as if they are the ghosts of those who took their own lives. The viewer has no idea what each letter says; even if they were legible, such letters can never fully explain why a person chose to end their life.

ABOVE · Nicky Hirst
Lorem Ipsum (detail at right), 2017
Printed paper, pinned to wall of
Helsinki Contemporary
Dimensions variable

OPPOSITE · Edgar Martins
Letter of Departure, from the series
'Siloquies and Soliloquies on Death,
Life and Other Interludes', 2016
C-type print · 50 × 40 cm (19¾ × 15¾ in.)

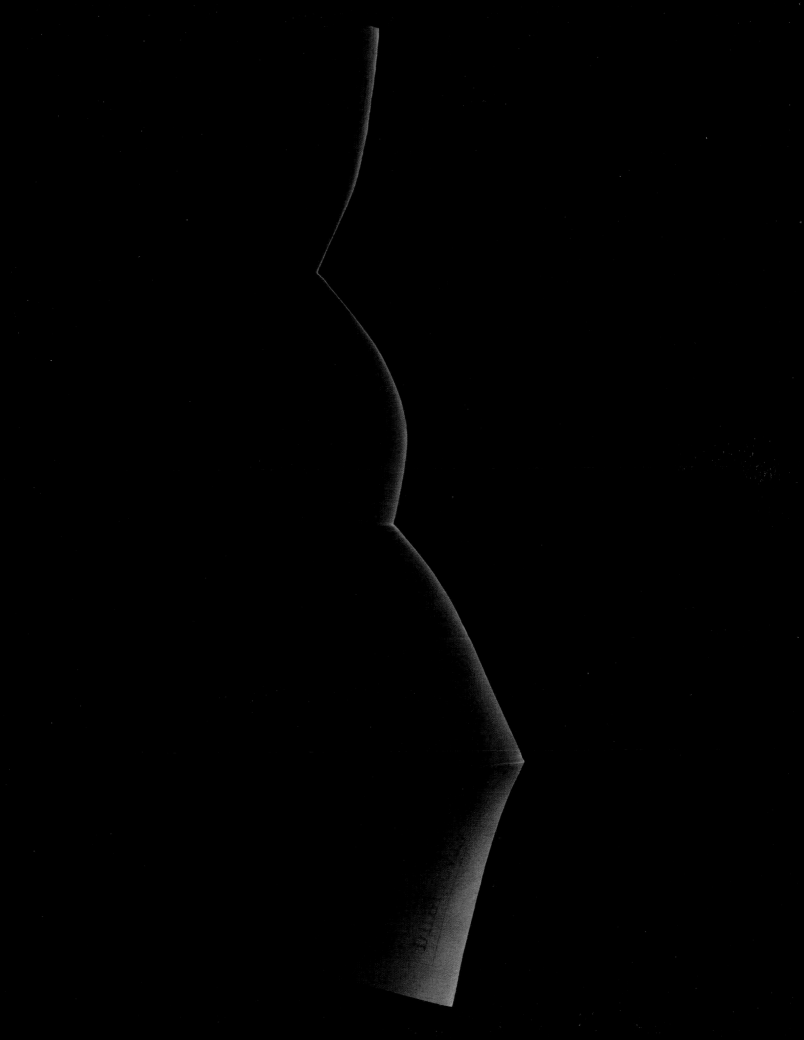

In addition to many neon works (see pp. 112–13), the Parisian collective artist known as Claire Fontaine has created numerous performance pieces involving matches and fire. *They Hate Us for Our Freedom* (left), shown in 2013 at 'Le Pont' exhibition at the Musée d'Art Contemporain in Marseilles, consisted of thousands of matches inserted into the gallery wall and then lit. The wording is based on a speech given by President George W. Bush after the 9/11 terrorist attacks. The huge combustion, resultant smoke and scorched walls altered the text, its form changing radically from almost minimalist accuracy to chaotic destruction. The work hints at the violent power of hate and the way in which it can spread as easily as wildfire.

For *Louvre Fire Poem* (opposite), Robert Montgomery was inspired by an episode from French history. In 1891 the artist Gustave Courbet caused outrage in some quarters by calling for the removal from the Place Vendôme in Paris of a column that had been erected to commemorate Napoleon's victory at Austerlitz in 1805. A few months later, Parisians revolted and destroyed the column. After the uprising, Courbet was sent to prison, even though he had played no part in the column's destruction, and was sent a huge bill for its replacement (which he never paid). Montgomery created a poem of wooden letters attached to a frame: 'WE WILL STILL ERASE THE WAR MONUMENTS EVEN IF WE ONLY HAVE PENCILS OF STICKS DIPPED IN RAINWATER. IMMEDIATELY EXONERATE GUSTAVE COURBET, REVENGE PROSECUTE PATRICE DE MACMAHON AND DESTROY THE VENDOME COLUMN.' The poem was set alight by Montgomery in Paris, its charred remains echoing the destruction of the column.

LEFT · Claire Fontaine
They Hate Us for Our Freedom, 2008
Matchsticks in plaster wall, internal corridor and digital video for projection or monitor · Dimensions variable

OPPOSITE · Robert Montgomery
Louvre Fire Poem, 2016
Oak, plywood, copper and fire
270 × 520 cm (106¼ × 204¾ in.)

The Romanian artist Mircea Cantor works with a variety of media, but is best known for his wall installations that incorporate dynamite blasting caps. *Sic Transit Gloria Mundi* (left) has been installed in many variations. The Latin title translates as 'So passes worldly glory', a phrase used at papal coronations from 1409 to 1963. It served to remind the new pope of the temporary nature of his power, and here, in the tradition of memento mori, reminds the viewer of their own mortality. Cantor inserts the caps into the wall and then lights each letter, causing the caps to ignite and burn the phrase into existence. The work, like a pupa becoming a butterfly, comes into being through its own extinction.

The French artist Mathieu Tremblin has made a series of works called 'Tag Clouds'. He finds a location, such as rue de Gaillon in Rennes (opposite), where there is pre-existing graffiti; to most viewers, these tags are illegible. He repaints the signatures in the same colour as the original graffiti, but in clearly defined letters. The tags of the street artists become something similar to the virtual tags, or keywords, used to navigate the internet. Tremblin explains: 'It shows the analogy between the physical tag and the virtual tag, both in form (tagged wall compositions look the same as tag clouds), and in substance (like keywords, which are markers of net surfing, graffiti is the marker of urban drifting).' He leaves the remade graffiti in place, but over time the street reclaims his intervention, as others re-tag the site.

LEFT · Mircea Cantor
Sic Transit Gloria Mundi (performance shown at top), 2012
Blasting caps and tape on wall,
FIAC 2012, Grand Palais, Paris
Approx. 200 × 300 cm (78¾ × 118⅛ in.)

OPPOSITE · Mathieu Tremblin
Tag Clouds 'Rue de Gaillon', 2010
Tags, font, stencils and spray paint on wall · 200 × 500 cm (78¾ × 196⅞ in.)

William Mackrell, a British artist, uses performance to make objects that involve his body activating a situation. In *Going to the Gallery* (left), Mackrell started out from his studio in Hackney Wick, east London, and travelled to the APT Gallery in the south-east of the city. He walked and took a train, all the while writing the phrase 'Going to the gallery' over and over on a white till receipt roll. The unravelling mass of paper dragged behind him, becoming dirty and gaining bodily form as it passed along the pavement and on to the train. On arriving at the gallery, Mackrell deposited the paper on the floor as the finished work. Passersby looked on throughout the duration of the written public performance, their expressions largely unchanged. However, one curious man at New Cross station asked the artist why he was doing this and followed him for a short time, offering his help as they left the station.

The American artist Tim Youd is in the middle of a ten-year project to retype 100 novels, each on the same make or model of typewriter used for the original, and in a location that held significance for the writer. Youd types each novel on a single sheet of paper, with a backing sheet. As the top sheet is repeatedly pulled through the typewriter, the text becomes illegible – but viewable as an artwork. When Youd finishes typing the novel, the two sheets are mounted and framed side by side. Completed diptychs include Philip K. Dick's *Flow My Tears, the Policeman Said*, 249 pages typed on an Olympia SG-3 at the CSUF Grand Central Art Center, Santa Ana, California (2013), and Virginia Woolf's *Orlando*, 333 pages typed on an Underwood Portable at Monk's House, Rodmell, East Sussex (2015). In 2017, to mark the fiftieth anniversary of the death of the playwright Joe Orton, Youd typed the whole of Orton's oeuvre for the exhibition 'What the Artist Saw' at MOCA London. Youd did the majority of his typing at the Queen's Theatre on Shaftesbury Avenue, where Orton's play *What the Butler Saw* had its world premiere in 1969.

OPPOSITE, TOP AND CENTRE · William Mackrell · *Going to the Gallery*, 2013 C-type prints · Each 21 × 30 cm (8¼ × 11¾ in.)

OPPOSITE, BOTTOM · William Mackrell *Going to the Gallery*, 2013 Performance with ink on till roll receipt, installation view at APT Gallery, London · Dimensions variable

RIGHT · Tim Youd · The artist retyping *Joe Orton's Complete Plays* at the Queen's Theatre, London, 2017

BELOW · Tim Youd · *Joe Orton's Complete Plays*, 449 pages typed on an Adler Tippa and an Adler Universal, Islington Public Library, Queen's Theatre and MOCA London, January–February 2017 Typewriter ribbon ink and acid-free masking tape on paper · 45.7 × 63.5 cm (18 × 25 in.), framed diptych

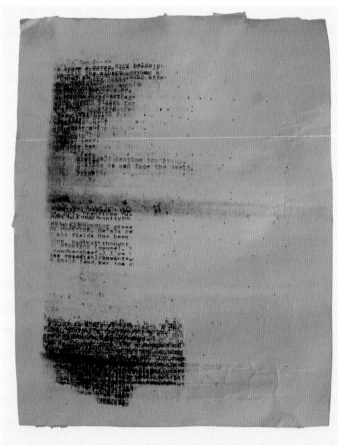

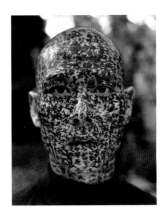 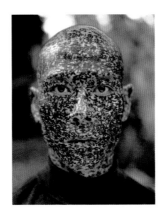 

Zhang Huan's *Family Tree* (left) has become emblematic of the new work that emerged from China as the country moved towards a capitalist economy. The work comprises nine photographs taken over the period of a day as calligraphers continuously wrote Chinese characters across Zhang's face. Zhang made the work after moving to New York, and the characters inked on to his face refer to his homeland, its culture and the names of people he knew. Many derive from physiognomy, the ancient Chinese art of judging personality on the basis of facial characteristics. Yet, rather than being illuminated, Zhang's character becomes obscured as more and more inkings are added. In a related work, *Shanghai Family Tree* (2001), the artist stands next to a woman and another man as their faces are gradually blackened, making it difficult to distinguish one from another. Zhang has commented: 'The body is the only direct way through which I come to know society and society comes to know me. The body is proof of identity. The body is language.'

Niels Meulman's most publicly recognized calligraffiti work might be *The Greatest Words* (opposite), a tribute to Muhammad Ali, which was used as the basis for an advertising campaign by Louis Vuitton in 2012. In a series of videos, Meulman writes a single word, including 'LIFE', 'WORD' and 'DREAM', on the canvas floor of a boxing ring, using a large broom dipped in black paint, while the hip-hop artist Yasiin Bey (formerly known as Mos Def) gives a spoken-word performance featuring some of Ali's poems and best-known quotes.

LEFT · Zhang Huan
Family Tree, 2000
9 colour photographs
Each 132 × 106 cm (52 × 41¾ in.)

OPPOSITE · Niels Shoe Meulman
The Greatest Words, tribute to
Muhammad Ali, Louis Vuitton
campaign, Toronto, Canada, 2012
Acrylic on canvas
Approx. 600 × 600 cm
(236¼ × 236¼ in.)

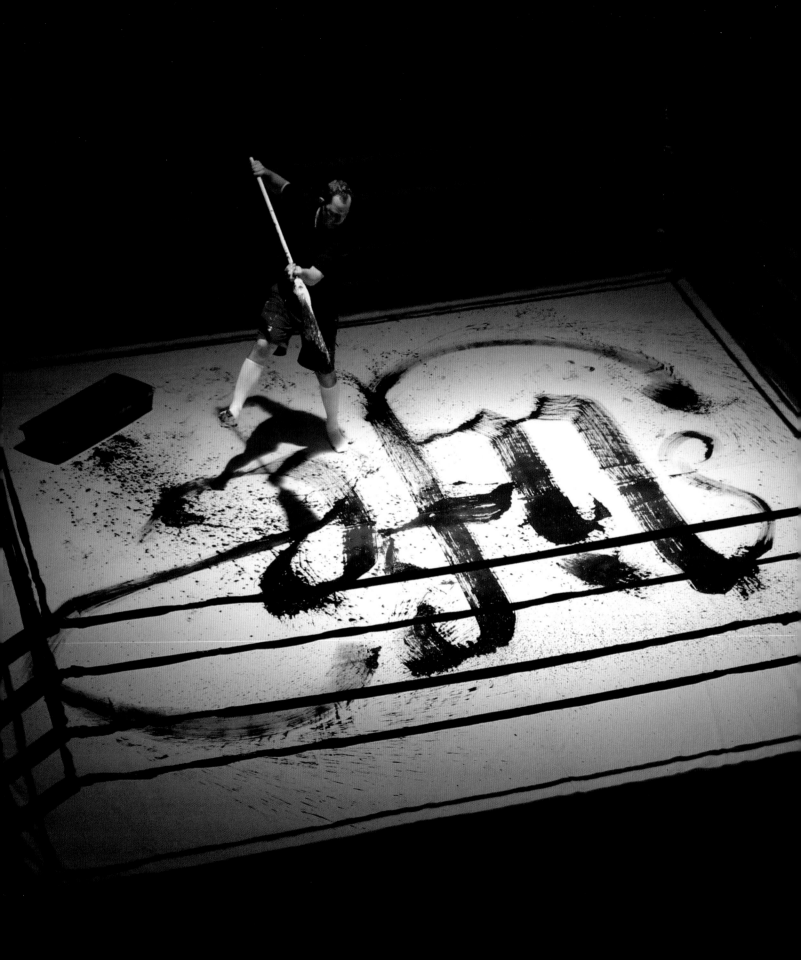

The Japanese artist Shinichi Maruyama has said: 'Once your brush touches paper, you must finish the character, you have one chance. It can never be repeated or duplicated. You must commit your full attention and being to each stroke.' In his 'Kusho' (meaning 'writing in the sky') photographs, he captures the completion – what he calls the 'decisive moment' – of each stroke. He has constructed a special brush that allows him to paint directly into the air. *Kusho #1* (2007) is a near-perfect circle, the symbol for *ensō*, which is used in Zen Buddhism to describe complete enlightenment; it represents the whole of the universe, as well as its opposite, the void. Calligraphers aim to create the perfect circle in one elegant stroke, which befits the minimalism that characterizes much of Japanese design. The 16th-century Italian writer Giorgio Vasari relates how Giotto was asked by Pope Boniface VIII to present a drawing showing his competence; he drew a perfect circle in a single stroke and thereby won a commission to create works for St Peter's Basilica in Rome.

OPPOSITE · Shinichi Maruyama
Kusho #1, 2007
Archival pigment print
137.2 × 111.8 cm (54 × 44 in.)
Edition of 10 and 3 artist's proofs

SOCIAL COMMENT

One might wonder if the words painted on protest signs or sprayed on to walls have ever had more than minimal effect. John Lennon and Yoko Ono might have claimed 'WAR IS OVER! IF YOU WANT IT' on billboards and posters in 1969 in protest against American involvement in the Vietnam War, but it did not bring an end to the conflict. From our perhaps more jaded perspective today, we see that most agitprop or protest pieces were often not particularly good art or effective in bringing about the changes that the artists desired. Lennon and Ono's *Bed-In for Peace* performance was a success as a work of art, but effected no reduction in global bloodshed.

How do contemporary artists comment on society, and how do they do so without being seen as naive, or worse, marginal? These are the core questions that this chapter seeks to address by presenting the work of artists who choose to make a social stand with their art. The works fall loosely into four main categories: work that is critical of the art world itself; work that deals with contemporary politics; work based on identity issues; and artworks that concern the world of work.

Bill Burns sends up planes with banners pleading for art-world dignitaries, such as senior curators and museum directors, to look down kindly on lowly artists, while Bob and Roberta Smith uses his work to oppose the closure of art schools. There is, of course, some overlap between the categories mentioned above, and the artists' collective Mil M2 creates imaginative projects that examine the politics of voting and education. Jeremy Deller is well known for his commitment to social change through his many works that consider where power is held within contemporary society. Massa Lemu, born in Malawi, makes work that explores his identity not only as an artist but also as a man of colour in the United States. Some artists, such as Betty Tompkins and Zachari Logan, look at their identity on the basis of their sexuality, and Paul Coombs's work deals with both queerness and the hatred that ISIS shows towards homosexuals.

In all of these works, text is at the heart of the matter, and the words that artists use need to be intelligent and indicate self-awareness. Artists must signal to the viewer that they are conscious that their comments come from a position of privilege (as artists), even if they are marginalized in other ways (for example, in terms of race, gender or citizenship). At the same time, the works have to be strong enough as art and sufficiently powerful in their message to compete with news media and advertising. It is a tough order, but I think the artists featured here rise well to the challenge.

Nari Ward uses a variety of found materials from his New York neighbourhood in his work to address issues of race, class and identity. In *We the People* (pp. 186–87), hundreds of multicoloured shoelaces spell out the opening words of the US Constitution in the style of the original calligraphy. The Constitution promised equality for all citizens, yet allowed slavery to continue. Ward's work functions within a background of police violence and the murder of young African-Americans (many wearing laced trainers). His intention is that the piece encourages community dialogue; he has said that it is 'not meant to be entertainment'. It has been installed several times, including at the New-York Historical Society in 2017, when visitors were invited to donate their laces to the work.

In 2015 the British artist Paul Coombs caused a media sensation when his *Flag of Dildosis* (right) was unveiled during the annual LGBTQ+ Pride in London march. The black-and-white banner was a deliberate lampooning of the ISIS flag. ISIS regularly throw gay men from buildings or stone them to death. Claiming an 'exclusive', CNN reported that an ISIS banner was paraded on the streets of London, failing to notice that the flag displayed not Arabic text but sex toys. Coombs said: 'It was important that I didn't try to replicate the writing on the flag, because the words and their subject – Islam – are not the target...I showed as little respect to this flag as ISIS shows to the religion and people they claim to represent...The flag was so clearly made of dildos that I never thought it could be mistaken for an actual ISIS flag.' The artist received death threats, and the police were so concerned for his safety that his phone was linked to a rapid-response team. Coombs has made different versions of the flag, which have been exhibited at ECKO projects, 'Silent Movies' at Cavendish Square Car Park, London, and Helsinki Contemporary.

The American artist Michelle Angela Ortiz engages with the people whose hardships she highlights, saying: 'I strive to counteract mainstream narratives that criminalize immigrants and devalue the contributions of communities of color...' In Philadelphia she made two installations for her 'Familias Separadas' (Separated Families) project of 2015. For *We Are Human Beings* (right), Ortiz and thirty members of the local community (mostly undocumented families) stencilled a text in chalk at the exit point of the Immigrations Customs Enforcement building, where people are taken during the deportation process. The words were those of Ana, an undocumented mother who was deported to Guatemala but subsequently had the deportation overruled. In LOVE Park (home of Robert Indiana's *LOVE* sculpture), Ortiz installed *Te Amo* (I Love You; right, below). The necklace depicted is similar to one worn by a Honduran woman to remind her of her eldest daughter, whom she was forced to leave behind. The woman was apprehended in Texas, but is fighting her deportation in Philadelphia.

PAGES 186–87 · Nari Ward
We the People, 2011
Shoelaces on wall, installed here at the Institute of Contemporary Art, Boston, 2017 · In collaboration with the Fabric Workshop and Museum, Philadelphia. Speed Art Museum, Louisville, Kentucky, Gift of the Speed Contemporary, 2016.1 Certificate of Authenticity included 243.8 × 823 cm (96 × 324 in.)

OPPOSITE · Paul Coombs
Flag of Dildosis, 2015
Hand-stitched cotton on cotton
150 × 90 cm (59 × 35⅜ in.)

RIGHT, ABOVE · Michelle Angela Ortiz
We Are Human Beings, from the project 'Familias Separadas' (Separated Families), 2015 · Chalk stencil on asphalt
6.1 × 27.4 m (20 × 90 ft)

RIGHT · Michelle Angela Ortiz
Te Amo (I Love You), from the project 'Familias Separadas' (Separated Families), 2015 · Outdoor vinyl on slate
7.6 × 12.2 m (25 × 40 ft)

In 2013–14 Shimon Attie made a series of site-specific works across Israel and Palestine called 'Facts on the Ground', which considered both the historic and the present situation. The installations consisted largely of light boxes with pertinent text, inserted into the landscape to be photographed; one, next to the concrete wall separating the two states, read 'A PROBLEM IN LOGIC'. Another intervention took the form of mirrored letters attached to the wall of a ruined mosque (above). Attie's concern was that the works be ambiguous and able to resist political interpretation; his primary aim was that they offer 'opportunities for reflection'.

ABOVE · Shimon Attie
Do unto others before, Laser-cut mirrored letters, Ruins of former Mosque attacked and damaged by rioting Israelis during second Palestinian Intifada, Tel Aviv, 2014
On-location laser-cut mirrored letters and digital C-type print
Mirrored letters: 1:1 architectural scale; print: 101.6 × 152.4 cm (40 × 60 in.)

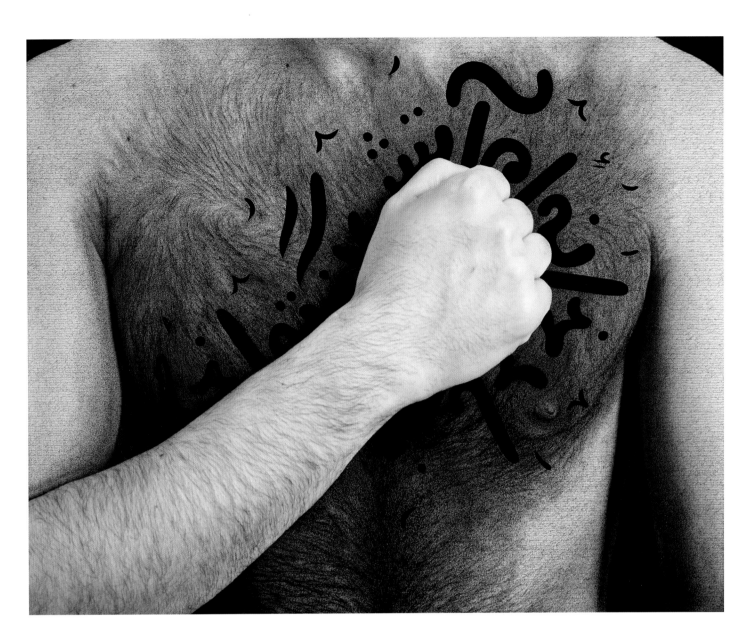

ABOVE · Shirin Neshat
My House is on Fire, from the series
'The Book of Kings', 2012
Ink on LE silver gelatin print
119.7 × 152.4 cm (47⅛ × 60 in.)

Shirin Neshat was raised in Tehran within a Muslim family who championed Western ideas of freedom and feminism. In the mid-1970s she moved to the United States to study, making a trip back to Iran only in 1990. The country Neshat found was at odds with her memory; it was under strict religious control, and gradually she began to make the work for which she is now renowned. Her black-and-white images of people feature handwritten calligraphic texts that often question strict, if not fundamental, interpretations of Islam. Other works address the ways in which men and women relate, regardless of their cultural or religious backgrounds.

The Cuban artist Tania Bruguera is involved in making highly political pieces that question where power is held and how it is wielded. She aims to turn 'viewers' into 'citizens'. Her work often touches on collective memory, as in the case of *Surplus Value/Plusvalía* (above), which was inspired by the theft of the sign *ARBEIT MACHT FREI* (Work sets you free) from the entrance to the Auschwitz concentration camp in Poland. Jewish people were worked or put to death at the camp. Bruguera positions her work within the context of the modern art market: the Spanish word *plusvalía* can be translated as 'capital gain' or 'surplus value', and the artist queries the value of labour in the highly seductive contemporary art world. The piece included an 'activated phase', during which an undocumented immigrant came into the space and welded or sandpapered the sign. It was not clear if he was there to repair or destroy the object, which in itself has value owing entirely to Bruguera's participation in the same market system that she critiques.

For his exhibition 'Minimalist Works from the Holocaust Museum' at Dundee Contemporary Arts in 2010–11, Jonathan Horowitz made a body of work critiquing the minimalist aesthetics of the art in the United States Holocaust Memorial Museum in Washington, DC. Horowitz explained: 'In the face of one of the worst things that's ever happened, art is represented as having nothing to say.' *Pink Curve* (2010) was a remake of an Ellsworth Kelly wall sculpture, but shaded pink in reference to the triangular badge that gay people were forced to wear by the Nazis. *Untitled (Arbeit Macht Frei)* (opposite) is a replica of the sign above the entrance gates at Auschwitz just as it was found, cut into three pieces, after its theft by neo-Nazis in 2009. Horowitz (and Bruguera) attempt to convey the immense tragedy of the Holocaust and offer an insight into how easily it happened and may do so again. Sadly, in 2017 news media confirmed reports of concentration camps for gay men in Chechnya.

ABOVE · Tania Bruguera
Surplus Value/Plusvalía, 2010
Activated Object; reproduction of a stolen object at a 1:1 scale, metal, tools and worker
80 × 520 × 5.1 cm (31½ × 204¾ × 2 in.)
Edition of 3 and 1 artist's print

OPPOSITE · Jonathan Horowitz
Untitled (Arbeit Macht Frei), 2010
Oil paint on steel
ARBEIT: 200 × 38.5 × 24 cm (78¾ × 15⅛ × 9½ in.),
MACHT: 15 × 160 × 52 cm (5⅞ × 63 × 20½ in.),
FREI: 40.5 × 186.3 × 20 cm (16 × 73⅜ × 7⅞ in.),
200 × 200 × 150 cm (78¾ × 78¾ × 59 in.) overall

Hank Willis Thomas is known for his investigations into what it means to be a black man in America. *I Am a Man* (opposite, bottom) comprises twenty small paintings, each with black-on-white text based on Civil Rights-era protest signs. Each painting offers a variation of the titular phrase, including 'BE A MAN', 'YOU THE MAN' and 'I AM I AM'. They question the visibility of others in what is still predominantly a white society, where, arguably, open racism has become acceptable once more. Other works by Thomas explore the nature of truth and understanding across different cultures and ethnicities. For his installation 'The Truth is I See You' at MetroTech Commons, Brooklyn, in 2015, he created a sculpture that takes the form of a pair of benches in rolled steel shaped like cartoon-style speech bubbles (above). Thomas extended his investigation with twenty-two temporary speech-balloon signs, one for each language spoken in Brooklyn, featuring statements about truth taken from a poem co-written with the artist Ryan Alexiev. An additional touring work, *In Search of the Truth (Truth Booth)* (opposite, top), is an ongoing collaboration with Alexiev, Jim Ricks and William Sylvester, in which visitors are invited to enter a mobile recording booth and complete the statement beginning 'The truth is...'.

ABOVE · Hank Willis Thomas
Ernest and Ruth, 2015
Steel plate and pipe, installed at
MetroTech, Brooklyn, New York
210.8 × 243.8 × 121.9 cm (83 × 96 × 48 in.)

OPPOSITE, TOP · Ryan Alexiev,
Jim Ricks, William Sylvester and
Hank Willis Thomas
In Search of the Truth (Truth Booth), 2013
Vinyl, installed here at Bamiyan,
Afghanistan · 426.7 × 792.5 × 365.8 cm
(168 × 312 × 144 in.)

OPPOSITE, BOTTOM · Hank Willis Thomas
I Am a Man, 2009
Liquitex on 20 canvas panels
Each panel 64.1 × 48.9 × 5.7 cm
(25¼ × 19¼ × 2¼ in.), 141 × 579.1 × 5.7 cm
(55½ × 228 × 2¼ in.) overall

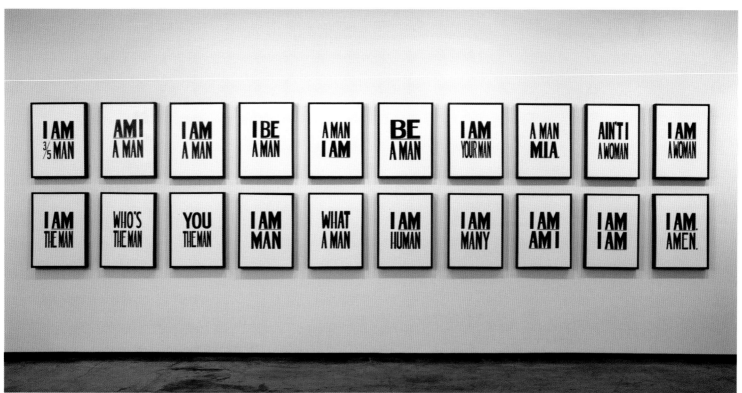

The work of the Chilean collective Mil M2 (One Thousand Square Metres) seeks to provoke debate about the nature of the individual and her or his actions, and how these affect society as a whole. The group frequently makes use of vacant buildings, open plazas and even beaches for its interactions with the public. The *Proyecto Pregunta* (Question Project; above) began in 2013 and has involved Mil M2 approaching many communities to ask often difficult questions in public. The group has created a set of simple tools for the use of participants: white cards bearing a single letter in black type. The cards can be arranged to form any question, and so far these have ranged from 'Why does the University of Chile have no Faculty of Education?' to 'When will we learn to vote?' In one series, Mil M2 invited people to pose questions that they would like to ask their parents. One example, seen above, translates as 'Mother, after using your Visa credit card, are you still a communist?'

The British artist Jeremy Deller has engaged with social or political issues in the majority of his works, including *The Battle of Orgreave* (2001), a re-creation, with more than 1,000 participants, of the violent confrontation in 1984 between striking coal miners and police at the Orgreave coke works in South Yorkshire. *Hello, today you have day off* (opposite), seen at the 56th Venice Biennale in 2015, is a banner displaying a text message sent to a British worker. Under UK law, employers are allowed to contract workers on a zero-hour basis, which means that the worker is on call for the employer when required, but is not guaranteed any work. The unironic text presented the worker's lack of employment that day as an unexpected bonus holiday.

ABOVE · Mil M2
PROYECTO PREGUNTA/ VALPARAÍSO/¿QUÉ LE PREGUNTARÍAS A TU PADRE O A TU MADRE? (Question Project/Valparaíso/ What Would You Ask Your Father or Mother?), 2014 · Digital photograph 3288 × 2544 pixels

OPPOSITE · Jeremy Deller
Hello, today you have day off, 2013 Wording of text message sent to a worker on a zero-hour contract, informing him his labour would not be required that day; fabric banner made by Ed Hall
Banner: 240 × 180 cm (94½ × 70⅞ in.), 240 × 200 × 3 cm (94½ × 78¾ × 1⅛ in.) overall · Edition of 3 and 1 artist's proof

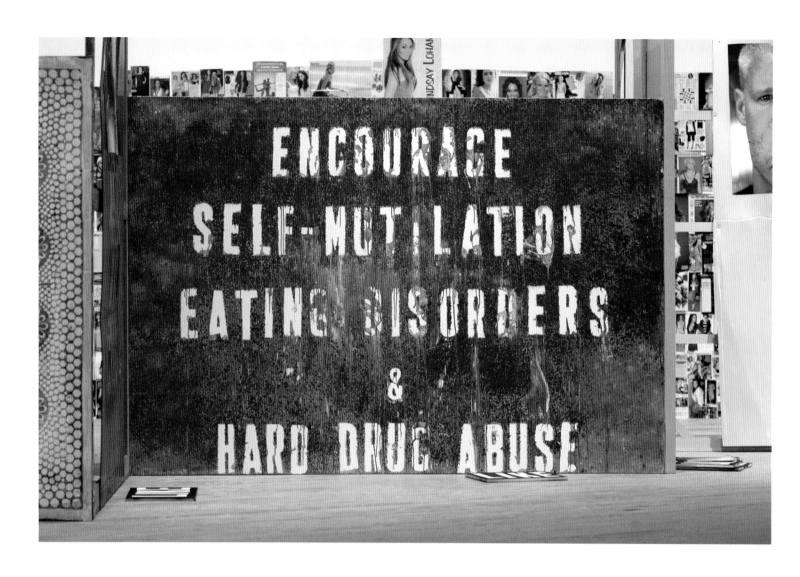

For more than three decades, the American artist Mark Flood has explored the corporate and commercial worlds and their relationship to the visual arts. In 2016 the retrospective 'Mark Flood: Gratest Hits', at the Contemporary Arts Museum Houston, Texas, presented a variety of artworks. The stencilled-word works often go against the American grain, as in the case of *Community Standards* (above), which, in white capital letters against a blood-red background, commands viewers to 'ENCOURAGE SELF-MUTILATION EATING DISORDERS & HARD DRUG ABUSE'. Other paintings advise, 'ASK YOUR DRUG DEALER IF YOUR HEART IS STRONG ENOUGH FOR SEXUAL ACTIVITY', or speak of 'WHORE MUSEUMS', 'GUTLESS COLLECTORS', 'BLIND DEALERS' and 'ALLEGED ARTISTS'. The rough-and-ready aesthetic of the word pieces was in stark contrast to Flood's elegant lace paintings, also on display. The unconventional installation encouraged visitors to place one of 5,000 small black-and-white 'LIKE' paintings in front of works they liked best (opposite). In this real-world version of Facebook, Flood showed how approval is deeply rooted in modern culture.

ABOVE · Mark Flood
Community Standards, 2014
Acrylic on canvas
182.8 × 266.7 cm (72 × 105 in.)

OPPOSITE · Mark Flood
5000 LIKES, 2015–16
Spray paint on canvas
5,000 parts, each 30.5 × 40.6 cm
(12 × 16 in.)

From 2010 to 2012 the Malawian artist Massa Lemu made a series of street performances called 'Passages for the Undocumented' in Houston, Texas. He held up home-made cardboard signs at the side of the road so that they could be read by passing motorists or pedestrians. The signs resemble those that many destitute people present, asking for food, money or work. One read 'A PORTRAIT OF THE ARTIST AS A DUNG BEETLE', and another asked, 'HOW DO YOU DESCRIBE A COLOR TO THE BLIND?' While these particular signs may have signalled to onlookers that they were witnessing performance art, other examples, such as 'IN PURSUIT OF FULFAILMENT' (opposite), were more poetic statements, commenting on immigration and dispossession. In one photograph documenting the series, Lemu gingerly stands at the roadside with a sign saying 'NIHILIST NEEDS TENURE'; he is now an assistant professor at Virginia Commonwealth University. These works are subtle provocations, challenging the assumptions of passers-by who, having seen so many similar signs before, simply drive or walk on, not reading the words on the card or thinking about the person who holds it.

In 2017 the British artist Ralph Dunn participated in a two-person show, 'I Want to Be Your Dog' (with Ryan Riddington), at MOCA London. He presented three works, including *Doormat* (2009/17), which welcomed visitors to the museum. The mat read: 'COME IN / I SUCK N / SWALLOW YOU / YOU GO'. Also exhibited was *Aroma* (above), which featured three columns of names in seven rows. Words such as 'THROB', 'VOLTAGE' and 'RUSH' could together be read as concrete poetry; they are, however, brand names of poppers (amyl nitrate), which many gay men use to increase sexual pleasure.

The Swedish artist Roberto Ekholm has created his own language, merging medical, spiritual and art references with the jargon of pseudoscience. For *CASE STUDY #34 (PRANA)* (opposite), he placed a sealed, silvered scientific glass flask alongside a word of his own making. The new word is 'a fusion of the Om sign and Duchamp's *Air de Paris* bottle neck', and refers to inedia, or breatharianism, which is the belief that it is possible to live off air alone. In Hinduism, *prana* is the life-giving force, said to originate from the sun, and relates to the energy on which inedia relies and which Ekholm contrasts with the modern idea of air as a commodity.

ABOVE · Ralph Dunn
Aroma, 2017 · Vinyl on glass
300 × 459 cm (118⅛ × 180¾ in.)

OPPOSITE · Roberto Ekholm
CASE STUDY #34 (PRANA), 2014
Found lab glass, aluminium oxide, cork, steel and vinyl
25 × 25 × 11 cm (9⅞ × 9⅞ × 4⅜ in.)

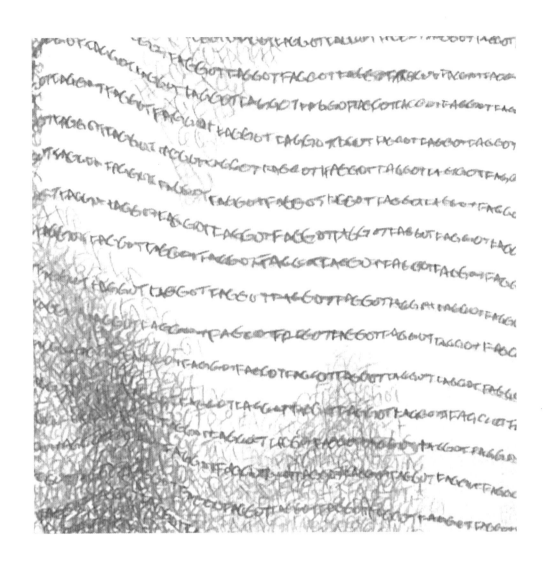

OPPOSITE AND ABOVE · Zachari Logan
26 Months (detail above), 2011
Blue pencil on Mylar
76.2 × 38.1 cm (30 × 15 in.)

Many of the Canadian artist Zachari Logan's works are intricate queer fantasias. He often uses his body as the starting point for investigations into masculinity, combining its drawn depiction with flora and fauna to hint at notions of nature, naturalism and the question of what is natural. In *Advice 1: Don't Be Gay* (2011), he built up a self-portrait by repeatedly writing this phrase in red pencil, thereby suggesting that he is himself constructed from this negative command. His deft drawing visually softens the impact, but makes the point that many LGBTQ+ people sublimate such commands. Logan says he chose red because it is 'the colour commonly associated with correction...I use the same phrase or word to create self-portraits that embody uncomfortable experiences...and imposed societal conformity.' In *26 Months* (opposite), he used blue pencil to draw a portrait of himself as a child. He wrote the word 'faggot' over and over again to create the image as a 'gesture of remembrance, or solidarity with an earlier self, one that might not have understood the weight of that word, thus obliterating its power to damage [one]self'.

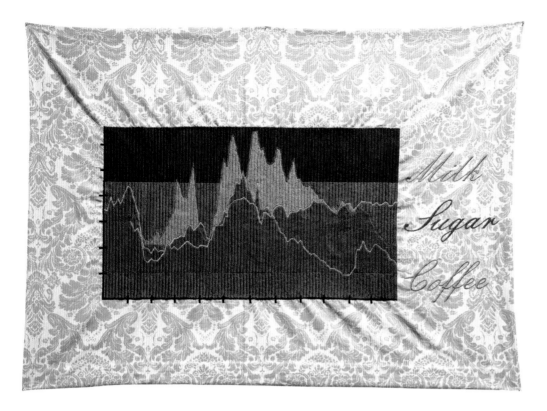

Maja Bajevic was born in the former Yugoslavia (now Bosnia-Herzegovina) but is now a French national. For the group exhibition 'All the World's Futures' at the 56th Venice Biennale in 2015, she made a series of embroidered works, 'Arts, Crafts and Facts', incorporating economic graphs. One piece shows oil, coal and gas prices over time; another, rice, corn and wheat prices; and the one shown above depicts those of milk, sugar and coffee. In each case, the names of the commodities are stitched on the right-hand side of the cotton ground. Bajevic highlights the fluctuations in price, making colourful but worrying visual representations of data. She questions the position of women in the art world and the global economic system by basing such works on traditional embroidery.

The Australian artist Michelle Hamer uses photography (found and her own) as the basis for her tapestries of daily life. Burger joints, exit signs on freeways and advertising billboards find their way into works that distil those moments that rush past, almost never noticed. Hamer's painstaking needlework, as in *My hurt hurts* (opposite, top), combines texts, yarn and the digital world, where the pixel is the norm. The works are located in historic art-making practice, yet seem completely up to date, commenting on the digital as much as the physical environments we inhabit. In this particular piece, sign upon sign seems just about to flash by, as the driver (or passenger) is comfortably seated in a speeding car. Hamer took the photograph on which the tapestry is based while she was in Los Angeles investigating the impact of the financial crisis on language. *Love Knows All Barriers* (opposite, bottom), stitched in barrier tape, reads 'You are my past, I am your future'. Hamer explains that it 'explores barriers and boundaries with physical materials often associated with such zones'.

ABOVE · Maja Bajevic
Arts, Crafts and Facts (Income of Top 1%, Productivity, Average Wages), 2015
Embroidery on cotton
90 × 120 cm (35⅜ × 47¼ in.)

OPPOSITE, TOP · Michelle Hamer
My hurt hurts, 2013
Hand-stitching, mixed yarn
on perforated plastic
51 × 68 cm (20⅛ × 26¾ in.)

OPPOSITE, BOTTOM · Michelle Hamer
Love Knows All Barriers, 2016
Hand-stitching, barrier tape
on construction mesh
115 × 300 cm (45¼ × 118⅛ in.)

Los-Angeles based Lisa Anne Auerbach uses knitting to make political statements about her native country. In 2008, for the Aspen Art Museum in Colorado, she made a series of 'Election Sweaters', all knitted in red, white and blue wool. Emblazoned across the front of each sweater was a slogan formerly used in a US political campaign, such as 'Save America from Socialism' (opposite) and 'Let America Be America Again'. A non-partisan project, it was intended to encourage people to vote in the forthcoming presidential election. In 2016 details from three knitted slogans were featured on billboards in Cincinnati as part of the 'I-71 Project' of the city's Contemporary Arts Center: *Let the People Rule!* was the slogan of both Andrew Jackson in 1828 and Theodore Roosevelt in 1912; *The Times Are Sadly Out of Joint* was a song written for the 1876 campaign of the Democratic candidate Samuel Tilden; and *The Stakes Are Too High for You to Stay at Home* was used in Lyndon Johnson's campaign in 1964.

ABOVE · Lisa Anne Auerbach
Photomural for window installation at the artist's exhibition 'Take This Knitting Machine and Shove It', Nottingham Contemporary, 2009
Photograph · Dimensions variable

OPPOSITE · Lisa Anne Auerbach
Roosevelt/Landon 1936 Campaign Sweater, 2008 · Wool · 53.3 × 45.7 cm (21 × 18 in.; size medium)

The American artist Raymond Pettibon has been making work that satirizes his country's popular culture and sensibilities since the late 1970s. A sometime member of his brother's punk group, Panic, Pettibon suggested the new name Black Flag when the band had to change their identity, and designed their distinctive logo. Many of his works have the appearance of adult comics and are made with ink on paper, as in the case of *No Title ("Why press him?")* (2007). They are often funny yet simultaneously disturbing. Pettibon works at a prolific pace and issues many pieces in comic-book or zine form, which he calls 'Superflux Pubs'.

ABOVE · Raymond Pettibon
No Title ("Why press him?"), 2007
Pen, ink, gouache and graphite
on paper · 40.6 × 57.2 cm (16 × 22½ in.)

OPPOSITE, TOP · Tom Fecht
*Open Square I – Names and Stones
(Mémoire nomade – National Gallery
Berlin – Hamburger Bahnhof, Berlin)*, 1996
97 engraved stones; 28 additional
stones outside, 2017 · 200 × 200 cm
(78¾ × 78¾ in.)

OPPOSITE, BOTTOM, AND PAGES 212–13 ·
Betty Tompkins
Installation views of 'WOMEN Words,
Phrases, and Stories' at the FLAG Art
Foundation, New York (detail opposite),
and Gavlak Los Angeles (pp. 212–13), 2016
1,000 paintings, acrylic on canvas
Individual canvases vary from
10.2 × 10.2 cm (4 × 4 in.) to 45.7 × 40.6 cm
(18 × 16 in.), 1.2 × 32 m (4 × 105 ft) overall

The German artist Tom Fecht started his 'Names and Stones' series in 1992 as a response to the AIDS crisis. The works feature cobble stones carved with the names of those who died from the disease. The first installation, *Homage* (p. 23), was presented at documenta IX in Kassel, where 250 stones, set into the paving at the bottom of the steps to the Museum Fridericianum, commemorated predominantly artists. The project was originally conceived as a *Mémoire nomade*, temporary installations travelling from town to town; however, it developed into a series of permanent installations in cities across Germany and elsewhere in Europe. *Open Square I* (right) is situated in front of the Museum für Gegenwart, part of the Nationalgalerie, at Hamburger Bahnhof in Berlin.

The American artist Betty Tompkins is known for her 'Fuck Paintings' (from 1969), depicting sexual intercourse in close-up. In 2002 (and again in 2013) she sent out a request for words used to describe women. She received more than 3,500 words and phrases in seven languages, many affectionate, but also many derogatory. Tompkins made 1,000 paintings of these words for an exhibition called 'WOMEN Words, Phrases, and Stories'. Each painting contains one word or phrase. Many words are painted on top of simulated works of 'old-boy painting', the term Tompkins uses to reference such artists as Willem de Kooning and Jackson Pollock. For every term of endearment, such as 'my old lady', there is a 'feminazi' and much worse. Tompkins read 500 of these words at a performance in Vienna in 2012, to powerful effect.

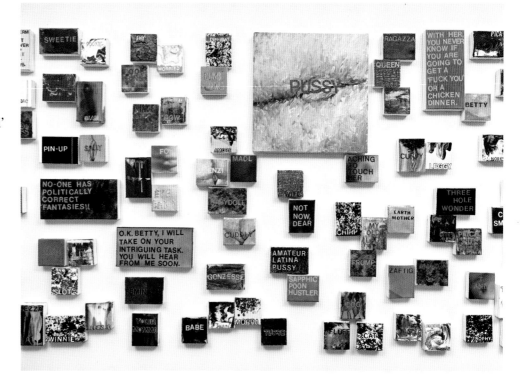

The Macedonian artists Hristina Ivanoska and Yane Calovski represented their country at the 56th Venice Biennale in 2015 with a pavilion titled 'We are All in This Alone'. Ivanoska exhibited the embroidered work *Untitled (Artist is not a civil servant)* (2013), which features two phrases. The phrase used in the title was inspired by the Brazilian architect Lina Bo Bardi; the other is borrowed from the French philosopher Michel Foucault: 'L'histoire, c'est ce qui transforme les documents en monuments' (History is what transforms documents into monuments). The words were stitched on to a woollen felt base in reference to the troubled birth of the various independent states that were once part of Yugoslavia, including the Republic of Macedonia, which came into being in 1991. Ivanoska and Calovski's collaborative work for the Pavilion of Macedonia referenced a 12th-century fresco by an unknown artist in the church of St George in Kurbinovo. The project included text pieces on paper by Ivanoska based on the writings of the French philosophers Simone Weil and Luce Irigaray, and Calovski's type-drawings based on the personal communications of the American artist Paul Thek. The works addressed questions concerning the past, the present and notions of faith.

ABOVE · Hristina Ivanoska
Untitled (Artist is not a civil servant), 2013
Thread and graphite on woollen felt
40 × 180 cm (15¾ × 70⅞ in.)

ABOVE · Bill Burns
Glenn Lowry Remember Me, 2013
Air advertising banner (study)
Length 10 m (32 ft 9¾ in.)

The Canadian artist Bill Burns has made a series of sardonic works that call into question the unwritten but well-known pecking order of curators and artists. His sculpture *Log Piles and Bespoke Log Bags* (2011–13) features the names of famous art-world movers, including the art dealers Jay Jopling and Barbara Gladstone, carved on to logs piled on the floor. The names came from the *Art Review* Power 100 list, and the logs were coated with milk and honey. Burns's air advertising banners have been flown over art fairs and exhibitions, pushing the work into a much more biting form of criticism. He hires commercial plane operators to circle these events with banners such as *Hans Ulrich Obrist Hear Us* and *Glenn Lowry Remember Me* (both 2013). While the banners are humorous calls to famous curators and museum directors (Obrist is artistic director of the Serpentine Galleries, London; Lowry, director of the Museum of Modern Art, New York) to pay attention to lesser-known artists, there is a sad recognition that, even by flying a plane over their heads, one is unlikely to succeed in gaining their ear or protection.

In 2007 Elizabeth Croft moved from Britain to Norway, where the law states that foreigners applying for residency must learn the national language. Croft has made a series of text works about her experience of adapting to a new society and learning the language. *Takk* (Thanks; left) is an exaggerated thank you, written in the colours of the Norwegian flag. Foreigners are often encouraged to express their gratitude for living in Norway. In *Det er så spennende* (It's So Exciting, 2013), she prepared an acceptance speech, to be used at the end of an unspecified project. The text includes corrections added by a female artist friend, reflecting the culture for positive thinking among Norwegian women, which simultaneously could be seen as a form of social control, as women are discouraged from 'whinging'. The text, translated into English, ends: 'Thank you for who you are and thank you from me. Thank you from me.'

The British artist Nick Jeffrey has made a series of 'Sorry!' paintings that repeat the phrase 'OH, I'M REAL SORRY!' over and over again. Like Croft, he is aware of the British dislike of causing embarrassment or disruption. People often say 'I'm sorry' if they bump into someone on the street or in a shop. They are expected not to push in or jump any queue, and if someone does, those in the line most likely will say, 'I'm sorry, didn't you know there's a queue?', almost as if they were taking the blame for another's incivility. *Untitled (we get in each other's way once in a while)* (opposite) draws on such learned social discomfort, yet offers some relief by mocking it ever so nicely – a very British trait.

LEFT · Elizabeth Croft
Takk (Thanks), 2013
Digital print on 100% cotton paper
59.4 × 42 cm (23⅜ × 16½ in.)
Edition of 20

OPPOSITE · Nick Jeffrey
Untitled (we get in each other's way once in a while), 2015 · Textile ink, ink, acrylic, spray paint and wax on canvas
195 × 155 cm (76¾ × 61 in.)

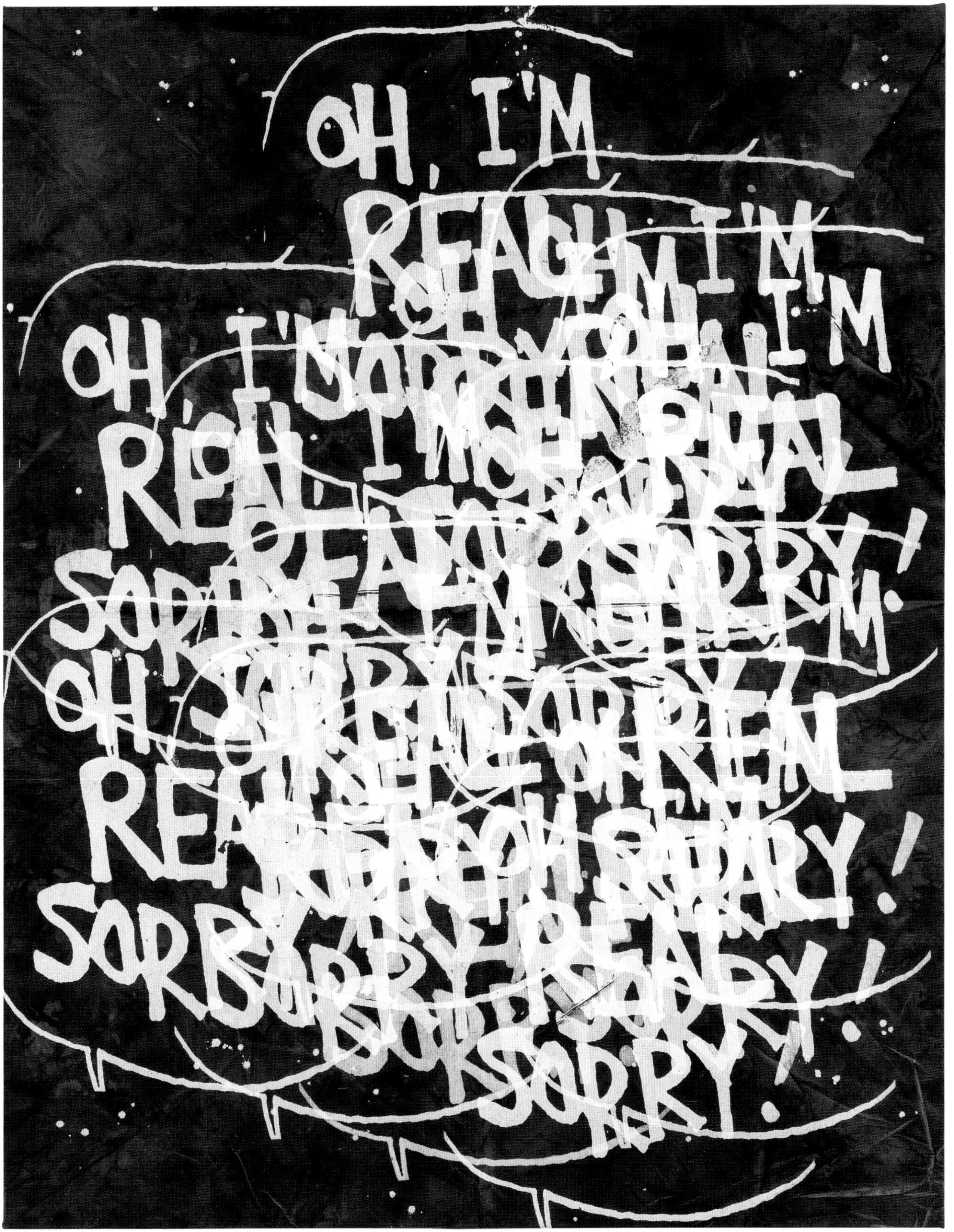
OH, I'M
SORRY!

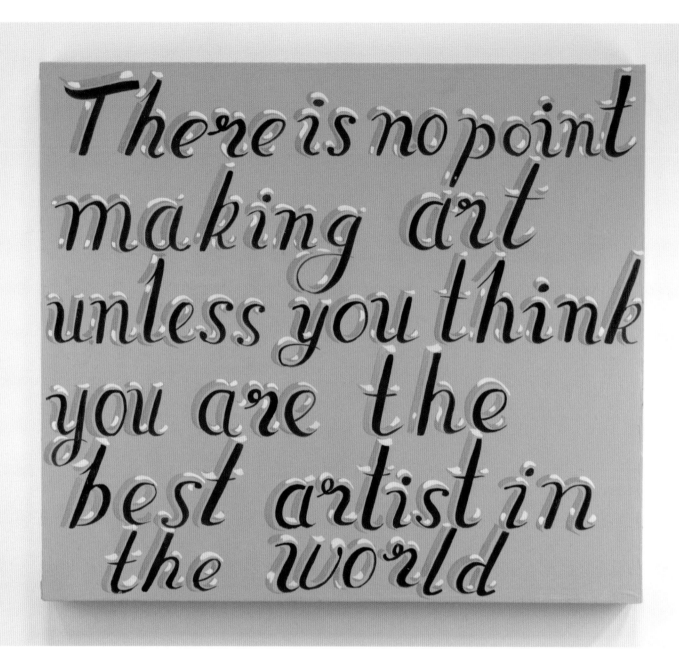

The British artist Bob and Roberta Smith is known for text paintings such as *There is no point making art unless you think you are the best artist in the world* (2006). Here the text floats on a field of light blue; in other works, various bright backgrounds are the base for political comments. Smith has fought the closure of art schools and made work about the subject, and in 2015 he ran for election as a Member of Parliament, calling for more creative subjects to be taught in schools. For his campaign, he produced works with slogans such as *This Campaign is an*

Art Work and *Art Makes People Powerful*. While Smith did not win (he stood against Michael Gove, the Conservative politician who was formerly Secretary of State for Education), he says, 'People might accuse me of a sort of political naivety, but I think it's a different kind of politics, and I do genuinely believe that there's a lot more that unites human beings than divides us.'

ABOVE · Bob and Roberta Smith
There is no point making art unless you think you are the best artist in the world, 2006 · Oil on board
58 × 66.5 cm (22⅞ × 26¼ in.)

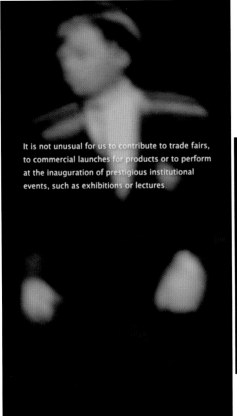

ABOVE · Elizabeth Price
Stills from *K*, 2015
2-screen video installation
Full duration: 7 minutes, 15 seconds

The British artist Elizabeth Price has made a variety of video installations that draw on such references as those she describes as 'architectural sites, social and political histories'. *The Woolworths Choir of 1979* (2012) features an anonymous choir who sing, 'We know. We are the chorus.' The video presents text, news footage of a department-store fire in 1979, photographs of church architecture, internet clips of dancers and a pulsating soundtrack. Price's two-screen installation *K* (above) features on one screen a stop-frame animation of the sun compiled from glass-plate slides made between 1870 and 1948; the other screen shows a CGI animation of the production and packaging of 'K'-brand nylon stockings. Images of dancers and singers 'migrate' across the two animations, linked by Price's narrative, which is attributed to a fictional group of professional mourners called The Krystals. The Art Institute of Chicago, where the work was shown in 2017, described *K* as a 'witty and emotional exploration of lamentation, commerce, and labor'.

THE DRAWN WORD

This chapter looks at drawings or paintings that feature text as a vital component. While words in this context are of course meant to be read in a traditional sense, they are also visual marks on the canvas or paper and, as such, they have an autonomy from their meaning as text; they are graphic elements that fit within the overall design of the composition, and it is in their liminal, fluid state between letters and marks that they differ from the other works in this book. They cannot readily be pinned down as one thing or the other, nor should they be.

The letters of the words that form John Robertson's series of paintings fill the entire transparent polythene ground. The works not only demonstrate the artifice of painting (we see the wooden stretchers behind the polythene), so that we can understand how Robertson makes an image, but they also betray the artifice of letters themselves and how they are joined together to make words and provide meaning. Likewise, Bryan Mulvihill presents the process as an integral part of the artwork by overpainting Chinese characters in all four cardinal directions in glaze on porcelain tiles. Layer upon layer of meaning fuses in the heat of the kiln to reveal a unique painterly work that can be read as an image rather than text.

Other artists make more legible use of letters and words in their paintings. For example, Harland Miller paints fictional covers of Penguin paperbacks, and Carl Ostendarp renders his name as if it were a logo. The paintings of Tim Ayres might even be seen as very large and colourful concrete poems. Maria Chevska builds up layers of paint as she presents and obscures sections of letters by the revolutionary Rosa Luxemburg, turning the words into images in the same way that we might picture characters and scenes in our heads when we read books. Lukas Göthman uses incredibly thick paint to almost carve out three-dimensional words that appear to leap off the surface of the canvas. Paint has such an allure for these artists (and many viewers), and it can be handled in so many different ways to form words and images.

However artists paint or draw words, those that make such works are aware that seeing is very different from reading. A painting needs to be seen as a whole, which encompasses its construction as a physical object as well as its content, including any marks that may contain meaning. Reading a painting for meaning is not the same as seeing it as an artwork, and that tension is what holds these works together.

Harland Miller's work explores the relationship between image and text, marrying aspects of Pop art, abstraction and figurative painting with his writer's love of words. His writing and painting have developed synchronously and come together in his most iconic artworks, 'The Penguin Books Series'. The Penguin paintings combine Miller's text works, in the form of the book titles, with his signature expressive brushwork. Some works reference such prominent writers as Ernest Hemingway and D. H. Lawrence alongside Miller's own titles, such as *I'm So Fucking Hard* (2003) and *Dirty Northern Bastard* (2009), while others bear Harland's name as the author. The works are humorous, sardonic and nostalgic at the same time, while the painting style mirrors the scuffed covers of the Penguin Classics themselves. Miller continues to be inspired by book covers, his more recent work recalling the abstract geometrical covers of popular psychology books of the 1960s and '70s. Miller's phrases are open enough to imbue every work with a different idiosyncratic significance to each individual viewer. These iconic titles work alongside the looseness and freedom of Miller's painting to create nuanced works that echo Miller's unique character.

ABOVE · Harland Miller
Health and Safety is Killing Bondage, 2016
Oil on canvas · 240 × 155 cm
(94½ × 61 in.)

OPPOSITE · Harland Miller
I am the One I've Been Waiting For, 2015
Watercolour, acrylic and oil on paper
153 × 122 cm (60¼ × 48 in.)

PENGUIN
BOOKS

I AM THE ONE
I'VE BEEN
WAITING FOR

HARLAND MILLER

6ᵈ

6ᵈ

Tim Ayres is a British artist who makes what at first appearance are minimalist text works. In pieces such as *Sad* (2013) or *Dead is easy* (2015), the words of the title stand out against a single-coloured ground. Other works present longer fragments of text from overheard conversations or misheard song lyrics. The 'N-N-N Paintings' feature a list of negative words, including 'no, not, nil, nope, never, neither, nor, nothing, none'. In all his word paintings, Ayres uses the mid-20th-century font Eurostile Extended 2, which is very evocative of that period, lending the works a crisp, machine-like aesthetic associated with mass production and public signage. The large scale of the paintings obliges the viewer to confront their physicality and places text at the heart of the experience.

The American artist Ed Ruscha has made a series of mountainscapes in which phrases are superimposed on various snow-covered peaks. In *Bliss Bucket* (2010), the words are in white against a blue mountain scene. In *Jet Baby* (2011), white words are set against a brown-and-white mountain with a dark sky. *Periods* (2013) features the abbreviations 'SECS. HRS. WKS. MOS. YRS.' in black capitals that increase in size as they march down the mountainside towards the viewer. Images and timescales conflate to evoke a sense of scientific, geological history, as in the case of *History Kids* (opposite), in which the words of the title float in front of an almost psychedelic scene. The work can be read in many ways; one possible reading is that mountains have history, and only those who doubt evolution do not see the geological timescale in billions of years.

RIGHT · Tim Ayres
And all that poetry shit means nothing now to me (GVN), 2014
Acrylic on linen
225 × 150 cm (88⅝ × 59 in.)

OPPOSITE · Ed Ruscha
History Kids, 2013
Lithograph
73.7 × 71.1 cm (29 × 28 in.)

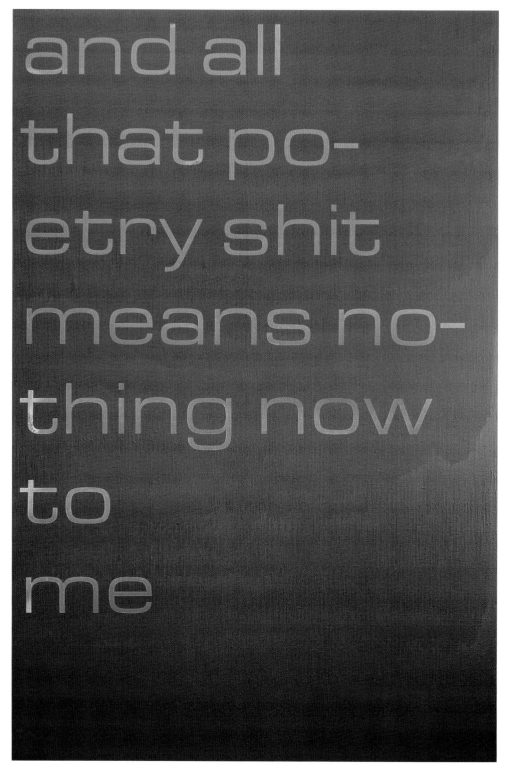

For her show 'Can't Wait [Letters RL]' at the Andrew Mummery Gallery, London, in 2004, the British artist Maria Chevska made a series of works touching on her Polish roots and also the act of painting. The paintings in the exhibition were created by the application of layer upon layer of paint, forming partially legible words. The source texts were extracts from letters that Rosa Luxemburg sent to her fellow revolutionary and sometime lover Leo Jogiches. Luxemburg (1871–1919), a Jewish Marxist, fled her native Poland (then part of the Russian Empire) for Switzerland and later settled in Germany. She was one

of the few female leaders of anti-war sentiment in Berlin, and was executed for her role in a communist uprising. Jogiches was murdered only a few weeks later. While the correspondence between the two (much of which is missing) is at the heart of Chevska's work, she provides only hints as to meaning. Letter 1 (1893), dating from a period when the lovers were in Switzerland, is the basis for *'Can't Wait [Letters RL]' (dream red)* (2004). The line 'I rushed up stairs only to see that my nights vision was merely a dream' emerges in white letters from a red-and-black field, recalling the nickname 'Bloody Rosa'.

ABOVE · Maria Chevska
'Can't Wait [Letters RL]' (dream red), 2004
Kaolin and oil-based paint on canvas
122 × 122 cm (48 × 48 in.)

ABOVE · Lukas Göthman
rotten, 2016 · Oil on canvas
19 × 24 cm (7½ × 9½ in.)

The Swedish artist Lukas Göthman develops his paintings through a long process of solitary travel, during which he jots down notes and phrases that are then distilled into his word works. He settles on words that will have a visual effect, either sculpturally or by way of content, but they all relate to his journals, which may contain truth, fiction or dream. Göthman likes to paint words that are disruptive to the gallery context, as in his lush grey oil painting *scabies* or the messy black-and-white *virus everyday* (both 2016). These are not works that shout 'Come, buy me', but they hint at some story that the artist alone knows.

The mouldy green painting *rotten* (above) almost bursts off the canvas like a bag of rotting garbage. It reads across two lines: 'rot', with 'ten' underneath. 'Ten' could be mistaken for 'ton', a reference to the weight of the rot, the weight of the deep pain suggested by the sculptural gouges of paint, and the weight of painting itself. The work is rotten in a most splendid way and, like the punk aesthetic of the 1970s, it compels the viewer to reassess what a painting might look like. Göthman claims, 'It's good to have heavy paintings. It's good for you.'

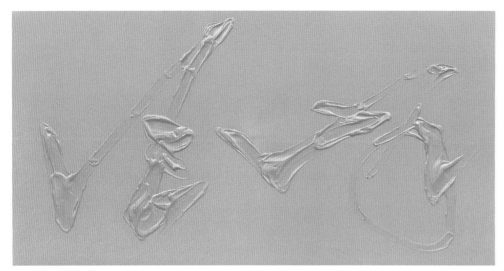

The paintings of the Chinese artist Tian Wei reference calligraphy and Western notions of Chinese characters. In fact, Tian uses the Latin alphabet. In *Hello* (left), the word is spelled out in marks across a yellow ground, but it does not look like English text; the eye has to follow the flow of the marks to make out the word. In *Verde* (2013), the Spanish and Italian word for 'green' is painted in dark green on a lighter green ground in a similar calligraphic form. Tian says: 'What I am attempting to do is to innovate and create the Chinese Way of Abstraction…I am constantly searching for the meaning of words and reflecting on their beauty, exposing their power and finally reflecting upon the invisible.'

The Canadian artist Bryan Mulvihill is one of few Westerners who have trained to perform the complete, elaborate Japanese tea ceremony. His interest in Eastern cultures extends to India and to China, where he is known for his calligraphic works, many on porcelain. Mulvihill knew Brion Gysin and has adopted the latter's cut-up techniques in his calligraphy. For his porcelain works, made in Jingdezhen, Jiangxi province, he uses glaze to write Chinese characters on large white tiles that have been specially prepared for him. He paints each character at least four times, so that it can be read from each cardinal direction. The result is that the character is almost illegible as text, but perfectly legible as an image. The work *Chung: Middle Way* (opposite) uses green, brown and purple glazes. *Chung* translates as 'middle' or 'centre'; it can also be used to mean 'within', 'to hit the mark' or 'to be successful'.

LEFT, ABOVE · Tian Wei
Hello, 2016 · Acrylic on canvas
152 × 298 cm (59⅞ × 117⅜ in.)

LEFT · Tian Wei
Line of the Line, 2017
Acrylic on canvas
223 × 177 cm (87¾ × 69¾ in.)

OPPOSITE · Bryan Mulvihill
Chung: Middle Way, Centre 4 Directions,
2015 · Lao Yu Tan Porcelain ceramic
glazes on Lao Yu Tan Porcelain,
Jingdezhen, China
57.1 × 55.8 cm (22½ × 22 in.)

The French artist Fabienne Audéoud has made a series of paintings featuring words that many would find startling. The titular phrases are painted across canvas or paper in *J'adore le cul* (I Love Arse, 2002), *Erection* (2014) and *Praying for North Korea* (2014). *Mohamed je t'aime* (Mohamed, I Love You; above) is an open-ended work that can be read in many ways. The artist has also used the same phrase on a stage curtain for a live performance. Audéoud pushes the boundary of what is acceptable within a fine-art context. Other works are more obviously humorous, as in the case of *Bijoux de gauche* (Leftist Jewelry, 2012), which displays the slogan 'Je vote Hollande' (I vote for Hollande).

The Iraqi artist Hassan Massoudy trained in classical calligraphy and contemporary Western fine arts, and combines elements of both in his work. Between 1972 and 1985 he toured Europe with his *Arabesque* performance, which brought his calligraphy to life via music. Massoudy's works often present phrases written by poets and philosophers, as in the 2015 painting *Even if happiness forgets you occasionally, never forget it completely. Jacques Prévert (1900–1977). Untitled* (opposite) features two large central red strokes, their elegant, abstracted movement floating above Arabic script that reads, 'O Friend! Do not go to the flower garden, the flower garden is within you. Kabir 16thC.'

ABOVE · Fabienne Audéoud
Mohamed je t'aime (Mohamed, I Love You; detail), 2012
Oil on canvas
180 × 200 cm (70⅞ × 78¾ in.)

OPPOSITE · Hassan Massoudy
Untitled, 2011
Ink and pigments on paper
74.9 × 55.1 cm (29½ × 21¾ in.)

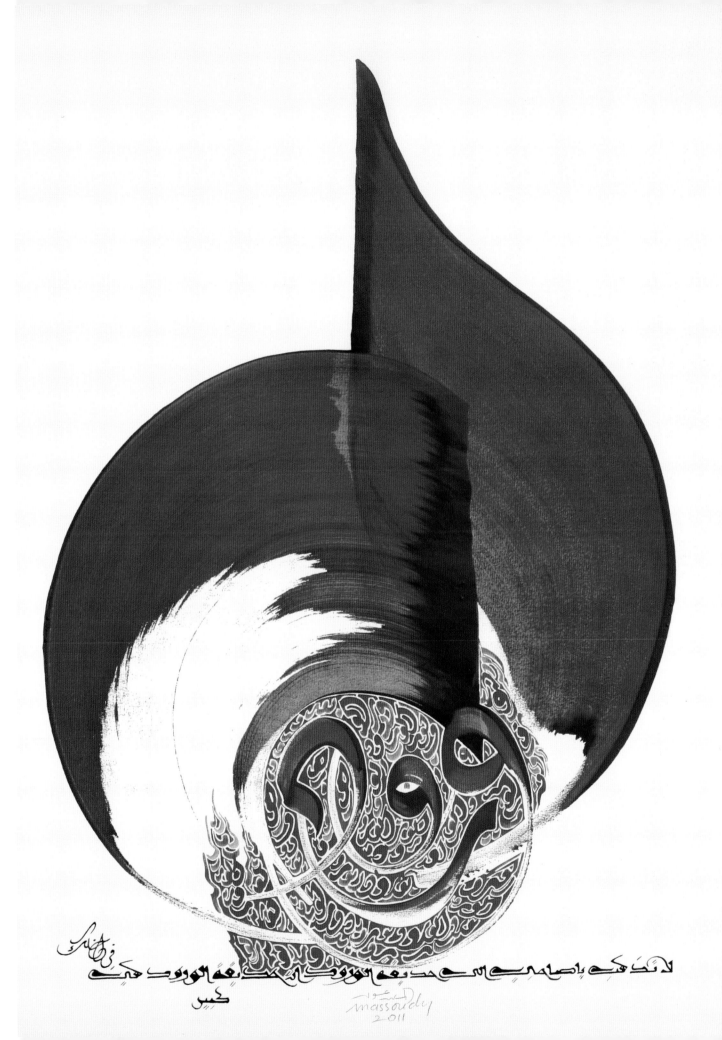

The sewing projects of the Mexican artist Tania Candiani have included embroidered latex balloons (*Leer de corrido* [Read Fluently], 2010). *Tejer el sonido* (Weaving Sound, 2015) is a video collaboration with traditional weavers in which the word *sonido* appears on a tapestry of Candiani's design. *Acerca del rojo, del azul y el amarillo* (About Red, Blue and Yellow) consists of a series of single-colour embroidered texts, all related to that particular colour. One of the red texts (above) translates as: 'For Kandinsky, red evoked the sound of trumpets.' For the 'Refranes' project (2008–11), Candiani fly-posted black-and-white posters across several cities with such proverbs as *En boca cerrada no entran moscas* (A Closed Mouth Lets in No Flies).

Ghada Amer's embroideries of women incorporate text, thereby introducing another layer of meaning to works such as *The Virgin without the Child* (opposite). The canvas depicts a woman's face with flowing, multicoloured hair. Closer inspection reveals embroidered letters that spell out 'THERE IS NO GREATER PILLAR OF STABILITY THAN A STRONG FREE AND EDUCATED WOMAN'. The phrase repeats across the whole of the image, and the ends of the threads are left dangling. In other works, Amer uses Arabic text, and in some pieces there is no overall image, simply repeated text. For example, *The Person Inside-RFGA* (2016) states repeatedly, 'I AM JUST A PERSON TRAPPED INSIDE A WOMAN'S BODY'.

ABOVE · Tania Candiani
Acerca del rojo, del azul y el amarillo (About Red, Blue and Yellow), from the series 'Cromática', 2015
Embroidery hoops, thread on cotton
Dimensions variable, diameter 15–40 cm (5⅞–15¾ in.)

OPPOSITE · Ghada Amer
The Virgin without the Child, 2016
Acrylic, embroidery and gel medium on canvas
127 × 106.7 cm (50 × 42 in.)

In 2012–13 Roni Horn made a series of works on paper called 'Remembered Words'. Each work consists of nine parts: three rows of three abstract images with words inserted into them. In *Remembered Words – (Sourpuss)*, one image comprises thirty blue circles, each with a single word written beneath, appearing to form a narrative from seemingly unrelated terms: 'MOHAIR', 'BLOWPIPE', 'RAG', 'FLINT' and 'JUNK'. *Remembered Words – (Bondage)* takes the same compositional format, except that the circles are predominantly yellow, with at most two words or phrases per panel. Horn said, 'The unknown is where I want to be.'

ABOVE AND OPPOSITE · Roni Horn
Remembered Words – (Bondage)
(detail above), 2012–13
Gouache, watercolour, graphite
and gum arabic on paper
9 parts, each 38.1 × 27.9 cm (15 × 11 in.);
42.2 × 32.2 × 3 cm (16⅝ × 12⅝ × 1⅛ in.),
framed

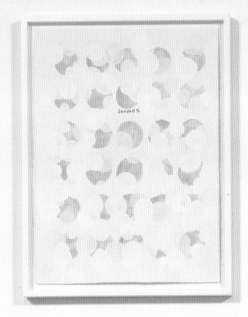

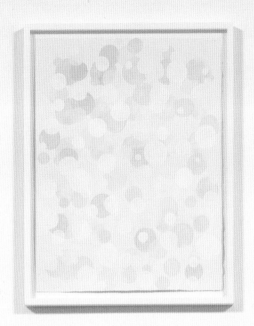

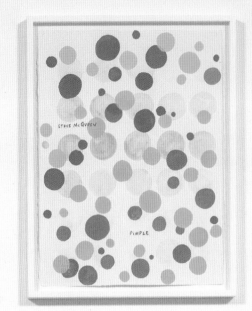

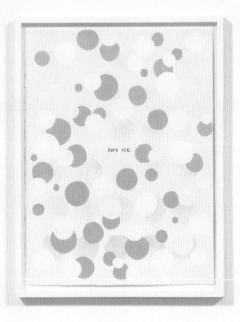

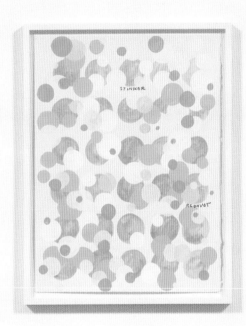

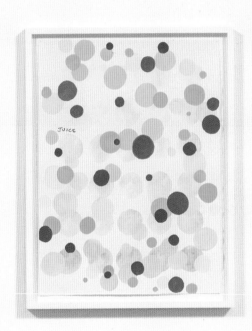

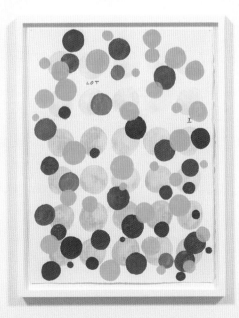

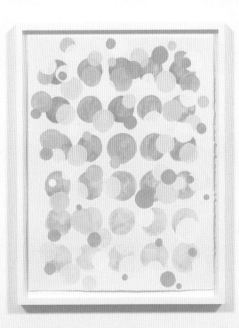

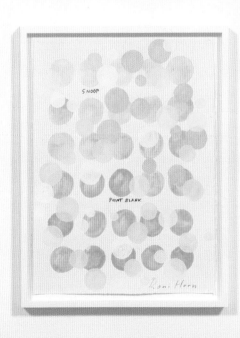

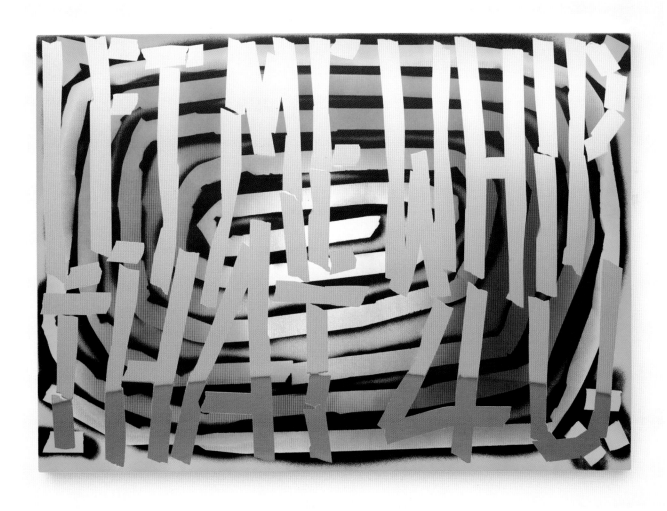

OPPOSITE, TOP · Mark Dutcher
Halcyon, 2014 · Oil and pencil on canvas
193 × 287 cm (76 × 113 in.)

OPPOSITE, BOTTOM · Mark Dutcher
Colby Keller, 2014 · Oil on canvas
78.8 × 63.5 cm (31 × 25 in.)

ABOVE · Eddie Peake
Let Me Whip That For You, 2014
Lacquered spray paint on polished
stainless steel · 100 × 140 cm
(39⅜ × 55⅛ in.)

Mark Dutcher's paintings recall queer poetry and reference LGBTQ+ artists or writers from the past (such as the poet Hart Crane), but also twist expectations. Adult subject matter and an almost childlike enjoyment in the application of paint create a type of disconnect between form and content, as in *Colby Keller* (opposite, bottom), in which the name of the well-known gay adult-film performer (and visual artist) is painted across the canvas, combining with other dynamic marks to make a passionate portrait. Other works have the appearance of layers of graffiti plastered on the side of a building or inside a toilet, their density making any particular line almost impossible to read; yet words like 'COCK' and 'SUCK' seem to stand out, as in *Halcyon* (opposite, top).

The British artist Eddie Peake was first recognized for his distinctive nude performance-art events, including *Touch* (2012). He is also known for his acid-coloured paintings, which often feature texts that have been layered into the imagery. Using tape to mask out the words, Peake applies lacquered spray paint on to polished steel, as in the case of *Crushingly Hopeless*, *Dead Your Lovers* (both 2013) and *Let Me Whip That For You* (above). For the Olympic Games in Rio in 2016, he made a screenprint called *Sweat* that sums up the beauty of toned bodies in competition; it reads, 'JOLTING BODY W. SWEATY SKIN. A SHEEN OF SWEAT, IRIDESCENT IN TWILIGHT.' These words might be a paean to sex or a night in a disco, as Peake is also a DJ, and his works and exhibitions combine all his interests.

The American artist Dan Colen is best known for his paintings composed of used chewing gum, but before he made those works, his 'Portraits of God' series investigated, in a realist style, how painting is socially constructed. In a piece based on the workshop of Geppetto, the creator of Pinocchio, the smoke from an extinguished candle spells out the title *Fuck* (above). In *Holy Shit* (opposite), the red-painted words are shown upside down, as if it were a graphic work by Georg Baselitz. The words of *No Sex No War No Me* (2006) fill the canvas from edge to edge. The letter 'M' in 'ME' is faint in comparison to the thickness of the other letters.

ABOVE · Dan Colen
Fuck, 2004 · Oil on canvas
22.6 × 21.6 cm (8⅞ × 8½ in.)

OPPOSITE · Dan Colen
Holy Shit, 2003
Enamel and moulding paste on wood
121.9 × 88.9 cm (48 × 35 in.)

HOLY
SHIT

SUSO33, from Spain, began his career working with well-known graffiti artists. He classifies his art as 'Live Action Painting', and he creates his works in the venues where they are shown. The painting *NOW (in/out)* (above) is a comment on the way in which graffiti art has moved from the streets ('out') into the formal setting of museums and galleries ('in'). The words 'IN' and 'OUT' are sprayed on the canvas in white and silver on a black ground. On top of them, in black, the artist has sprayed 'now' (with the 'n' inverted). The piece questions how any artwork is accepted in the market, and how certain works or artists fall in and out of fashion or critical favour.

The American artist Christopher Wool made paintings throughout the 1990s (1988–2000) featuring black words stencilled on to a white ground. *Untitled* (1992) features the word 'SEX' floating above 'LUV'; black drips run down the image. A series of paintings uses the words 'RIOT' and 'FOOL', painted so that the first two letters of each word sit atop the last two. *If You* (1992) states, 'IF YOU CAN'T TAKE A JOKE YOU CAN GET THE FUCK OUT OF MY HOUSE'. *Untitled* (2000; opposite) reads, 'THE HARDER YOU LOOK THE HARDER YOU LOOK'. The spacing of the letters across the frame requires the viewer to take in the image as a whole before decoding the individual words. Wool says: 'If you take text and image and you put them together, the multiple readings that are possible in either poetry or in something visual are reduced to one specific reading. By putting the two together, you limit the possibilities.'

ABOVE · SUSO33
NOW (in/out), 2011
White, black and silver spray paint on canvas
140 × 230 cm (55⅛ × 90½ in.)

OPPOSITE · Christopher Wool
Untitled, 2000
Enamel on aluminium
274.3 × 182.9 cm (108 × 72 in.)

THEHARDERYOULOOK

THEHARDERYOULOOK

The American artist Harvey Opgenorth has created a number of word-based performances, some with the permission of museums and others that were guerrilla interactions. *Gallery Graffiti* (2010) was a collaboration with Joe Bruns, who sprayed the word 'GRAFFITI' in black paint on to the white gallery wall at the Institute of Visual Arts in Milwaukee. Opgenorth was standing against the wall in an all-white outfit, and when he moved away he took part of the graffiti with him. The work was remade in 2017 at Helsinki Contemporary (opposite). In Opgenorth's earlier 'Museum Camouflage' performances (1998–2001), he wore clothes specially designed to blend into existing artworks. He stood motionless and completely silent for an hour in front of paintings by artists including Ellsworth Kelly, Henri Matisse and Christopher Wool (left). Through such works, Opgenorth investigates how museums, as institutions, function and relate to visitors and artists.

LEFT · Harvey Opgenorth
Museum Camouflage: Christopher Wool,
2001 · Hour-long performance at the
Milwaukee Art Museum, Wisconsin
Dimensions variable

OPPOSITE · Harvey Opgenorth
Gallery Graffiti, 2010/17
Performance, here at Helsinki
Contemporary, 2017
Dimensions variable

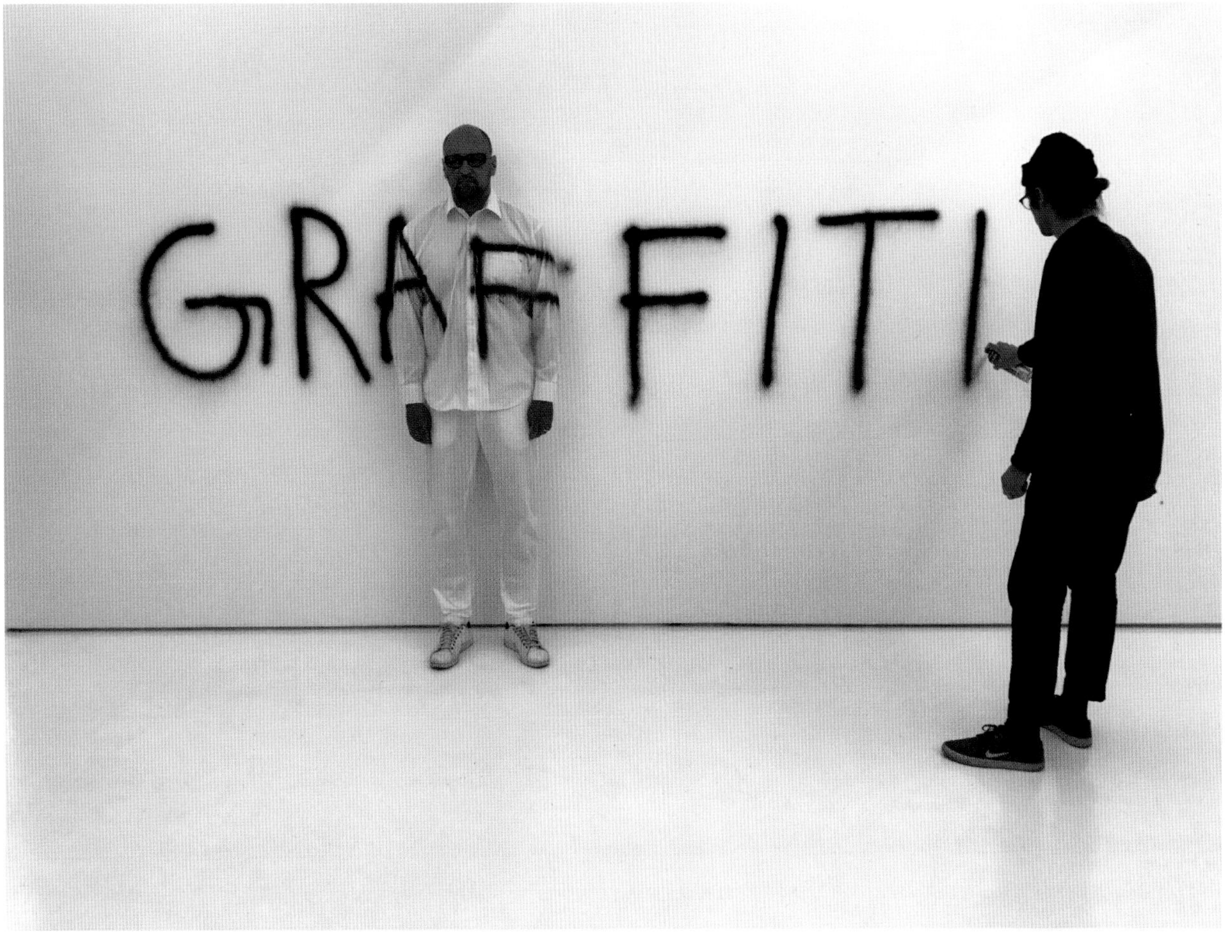
GRAFFITI

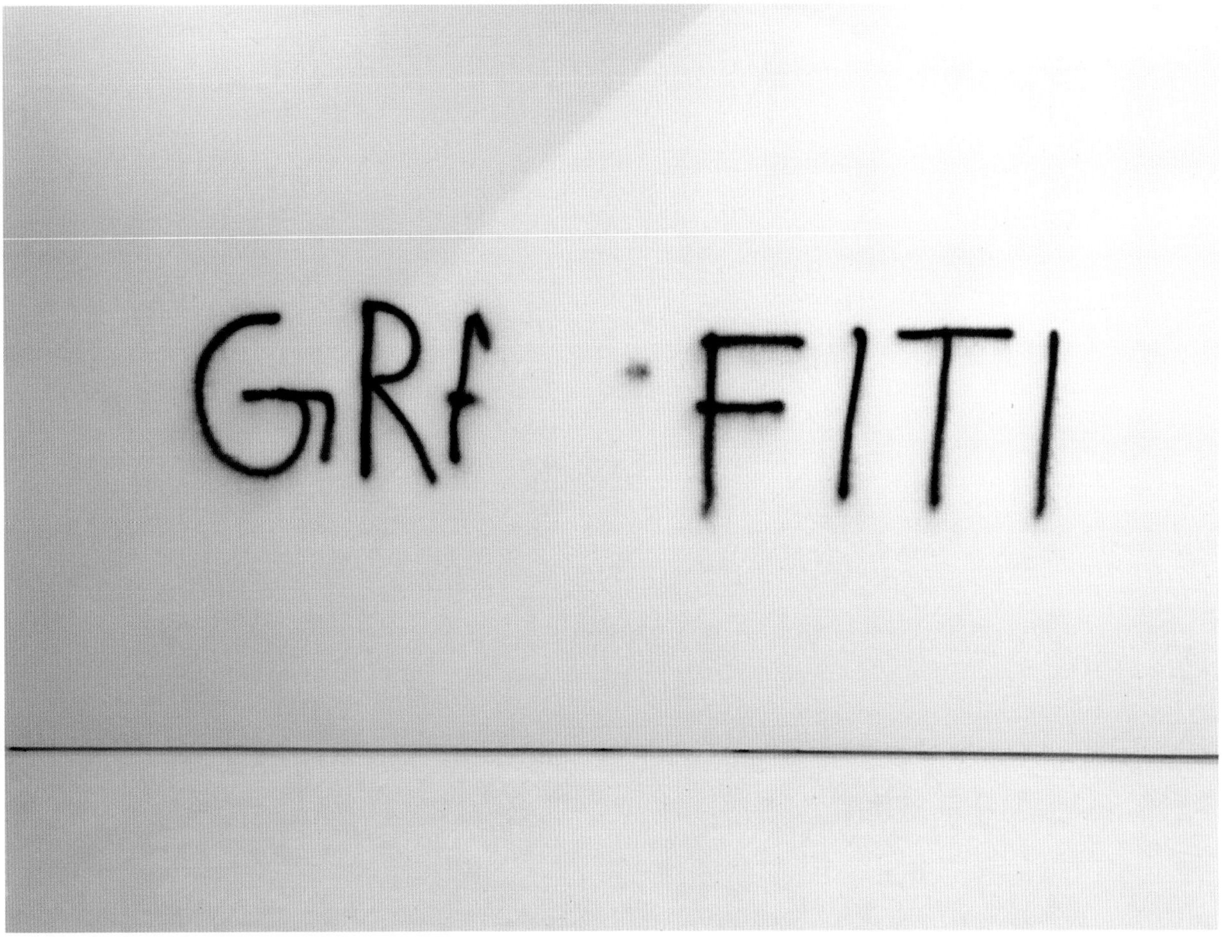
GRf FITI

- and my point was - it's - it's not that I'm necessarily right - I just feel
with it - just - this feeling - of every time - I mean I still live there - every ti
- the whole thing - has to - just has to change - it threw everyone - into
uppressed it all - or - perhaps I just wrote it down - and that made me feel bet
the table - listening to the caged bird - I had nothing - to go by - I just wer
ny of us - find it very difficult - to admit to - there has to be - seeing there
cause of what preceded it - and followed it - in a year - I remember - so cle
and of course - they are just - forever -. No, quite honestly I wouldn't - so
ver the years - I do have to say - there is a difficulty - it's very easy - to los
't - I just don't know - I mean - I would like to try - but - one of the probl
ow can you do - that - ? - all the way through - it would depend on you - hor
RY OLD" - she speaks - to the tiny bird - A DREAM - a ma
ve so much - to say - but is speaking from itself - of itself - as a limit
ne - but - a constant revelation - I never quite knew what was going to
it was true - and I found myself adjusting - in my mind - all over again
no words - could describe it - if I needed - to be reminded - and leave -
a great change - but - it doesn't change my life fundamentally - at a dee
see - the pattern - something much closer - a share - would that - b
NOTHING THERE - there's nothing there" - and I would ask - risk
believable - what an impact this is having - no - no, not at all - I mean it
future - to see - a threat - a way - return - but an uphill struggle - how
y. I had a sense it would be difficult - inevitably - I was doing things for
ot of myself into it - for it - to come alive - again - yes, and this is - and
re - then I would have something which would be - very strong - and
- of that - so - there is something - about - just keeping something - a
oncern - but - I started thinking - then - I was very - isolated - and er
to do anything like that - at all - no - so that was just something that I
re competing values - choices - the reality is - you can't know - but -

Simon Lewty, a British artist, has been writing pictures since the 1970s. His distinctive handwriting – applied to various media, including gesso and tissue – is sometimes integrated with imagery and at other times appears on its own, as in *Passing Days and Nights of Oblivion Will Drain Reason Before the Strength of the Flower* (2008). Many of the texts comprise overheard conversations or are taken from the artist's copious diaries. He uses block writing (more legible for the viewer) and also cursive script, which gives the appearance of being centuries old. The tension between the styles in these seemingly stream-of-consciousness works further distances the viewer from what Lewty calls the 'rhymes' of text and imagery over time.

OPPOSITE AND LEFT· Simon Lewty
Passing Days and Nights of Oblivion Will Drain Reason Before the Strength of the Flower (details at left), 2008
Ink and acrylic on paper
112 × 121 cm (44⅛ × 47⅝ in.)

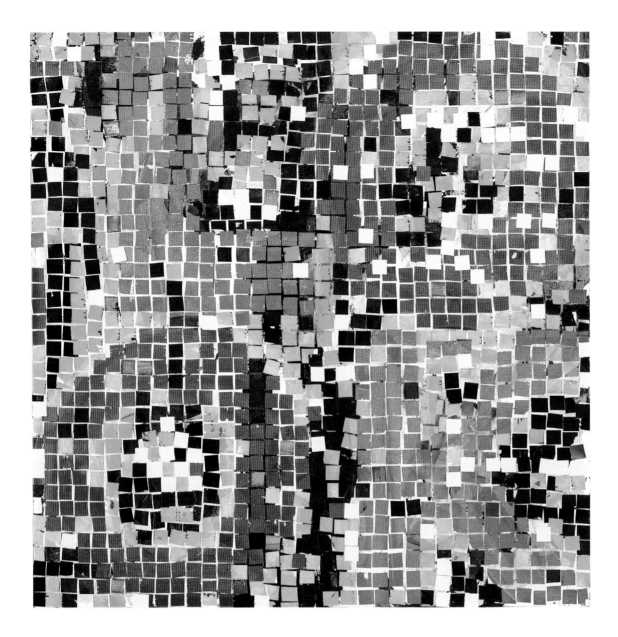

In his effort to deconstruct the modernist ideal, the Austrian artist Heimo Zobernig works across many media, often employing grids and monochrome in his paintings, sculptures and installations. A large body of paintings uses a single word – for example, 'REAL', 'RAGE' or 'LOVE' – as the basis for complex graphic compositions in which the letters are repeated in different layers of colour. *Untitled* (above) uses a grid structure and squares of colour to spell out the word 'LOOK'. It is as much a suggestion as a command to the viewer, who must attempt to read both the image as a whole and its constituent parts.

Mel Bochner was one of the forerunners of conceptualism. Since the 1960s, using painting and large-scale installation, he has developed systems that investigate how art is understood as a visual and linguistic language. His works ask the viewer to question the way in which they receive and comprehend information. The 'Thesaurus' paintings start with one word, such as 'AMAZING', and then continue with synonyms (for example, 'AWESOME', 'BREATHTAKING'). In other paintings, the phrase 'BLAH' is repeated over and over. The works are open-ended and can be read in many ways. Bochner says, 'You put these things out in the world and you just back off, let people make of it what they want.'

ABOVE · Heimo Zobernig
Untitled, 2014
Acrylic on canvas
200 × 200 cm (78¾ × 78¾ in.)

OPPOSITE · Mel Bochner
Going Out of Business, 2014
Oil on velvet in 2 parts
235 × 176.5 cm (92½ × 69½ in.) overall

GOING OUT
OF BUSINESS!
CALLING IT
QUITS! LOST
OUR LEASE!
EVERYTHING
MUST GO! ALL
SALES FINAL!
NO GOOD OF-
REFUSED!

Kendell Geers's painting *Tainted Love XIII* (2012) features the Afrikaans word 'VOETSTOOTS'. It can be translated as 'offhand' or 'straight away'. But perhaps its secondary meaning, which is 'without picking or choosing' or 'with all defects', best suggests what Geers is hinting at here. The word sits on top of a wild splash of acrylic paint and oxidized copper, recalling Andy Warhol's 'Piss' (or Oxidation) paintings. The explosion of feeling and emotions that love, tainted or not, engenders is visually explored in the work, and made more complex by the addition of the bold text.

ABOVE · Kendell Geers
Tainted Love XIII, 2012
Acrylic and copper oxidized on canvas
100 × 120 cm (39⅜ × 47¼ in.)

ABOVE · Liu Ye · *BAUHAUS No. 1*, 2013
Acrylic on canvas
15 × 19 cm (5⅞ × 7½ in.)

The Chinese artist Liu Ye has a deep interest in Western modern art, especially the work of Piet Mondrian (1872–1944). He has made several bodies of work that subtly reference the Dutch artist's approach to painting. Grids and semi-architectural structures, as seen in *Bamboo Bamboo Broadway* (2012), are often the basis for the addition of disparate objects. *Composition with Votalin 25* (2009) shows a box of pills in the centre of a grid or tablecloth. Many of Liu's works hint at a narrative. *BAUHAUS No. 1* (above), for example, depicts a book open at the title page. The viewer sees it upside down, as if the reader has walked away, leaving the image and text as a clue or a starting point for the imagination.

Capital Investments

Gardar Eide Einarsson is a Norwegian artist who often uses appropriation to recontextualize power structures that appear to be benign. In 2016 he named a series of paintings after the titles of IBM instruction manuals from the 1960s: *Capital Investments* (left), *General Ledger and Financial Control* and *Inventory Control and Material Accounting*. The manuals provided information on how to codify data into power structures. IBM played a leading role in the emergence of digitized computing power, and its marketing material of the time foretold of a bright future of equality for all – a future that Einarsson questions. The text is in crisp lettering on a messy field of black, yellow and white with black drips; it serves to ask, what ghosts are still in the machine?

The British artist John Robertson has made a series of word paintings on semi-transparent polythene. The wooden frames behind slowly come into the viewer's vision, exposing the fragility of words and their construction. Robertson paints the words on to the polythene in a variety of colours and orientations. In *Principle (GROUND)* (2012), orange paint spells out the word 'GROUND' in an anticlockwise direction, so the viewer sees 'GR' the right way up, then 'OU' turned to the right, and 'ND' on their heads. The letters are painted quickly in overlapping single brushstokes. In *Double Double Negative (NO NO NO NO)* (opposite), the letters 'NO' are painted to face each cardinal direction, green on pink on blue on yellow. We detect an echo of Duchamp's *First Light* (1959), an etching of the word 'NON'. Duchamp's *non* illustrated the poem of the title by Pierre-André Benoit and is considered a pun on the word *nom* (name). Robertson is also painting non-images and words that barely retain their meaning.

LEFT · Gardar Eide Einarsson
Capital Investments, 2016
Acrylic, gesso and graphite on canvas
220 × 180 cm (86⅝ × 70⅞ in.)

OPPOSITE · John Robertson
Double Double Negative (NO NO NO NO),
2012 · Oil on polythene
49 × 42 cm (19¼ × 16½ in.)

The British artist and author Simon Morley has been occupied with words, text and books for more than thirty years. His *Writing on the Wall: Word and Image in Modern Art* (2003) is a foundational text on the topic. In his series of 'Book Paintings', Morley paints the covers of books in monochrome colours. He explains: 'The text is always painted only a tone darker than the ground in order to confuse the figure-ground relationships and to slow down perceptual-reading response.' The series includes the painted cover of Albert Camus's *L'Homme révolté (1951)* (above) in grey. It was made for a solo exhibition at Galerie Scrawitch in Paris in 2014 called 'Albert Camus: Oeuvres'. Morley painted several first editions of Camus's books in the characteristic cover design of the publisher Gallimard, for which Camus also worked as an editor. The cover colours that Morley chose are evocative of the mid-20th century.

ABOVE · Simon Morley
L'Homme révolté (1951), 2014
Acrylic on canvas
40 × 30 cm (15¾ × 11¾ in.)

OPPOSITE, TOP · Carl Ostendarp
'BLANKS' exhibition, installation view at the Elizabeth Dee Gallery, New York, 2014

OPPOSITE, BOTTOM · Carl Ostendarp
Charles Kynard, 2014
Acrylic on canvas
126.7 × 147 cm (49⅞ × 57⅞ in.)

In a sense, the American artist Carl Ostendarp paints self-portraits, his initials or first name providing not only graphic imagery and text but also context. All paintings in his 'BLANKS' exhibition in 2014 at the Elizabeth Dee Gallery, New York (above) – for example, *Charles Kynard* (right) – were named after popular Hammond Organ players of the 1960s and '70s. The works look very flat, and some of the larger ones could almost be advertising hoardings for a company called CO (their size depends on the proportions of the space in which they are shown). Ostendarp is critical of the corporate nature of the art business, including art fairs and publishing. According to the artist, the floating Cs and Os can also be read as meaning 'care of', leading to the question, who is taking care of art in this global age of trading, flipping and temporary collecting? The letters disrupt their monochrome backgrounds, which emanate a 1960s chic and a minimalism that is now all too easy to digest. The works seemingly ask, is good taste killing good art?

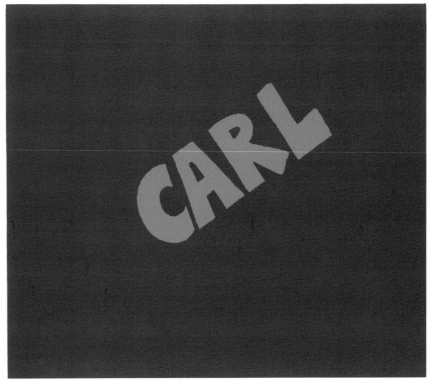

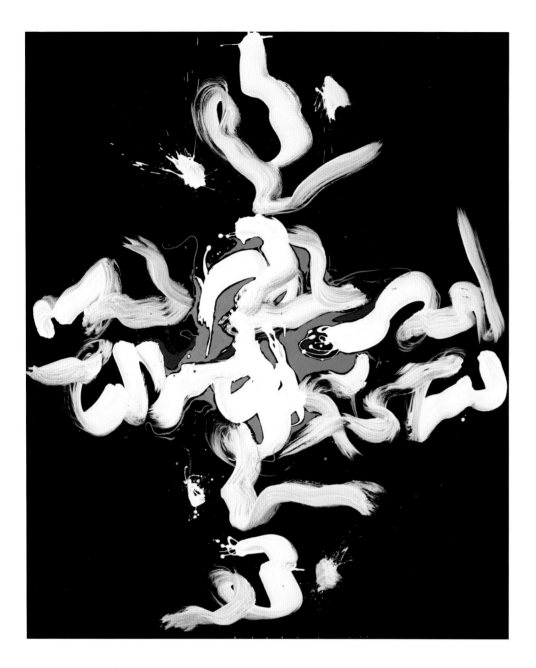

The Iranian artist Golnaz Fathi is one of
only a few women trained as a classical
Persian calligrapher. In her work she
simplifies and abstracts text and letters
into a private visual language that the
viewer may initially read as an image.
In earlier pieces, such as *Untitled (5)*
(2010), words that are clearly based on
Persian script morph into abstraction,
but in later work, such as *Broken Night*
(opposite), Fathi's writing is more akin
to Cy Twombly's 'blackboard' pieces.
It is evident that the base is rooted in
language but, in the artistic translation
into painting, the viewer is left with
marks that merely hint at meaning.

ABOVE · Golnaz Fathi
Does it need to be read? I doubt it...the forms
fascinate me more! they are woven into each
other, they have become one..., 2010
Acrylic on canvas
170 × 140 cm (66⅞ × 55⅛ in.)

OPPOSITE · Golnaz Fathi
Broken Night, 2013
Pen and acrylic on canvas
146 × 128 cm (57½ × 50⅜ in.)

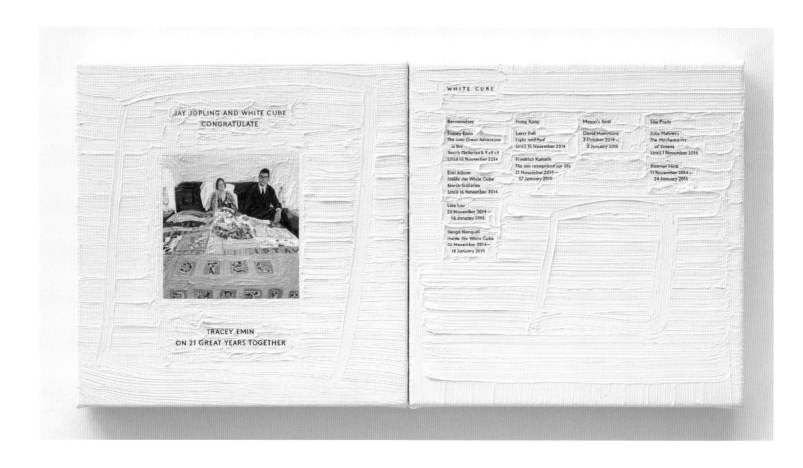

In the mid-1980s, the British artist Simon Linke began painting advertisements in *Artforum* magazine for the exhibitions of other artists. At that time, his works reproduced the predominately black-and-white adverts at varying scales, ranging from about 12 to 182 cm squared (5–72 in. squared). Recent works have the same dimensions as the magazine's pages. The pictorial structure of the paintings has grown in complexity, incorporating images and text found in the adverts; it could be argued that the series represents a history by proxy of the commercial art world centred on New York. In the 2000s, adverts for designer clothing started appearing in the magazine, and Linke followed suit with, for example, *Helmut Lang, Artforum (Label)* and *Prada, Artforum* (both 2006). His paintings question authenticity, identity and the significance of an artist's style as a brand. *Lawrence Weiner at Regen Projects* (opposite) is ironic, as Weiner's text-based works are usually flat, with no visible brushstrokes.

ABOVE · Simon Linke
Tracey Emin, 21 Years at White Cube, 2015
Oil on linen
26.5 × 53 cm (10⅜ × 20⅞ in.)

OPPOSITE · Simon Linke
Lawrence Weiner at Regen Projects, 2017
Oil on linen
26.5 × 26.5 cm (10⅜ × 10⅜ in.)

MADE TO BE

LAWRENCE WEINER

REGEN PROJECTS

LAWRENCE REGEN

7 MAY 2016

REGEN PROJECTS
TEL 1 310 276 5424

6750 SANTA MONICA BOULEVARD
FAX 1 310 276 7430

LOS ANGELES CA 90038
WWW.REGENPROJECTS.COM

This final chapter deals with artists who use books as the material for their installations or who rework them into a different kind of textual object. These artists differ from artists who make artist books. Artist books are works of art in their own right and are usually created as new objects, whether they are lithograph or etched editions or now computer-generated and digitally printed.

The artists Anouk Kruithof and Adam Bateman use thousands of second-hand books to build towering geometric installations. The colours of the spines, pages and covers come into play as elements in the construction process. Ana Fonseca also uses a large number of books in her installation, but they are all of an erotic nature, and they prop up furniture or act as a visual stuffing, falling out of an antique settee. Ishmael Randall Weeks embeds books into architectural columns of his own making, with grey concrete and steel rebar being physical manifestations of the ideas found in his books about building. By contrast, Eric Yahnker builds sculptures from books with titles that speak to one other and to the viewer, forming a distinct new object in a more visible fashion. Stacking books one on top of the other to make a new object recalls the way in which many of us live with books at home. When people own a lot of books, they often have to stack them against a wall or pack them tightly on shelves. Even if we don't possess an extensive book collection, we are still familiar with countless rows of books in bookshops and libraries. Sadly, many libraries are moving away from the storage of physical books, and soon we may have access to a digital library only; we risk losing these social spaces that historically have been part of our greater culture.

Other artists physically alter pre-existing books to make new art objects. For example, Christina Mitrentse shoots a hole through books and displays the mutilated results, along with the shell casing of each bullet used. Andrea Mastrovito cuts up illustrated books to make magical installations that display all manner of flora and fauna. These artists understand the psychic damage that may come from seeing the physical destruction or transformation of a book. The burning of books still has the ability to make the heart grow cold with fear, for, as history has often shown, repressive political regimes may start with the destruction of knowledge and then attempt to destroy those who generate or consume it.

As many readers move away from the physical book, and as text becomes mere information and data (which longs to be free), how will future generations look at that small printed package of wet type on paper?

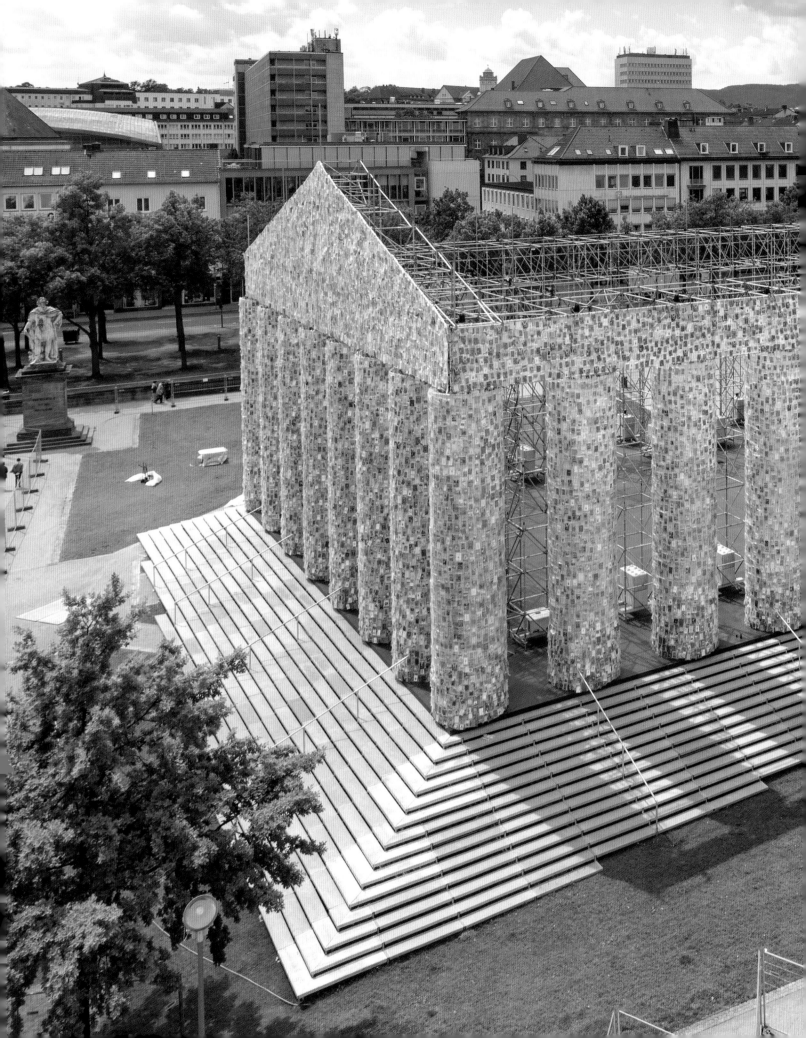

The Argentinian artist Marta Minujín first made her installation *El Partenón de libros* in 1983, after the fall of the military junta in her homeland. She chose to replicate the Parthenon because it is a symbol of democracy. To create her structure she used books that the junta had banned, and at the end of the event they were given away. For documenta 14 in 2017, Minujín built a full-scale version called *The Parthenon of Books* (pp. 260–61) for Friedrichsplatz in Kassel. Significantly, in 1933 more than 2,000 books were burned on this site as part of the Nazis' *Aktion wider den undeutschen Geist* (Campaign against the Un-German Spirit). Minujín asked people from around the world to donate over 100,000 banned books to be used in the work's construction; the books were strapped to the steel frame with plastic sheeting and, again, at the end of the exhibition they were freely distributed.

The Dutch artist Anouk Kruithof uses a wide variety of books in her monumental sculptural works. For *Enclosed content chatting away in the colour invisibility* (above), she gathered approximately 3,500 disused books, most dating from the early 20th century. Some, especially titles from Eastern Europe, were bought in 1 Euro discount stores. Many such books end up in paper banks, to be recycled rather than read. In Kruithof's installation, the books also go unread, instead becoming bricks in a great wall of colour. The installation sometimes features a video, projected 1:1, showing one version of the work (for each installation, the books are displayed in a different order). The digital wall of books eventually collapses with a loud bang, and is then rebuilt. Kruithof likens the individual books to pixels, representing the never-ending march of technology and its impact on reading, printed books, art and the viewer.

PAGES 260–61 · Marta Minujín
The Parthenon of Books, 2017
Steel, books and plastic sheeting
19.5 × 29.5 × 65.5 m
(63 ft 11¾ in. × 96 ft 9⅜ in. × 214 ft 10¾ in.)
Commissioned by documenta 14, with support from the Ministry of Media and Culture of Argentina

ABOVE · Anouk Kruithof
Enclosed content chatting away in the colour invisibility, ongoing since 2009
Approx. 3,500 found coloured books, installed here at Casemore Kirkeby, San Francisco, 2017
230 × 410 cm (90½ × 161⅜ in.)

ABOVE · Adam Bateman
Kittens, 2011 · Books
502.9 × 670.6 × 121.9 cm
(198 × 264 × 48 in.)

The monumental sculpture *Kittens* (2011), by the American artist Adam Bateman, was part of the 'Cantastoria' exhibition, curated by Aaron Moulton for the Utah Museum of Contemporary Art in 2012. The exhibition title is the Italian term for 'history singer' or for a story that is told in song. Such tales were performed for the inhabitants of small towns or villages at a time when most people were illiterate. The storyteller often pointed to a series of images as they sang. These performances were a means of passing on news and important cultural messages. *Kittens* renders the viewer illiterate, at least in terms of reading the thousands of books that Bateman used to create the 5-metre-tall (16½ ft) structure. The books were stacked without the use of glue, so there remains the possibility of the books once more becoming legible and being read – but that is not the point. The viewer is presented with a huge volume of hidden words; they are invited to imagine those words and to create their own stories (possibly including ones that involve small felines). The layers of different coloured covers recall geological strata and the passing of many varied histories.

The Portuguese artist Sofia Leitão has made a series of sculptural works consisting of stacks of books with golden springs spewing from them (above). The books date from the 19th, 20th and 21st centuries (the older books placed at the bottom), creating a timeline that may be associated with a cultural geology. Leitão explains that 'obsolete information, once representative of a bygone world, is lost through crystallizing or liquefying as a gold torrent', in much the same way that oil is generated within rock structures. Natural and artificial phenomenon are hinted at in the works, which allude to the wealth of knowledge potentially lost or yet to be rediscovered.

In 2010 Ana Fonseca, a Portuguese artist, created the site-specific installation *Jardim perfumado* (Perfumed Garden; opposite) at the Museu de Artes Decorativas, Fundação Ricardo do Espírito Santo Silva in Lisbon. In one of the grand drawing rooms she placed piles of books under an antique cream sofa and a similar chair. If they looked closely, viewers could make out the titles of some of the books, including *Jardin perfumado*, written sometime between the 12th and 15th centuries, and attributed to Muhammad al-Nafzawi. The Arabic text describes sexual positions, manners, techniques and pleasures. Other books that stood out from their storage place included *The Kama Sutra*, the famous ancient Sanskrit treatise on the art of sexual technique; *The Art of Love* by Ovid; an anthology of erotic poetry; works by the Marquis de Sade; and contemporary erotic novels. 'Whatever Lola Wants', sung by Sarah Vaughan, played softly in the background. Fonseca continually had to restack and tidy the piles, as – although the books were not meant to be touched – visitors and guard staff kept removing them to read and then misplaced them. Visitors were also not allowed to sit on the furniture.

OPPOSITE · Sofia Leitão
Matéria do esquecimento (Forgetfulness
Matter), 2011 · Books, sequins, steel
pins, foam, wire and black leatherette
256 × 190 × 130 cm
(100¾ × 74¾ × 51⅛ in.)

ABOVE AND LEFT · Ana Fonseca
Jardim perfumado (Perfumed Garden),
2010 · Second-hand and erotic books,
and sound; site-specific installation
at the Museu de Artes Decorativas,
Fundação Ricardo do Espírito Santo
Silva, Lisbon · Dimensions variable

In *The Castle* (left), Jorge Méndez Blake harnesses the power of words in both a symbolic and a physical way. Méndez Blake placed a paperback copy of Franz Kafka's unfinished novel (1926) of the same name in the middle of his work, at the base of a wall of red bricks. In the novel, the protagonist, K, attempts to deal with an unseen, stifling bureaucracy that crushes him, much like Méndez Blake's brick wall might do. The placement of the book disrupted the structure of the wall and, as each row of bricks was added, the bump in the wall became more pronounced. Méndez Blake's work is more hopeful than Kafka's, however, as it demonstrates the way in which one individual or text can make an impact on the world.

Five Thousand Trashy Romance Novels (opposite), by the American artist Thedra Cullar-Ledford, is a conceptual portrait of her mother, a 'serious' published author who secretly loves to read romantic fiction. Consisting of colourful paperbacks (with such titles as *Tears of the Moon*, *Rebel's Desire* and *Seasons of Love*) stacked into a square, it is topped by a concrete lid that presses down on – one could say, suppresses – the novels geared towards women. The work poses the question: what books are suitable for adults to be seen reading? The piece has been remade on several occasions, including at the National Academy Museum, New York, in 1998, and in 2016 at the Contemporary Arts Museum Houston, Texas.

LEFT · Jorge Méndez Blake
The Castle (detail at bottom), 2007
Bricks and 1 copy of Franz Kafka's
El castillo · 1.8 × 23 × 0.4 m
(70⅞ in. × 75 ft 5½ in. × 15¾ in.)

OPPOSITE · Thedra Cullar-Ledford
Five Thousand Trashy Romance Novels,
1997/2016 · Approx. 5,000 books,
concrete and graphite, installed here
at the Contemporary Arts Museum
Houston, Texas, 2016
114.3 × 114.3 × 121.9 cm (45 × 45 × 48 in.)

The Peruvian artist Ishmael Randall
Weeks seeks to address issues of
urbanization and its costs to populations
that might have no say over it. He
juxtaposes the architecture of High
Modernism, exemplified by the work
of Le Corbusier, and its aim of carving
out pure, usually white, space in the
built environment, with the architecture
of urban Latin America (such as *favela*
shacks and temporary adobe structures).
Randall Weeks's work often takes the
form of a visual landscape created from
books on architecture, and he critiques
the hidden values at their core by
emphasizing how their internationalist
language of the new contrasts with the
structures of the indigenous peoples of
his homeland. In *Pilares* (Pillars; right), he
presents four concrete columns that look
as if they have been abandoned during
the construction process – as was the
case with so many similar structures after
the economic crash of 2008. The pillars
are composed of reinforced concrete and
books on such topics as concrete, human
geography and economics.

In 2010 Fiona Banner was awarded
the Duveen Galleries commission at
Tate Britain, for which she installed
recently decommissioned Harrier and
Jaguar aeroplanes in the neoclassical
space, almost as if they were exotic
animal specimens. Her interest in war
planes extends to her work *1909–2011*
(opposite), which comprises a stack of
books of all the world's models from the
international authority, Jane's. It took
Banner nearly twenty years to gather all
the books into a single collection that
she then transformed into a sculpture,
where the information contained
within is now out of reach, yet remains
temptingly close.

RIGHT · Ishmael Randall Weeks
Pilares (Pillars), 2014
Reinforced concrete, carved books
and laminated photographs, installed
at Arróniz Arte Contemporáneo,
Mexico City · Dimensions variable

OPPOSITE · Fiona Banner
1909–2011, 2010
97 *Jane's All the World's Aircraft* books
375 × 35 × 22 cm (147⅝ × 13¾ × 8⅝ in.)

Exceptional Suicide (left), by Eric Yahnker, was included in the American artist's 2016 show 'Noah's Yacht' at Zevitas Marcus, Los Angeles, before the US presidential election of that year. The work comprises two very different books: the collaboration between Dick Cheney and his daughter Liz, entitled *Exceptional: Why the World Needs a Powerful America* (2015); and *Suicide* (1897), by the French sociologist Émile Durkheim. The Cheneys are on the right of the political spectrum, while Durkheim espoused left-wing beliefs. Yahnker studied journalism and suggests that much of his artwork 'is innately built upon language'; he says, 'I've always hinted my work was as much to be read as viewed.' *A Full Plate* (left, below), made for his solo show 'Nervous Surf' at Galerie Jeanroch Dard, Paris, in 2010, depicts the spines of the books *Breakfast with Mao*, *Lunch with Mussolini* and *Dinner with Mugabe*. According to Yahnker, the large colour drawing offers the viewer 'a hypothetical, casual "seat at the table" with a few of the 20th century's most infamous despots'.

The Chinese artist Yang Zhichao addressed his country's past when he presented an installation of thousands of diaries previously owned by ordinary citizens that he bought at Beijing's Panjiayuan, or Dirt, flea market. The work, *Chinese Bible* (opposite), recalls the fact that, under Mao Zedong's rule (1949–76), people were expected to carry a copy of, and be able to quote from, his 'Little Red Book', which contains such aphorisms as 'All reactionaries are paper tigers.' Yang's diaries date from 1949 to 1999, and they record fragments of everyday life, such as shopping lists, knitting patterns and song lyrics, as well as the more chilling 'self-criticisms' that those who broke the rules had to endure.

LEFT, ABOVE · Eric Yahnker
Exceptional Suicide, 2016 · 40 books
36.5 × 63.5 × 16.5 cm (14 × 25 × 6½ in.)

LEFT · Eric Yahnker
A Full Plate, 2010
Coloured pencil on paper
199.4 × 133.4 cm (78½ × 52½ in.)

OPPOSITE · Yang Zhichao
Chinese Bible, 2009
3,000 found diaries, installed here at Sherman Contemporary Art Foundation, Sydney, 2015 · Dimensions variable

THE LIBRARY OF
UNBORROWED BOOKS

OPPOSITE · Meriç Algün
The Library of Unborrowed Books.
Section I: Stockholms Stadsbibliotek
(detail at bottom), 2012
Site-specific installation at
Konstakademien, Stockholm,
with books, shelves, brass sign
and 2 contracts · Dimensions variable

ABOVE · Rachel Whiteread
Untitled (Novels), 1999
Plaster, polystyrene and steel
121 × 163 × 26 cm (47⅝ × 64⅛ × 10¼ in.)

The Turkish artist Meriç Algün asks, what happens to a library book that is never read? In her ongoing series of installations called 'The Library of Unborrowed Books', she displays those titles that no one has ever checked out from specific libraries. The first incarnation, in 2012 (opposite), featured books from Stockholms Stadsbibliotek. Further installations, in 2013–15, borrowed titles from libraries in New York, Sydney, Cuenca (Ecuador), Athens and Istanbul. Algün's work questions the validity of an unborrowed book, which has merely been catalogued into the vast global, continuously growing system of words, information and their storage. Neither the viewer nor the artist will ever know why these books were simply left on the shelf.

Since the late 1980s the British artist Rachel Whiteread has cast many objects – or, rather, their 'negative spaces' – ranging from the insides of wardrobes and the undersides of chairs to an entire building (*House*, 1993). She won the competition to design the Judenplatz Holocaust Memorial in Vienna with *Nameless Library* (2000). Its walls comprise eleven rows of cast library shelves, the spines of the books hidden, so that viewers see only the closed pages. The monument is as impenetrable as the concrete books are illegible. The inscription on the base reads (in German, Hebrew and English), 'In commemoration of more than 65,000 Austrian Jews who were killed by the Nazis between 1938 and 1945.' The monument may be seen as the culmination of Whiteread's cast-book works, among them *Untitled (Novels)* (above), in which the colour of the covers seeped into the plaster.

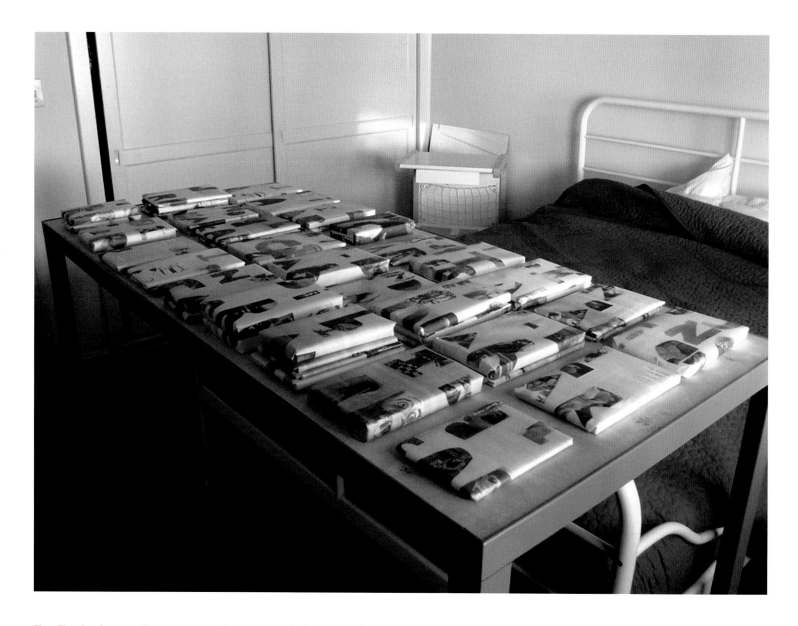

Eve Fowler has made a continually changing work that originated at the ONE National Gay and Lesbian Archives, at the University of Southern California, Los Angeles, where she bought sixty-two books, dating from the 1960s, '70s and '80s, as duplicates for clearance. The work gradually evolved as she wrapped the books in newspaper collages of her own making. Fowler has exhibited them, both hidden within and out of their covers, in a variety of venues, including the 2010 California Biennial at the Orange County Museum of Art; Printed Matter, New York, in 2013; Artspace, Sydney, in 2015; and the Center for Book Arts, New York, in 2016. The full name of the work covers six typed pages, and includes bibliographic information on all the books (title, author, publisher and year of publication) and a short story by Andrea Dworkin. Fowler provides a handout of the extended title when she exhibits the work in order to expand the viewers' knowledge of pioneers in lesbian and feminist writing. Fowler explains: 'As I looked closely at these books I realized that the women who wrote them took real risks to assert themselves. So the project is a show of appreciation for these writers who made the effort to change things, [to] state their opinions in obscurity.'

ABOVE · Eve Fowler
62 Books, ongoing since 2004
Books, printed title document
and newspaper, installed here at the
Apartment 2 Gallery, Los Angeles, 2010
Dimensions variable

ABOVE AND OVERLEAF ·
Andrea Mastrovito
The Island of Dr Mastrovito II
(detail above), 2012
1,200 cut-out books about botany
and zoology, installed at the Musée
de Design et d'Arts Appliqués
Contemporains (mudac), Lausanne,
2012–13 · Dimensions variable

The Italian artist Andrea Mastrovito uses assemblage and collage to make paintings and installations. *The Island of Dr Mastrovito* – first installed at Governors Island, New York, in 2010, with a new version shown in Lausanne in 2012–13 – features thousands of three-dimensional pictures of flora and fauna cut from the pages of zoology and botany books. The visually complex work sees a veritable Noah's ark of animals intermingle with flowers, plants and real-life members of the audience. The work rains down from the ceiling and spills across the floor, almost bombarding the viewer with brightly coloured images that pop up out of their book bases. The work references *The Island of Dr Moreau* (1896), a novel by

H. G. Wells, in which the eponymous doctor creates gruesome human–animal hybrids that are anything but the happy creatures in Mastrovito's installations. In biblical texts, before the Fall of Man, all animals, including humans, lived in perfect harmony in the Garden of Eden.

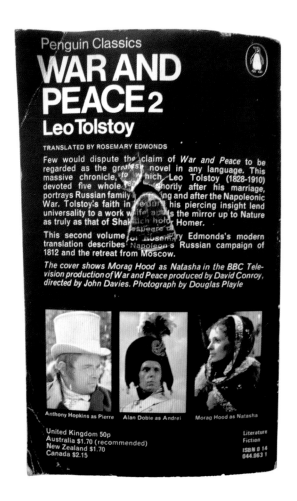

The Greek artist Christina Mitrentse has made multiple series of works involving the alteration of pre-existing books. Many are stacked, folded and sanded into new objects. Other works consist of several books merged together; in *Beethoven versus Mozart* (2010), two music scores are folded together. For the 'Wounded Books' series (above), Mitrentse took Penguin and Pelican paperbacks and titles from the Wiener Library in London (devoted to the study of the Holocaust) to the Imperial College Union Rifle and Pistol Club, and shot them with a Winchester 4.8 calibre rifle under licensed conditions. The books were then placed in clear plastic sleeves and exhibited. The front covers have a clean wound, while the backs display greater evidence of violence. Mitrentse's aim is that the viewer becomes a conceptual reader of books that are themselves endangered, as the digital age disrupts old models of information production, distribution and delivery.

Aleksandar Duravcevic's exhibition 'Memory Keeper', at Ordovas, London, in 2017, explored storytelling, the endless passage of time and the ways in which humans often repeat the mistakes of the past. Duravcevic was born in the former Yugoslavia and fled to Italy during the civil war of the early 1990s. Many of his works address war as a global phenomenon. His wordless book *Touch Me Not* (opposite) is carved from marble, and the only story within is that written by the grain of the stone. The obvious weight of the volume comes into focus, together with the weight of history, as it attests to more than one period of human conflict and our apparent inability as *Homo sapiens* to learn.

ABOVE · Christina Mitrentse
War and Peace (Wounded Book), 2013
Found book and bullet casing
18 × 11 × 4 cm (7⅛ × 4⅜ × 1⅝ in.)

OPPOSITE · Aleksandar Duravcevic
Touch Me Not, 2017
Travertine with steel base
82.5 × 89.5 × 70 cm
(32½ × 35¼ × 27½ in.)

This book is dedicated to my partner, Travis Barker, who has long supported all of my artistic and personal efforts.

I would like to thank all the artists and their representatives for their participation in the book.

This book would not exist were it not for the dedication and professionalism of Roberto Ekholm, Paola d'Albore, Amandine Carat, Alexandra Fraser, Elliot Higgs and Sara Medici.

I would like to thank the staff of Thames & Hudson, especially Amber Husain and Roger Thorp, and the editor, Claire Chandler, for their hard work. Special thanks to Jonathan Abbott for his wonderful design work.

I would also like to thank Constance Kaine for her continuing support of my writing for more than thirty years.

Further Reading

General

Dixon Hunt, John, David Lomas and Michael Corris, *Art, Word and Image: 2,000 Years of Visual/Textual Interaction*, London: Reaktion, 2010

Kalyva, Eve, *Image and Text in Conceptual Art: Critical Operations in Context*, Cham, Switzerland: Palgrave Macmillan, 2016

McLuhan, Marshall, and Quentin Fiore, *The Medium is the Massage: An Inventory of Effects*, New York: Bantam, 1967

Morley, Simon, *Writing on the Wall: Word and Image in Modern Art*, London: Thames & Hudson, 2003

Selby, Aimee (ed.), *Art and Text*, London: Black Dog, 2009

Artist Monographs and Exhibition Catalogues

Auping, Michael, *Jenny Holzer*, New York: Universe, 1992

Banner, Fiona, *The Nam*, London: Frith Street Gallery, 1997

Barbara Kruger: Believe + Doubt, exhib. cat., ed. Yilmaz Dziewior, Kunsthaus Bregenz, 19 October 2013–12 January 2014

Brown, Katrina M., *et al.*, *Nathan Coley*, Ostfildern: Hatje Cantz, 2014

Ceal Floyer: A Handbook, exhib. cat., ed. Susanne Küper, Kunstmuseum Bonn, 29 October 2015–10 January 2016; Aarau, Aargauer Kunsthaus, 30 January–10 April 2016

Cerith Wyn Evans, exhib. cat. by Hélène Cixous *et al.*, London, Serpentine Sackler Gallery, 17 September–9 November 2014

Christian Marclay: Action, exhib. cat., ed. Madeleine Schuppli, Aarau, Aargauer Kunsthaus, 30 August–15 November 2015

Christopher Wool, exhib. cat., ed. Katherine Brinson, New York, Solomon R. Guggenheim Museum, 25 October 2013–22 January 2014

Collins, Judith, and Iain Sinclair, *Gavin Turk*, Munich and London: Prestel, 2013

Dan Colen: Sweet Liberty, exhib. cat. by Francesco Bonami *et al.*, London, Newport Street Gallery, 4 October 2017–28 January 2018

De Oliveira, Nicolas, *et al.*, *Capitalism and Schizophrenia: Stefan Brüggemann*, Madrid: Turner, 2004

Deller, Jeremy, with Rufus Norris, *"We're here because we're here"*, London: Cultureshock Media for 14–18 NOW, 2017

Ed Ruscha and the Great American West, exhib. cat. by Karin Breuer, Kerry Brougher and D. J. Waldie, San Francisco, de Young, 16 July–9 October 2016

Fowler, Eve, *Anyone Telling Anything is Telling That Thing*, New York: Printed Matter, 2013

Ghada Amer, exhib. cat by Thérèse St-Gelais, Montreal, Musée d'Art Contemporain de Montréal, 2 February–22 April 2012

Glenn Ligon: Come Out, exhib. cat. by Megan Ratner, London, Camden Arts Centre, 10 October 2014–11 January 2015

Godfrey, Tony, and Hélène Cixous, *Vera's Room: The Art of Maria Chevska*, London: Black Dog, 2005

Golnaz Fathi: Liminal Subliminal, exhib. cat. by Gerard Houghton, London, October Gallery, 11 November 2009–22 January 2010

Heide, Ulrich, and Dietmar Kamper (eds), *Tom Fecht – Namen und Steine: Mémoire Nomade*, rev. edn, Vienna and New York: Springer, 2001

Joseph Kosuth: 'ni apparence, ni illusion', exhib. cat. by Henri Loyrette *et al.*, Paris, Musée du Louvre, 22 October 2009–21 June 2010

Kraynak, Janet, Alexander Alberro and Juliane Rebentisch, *Monica Bonvicini*, London: Phaidon, 2014

Kusho, exhib. cat. by Shinichi Maruyama, New York, Bruce Silverstein Gallery, 15 January–21 February 2009

Laure Prouvost: Hit Flash Back, exhib. cat. by Nick Aikens *et al.*, Dijon, Frankfurt and Lucerne, 2016–17

Lawrence Weiner: As Far as the Eye Can See, exhib. cat., ed. Ann Goldstein and Donna De Salvo, New York, Los Angeles and Düsseldorf, 2007–9

Liliane Lijn: Works 1959–80, exhib. cat. by David Alan Mellor, Warwick, Mead Gallery, 28 April–22 June 2005

Mark Flood: Gratest Hits, exhib. cat. by Bill Arning *et al.*, Contemporary Arts Museum Houston, 30 April–7 August 2016

Massoudy, Hassan, *Calligraphies of Love*, London: Saqi Books, 2017

Maurizio Nannucci, exhib. cat., Florence, Palazzo Vecchio, 22 October–4 December 1983

Mel Bochner: If the Colour Changes, exhib. cat., ed. Achim Borchardt-Hume and Doro Globus, London, Munich and Porto, 2012–13

Méndez Blake, Jorge, *Other Literature*, Mexico City: Ediciones MP, 2016

Miller, Harland, *International Lonely Guy*, contrib. Ed Ruscha *et al.*, New York: Rizzoli, 2007

Nari Ward: Sun Splashed, exhib. cat. by Diana Nawi *et al.*, Pérez Art Museum Miami, 19 November 2015–21 February 2016

Neri, Louise, Lynne Cooke and Thierry de Duve, *Roni Horn*, London: Phaidon, 2000

Noe, Christopher (ed.), *Liu Ye: Catalogue Raisonné, 1991–2015*, Ostfildern: Hatje Cantz, 2015

Rachel Whiteread, exhib. cat., ed. Ann Gallagher and Molly Donovan, London, Vienna, Washington, DC, and St Louis, 2017–19

Raymond Pettibon: A Pen of All Work, exhib. cat., ed. Massimiliano Gioni and Gary Carrion-Murayari, New York, New Museum, 8 February–16 April 2017; Maastricht, Bonnefantenmuseum, 1 June–30 October 2017

Shirin Neshat: Facing History, exhib. cat., ed. Melissa Chiu and Melissa Chiu, Washington, DC, Hirshhorn Museum and Sculpture Garden, 18 May–20 September 2015

Smith, Bob and Roberta, *I Should Be in Charge*, London: Black Dog, 2011

Szewczyk, Monika (ed.), *Meaning Liam Gillick*, Cambridge, Mass., and London: MIT Press, 2009

Tania Bruguera: Talking to Power/Hablándole al poder, exhib. cat., ed. Lucía Sanromán and Susie Kantor, San Francisco, Yerba Buena Center for the Arts, 16 June–29 October 2017

Terence Koh, 1980–2008: Love for Eternity, exhib. cat. by Bill Arning and Agustín Pérez Rubio, León, Museo de Arte Contemporáneo de Castilla y León, 27 September 2008–11 January 2009

TSANG Kin-Wah: Ecce Homo Trilogy, exhib. cat., ed. Markus Landert and Stefanie Hoch, Warth, Kunstmuseum Thurgau, 23 August–15 December 2015

Welchman, John C., and Carter Ratcliff, *Kwang Young Chun: Mulberry Mindscapes*, New York: Skira Rizzoli, 2014

Wobbe, Katharine and Henrik (eds), *Robert Montgomery*, Berlin: Distanz, 2015

Yablonsky, Linda, *Noble & Webster: 2000 Words*, Athens: DESTE Foundation for Contemporary Art, 2014

Zhang Huan, exhib. cat., ed. Yilmaz Dziewior, Kunstverein in Hamburg, 30 November 2002–9 February 2003; Kunstmuseum Bochum, 5 April–15 June 2003

A = ABOVE; B = BELOW;
C = CENTRE; L = LEFT;
R = RIGHT

2 · Photo: Chun Kwang Young studio
4 · Courtesy Björkholmen Gallery. Photo: Roger Björkholmen
9 AL · Art Institute of Chicago, Mr. and Mrs. Carter H. Harrison Collection, 1954.1193; AR · Philadelphia Museum of Art, Philadelphia, The Louise and Walter Arensberg Collection, 1950 (1950-134-26). Braque © ADAGP, Paris and DACS, London 2018; BL · Metropolitan Museum of Art, New York. Leonard A. Lauder Cubist Collection, Purchase, Leonard A. Lauder Gift, 2014 (2014.463); BR · Metropolitan Museum of Art, New York. Alfred Stieglitz Collection, 1949 (49.59.1)
13 AR · Private collection, Courtesy Tornabuoni Art; AL · Courtesy Archives Fondazione Nicola Del Roscio. Photo Mimmo Capone. © Cy Twombly Foundation; B · Courtesy Cheim & Read, New York. © Louise Fishman
14–15 · © Ed Ruscha. Courtesy the artist and Gagosian
17 A · The Estate of Stanisław Dróżdż, Courtesy Galeria Propaganda, Warsaw; B · Courtesy the author's collection. Photo: Hassan Massoudy
19 A · Photo: Richard Wilding 2015. Courtesy the artist. Collection of James Keith Brown and Eric Diefenbach; B · Collection Museum of Modern Art, NYC. Courtesy the artist
21 AL · Courtesy Galleria Fumagalli Milano. Photo: Musacchio & Ianniello; AR · Courtesy the artist and Gladstone Gallery, New York and Brussels. Photo: David Regen. © Mario Merz ; BL · Courtesy the artist and P420, Bologna. Photo Carlo Favero; BR · © Gilbert & George. Courtesy White Cube
23 AL · © Raymond Pettibon. Courtesy David Zwirner, New York/Hong Kong.

Photo: MOCA London; AC · Photo: FXP Photography; AR · Courtesy the artist and Gladstone Gallery, New York and Brussels. © Shirin Neshat; BL · Courtesy the artist and Hauser & Wirth. Photo: Wilfried Petzi; BR · Courtesy documenta Archive Kassel / German AIDS-Foundation, Bonn. Photo: Werner Maschmann
26–27 · Courtesy eL Seed. Photo: eL Seed
28 · Photo courtesy Moved Pictures Archive, New York. Weiner © ARS, NY and DACS, London 2018
29 · Courtesy St+Art India. Photo: Akshat Nauriyal
30 · Courtesy the artist. Photo: Sebastian Bieniek (B1EN1EK)
31 · Courtesy Futurecity Ltd. Photos: Ron Bambridge
32 A · Photo: Beni Bischof; B · Photo: Beni Bischof
33 · Courtesy Micah Lexier and Birch Contemporary, Toronto. Photo: Roger Smith
34 · Courtesy Mark Themann. Photo: David Brandt
35 · Courtesy Kay Rosen
36–37 · Courtesy Helsinki Contemporary. Photo: Jussi Tiainen.
38 · Photos: TSANG Kin-Wah
39 · Photo: Michael Petry
40 L · Photo: Anka Dabrowska; R · Photo: MOCA London
41 · Courtesy Bracknell and Wokingham College of Further Education and the artist. Photo: Stephen White
42 · Courtesy the artist and Frith Street Gallery, London. Commissioned by the De La Warr Pavilion as part of the ROOT 1066 International Festival. Photo: the artist
43 · Courtesy the artist. Photos: Injinaash Bor
44 · Courtesy The Glasgow School of Art. Photo: Alex Sarkisian
45 A · Courtesy the artist and Galeria Vermelho, Sao Paulo, Brazil. Photo: Klaus Stoeber; B · Courtesy the artist and Galeria Vermelho, Sao Paulo, Brazil. Photo: Aurélie Goetz
46 · Courtesy Contemporary Art Centre of Montenegro. Photo: Duško Miljanić
47 · Photo: Kate Murdoch
48 · Courtesy the artist and

Marian Goodman Gallery, New York. Photo: John Berens
49 · Photo: xpon-art gallery
50–51 · Courtesy Dvir Gallery, Tel Aviv. Photo: Elad Sarig
52–53 · Courtesy Mary Boone Gallery, New York. © Barbara Kruger. Photo: Cathy Carver.
56–57 Courtesy the artist. Photo: Alan Magee
58 · © Santiago Sierra Credit. Courtesy Lisson Gallery. Photo: Ken Adlard
59 · Photo: Nick Caro Photography
60 · Photo: Ryan Everson and Jason Garcia
61 · Courtesy the artist and VG Bild-Kunst. Photos: Jan Ralske
62 · Courtesy the artist / Artist Rights Society (ARS), New York, NY. Image courtesy the artist and Paul Kasmin Gallery. Photo: Elisabeth Bernstein
63 · Photo courtesy Fondazione Merz
64 A · Courtesy Cheim & Read, New York B · Courtesy Cheim & Read, New York
65 · Courtesy Cheim & Read, New York
66 · Courtesy the artist and Galeria Vermelho, Sao Paulo, Brazil. Photo: Tania Candiani
67 · Courtesy the artist. Photo: the artist and Exhibit320
68 · Collection of the City and County of San Francisco, San Francisco Arts Commission. Photo: Bruce Damonte
69 · Courtesy 303 Gallery, New York; Galerie Eva Presenhuber, Zürich; Victoria Miro Gallery, London; and Regen Projects, Los Angeles
70 A · Courtesy Becker Collection, Cologne. Photo: Achim Kukulies, Dusseldorf; C · Courtesy Becker Collection, Cologne. Photo: FORT; B · Courtesy Philara Collection, Dusseldorf. Photo: Achim Kukulies, Dusseldorf
71 L · Photo: Studiobarbosaricalde; AR · Photo: Studio-barbosaricalde; BR · Photo: Studiobarbosaricalde
72 · Courtesy the artist. Photo: Nigel Green
73 · Courtesy the artist and Barry Whistler Gallery. Photo: the artist
74 · Courtesy Rirkrit Tiravanija Studio. Photos: MOCA London
75 · Photo: Chun Kwang

Young studio
76 · Photo © Jake and Dinos Chapman (Image: Jonathan Middleton)
77 · Photo: Ghiora Aharoni
78 · Photo: MOCA London
79 A · Courtesy LABS Gallery, Bologna (I). Photo: Fabio Zonta; B · Courtesy the artist; Photo: Fiona Wang
80 · Courtesy the artist and Hauser & Wirth; Photo: Ron Amstutz
81 · Photo: Fiona Shaw
82 · Photo: Robert Glowacki Photography
83 · Courtesy the artist and Hannah Barry Gallery. Photo: James Balmforth
84 A · Courtesy Caroline Whitehead and Rick Yoder. Photo Matthew Booth; B · Courtesy EKCO London. Photo: Matthew Booth
85 · Photo: the artist
86 · Courtesy Corporate collection, USA
87 · Courtesy the artist. Photo: Mark Dutcher
90 · Courtesy Neue Berliner Raume and Anna Jill Lüpertz Gallery. Photo: Robert Montgomery Studio
91 · © Jenny Holzer. ARS, NY and DACS/Artimage, London 2018. Photo: Sang Tae Kim
92 · Photo © studioNathanColey
93 · Photo © studioNathanColey
94 · © Tim Noble and Sue Webster. All Rights Reserved, DACS 2018. Photo: Courtesy Blain|Southern, Photo Peter Mallet
95 · Courtesy the artist and VG Bild-Kunst. Photo: Mattias Givell
96–97 · Photo: Cisco and David Gallard
98 · © Cerith Wyn Evans. Photo © Stephen White Courtesy White Cube
99 · © Glenn Ligon; Courtesy the artist, Luhring Augustine, New York, Regen Projects, Los Angeles, and Thomas Dane Gallery, London
100 · Tur © DACS 2018. Photo: MOCA London
101 · Photo: Alexandre Ouairy
102 · Courtesy the artist. Photo: Andrew Catlin
103 · Courtesy the artist and MOCA London. Photo: Lewis Ronald

104 · Courtesy the artist / KUAD Gallery Istanbul / Sprüth Magers Gallery London © Joseph Kosuth. ARS, NY and DACS, London 2018

105 · Courtesy the artist. Photo © Tim Etchells

106 · Photo: Li Bo (李泊)

107 · Courtesy Galerie Nikolaus Ruzicska Salzburg. Photo: Zona Archives Firenze

108/109 · Courtesy David Roberts collection. Photo: Steve Payne

110 · Courtesy the artist and Hauser & Wirth. © Martin Creed. All Rights Reserved, DACS 2018. Photo: Hugo Glendinning.

111 · Courtesy the artist

112 A · Courtesy Claire Fontaine and Galerie Neu, Berlin. Photo: James Thornhill; B · Courtesy Claire Fontaine and Air de Paris, Paris. Photo: Florian Kleinefenn

113 · Courtesy Shi Yong and ShanghART Gallery. Photo: Shi Yong

114 · Courtesy CONNERSMITH, Washington, DC. Photo © Sheldon Scott

115 · Courtesy the artist and Lehmann Maupin, New York and Hong Kong

116 · Courtesy the artist and Devin Borden Gallery. Photo: Darryl Lauster

117 · Collection of Avo Samuelian and Hector Manuel Gonzalez. Photo: David Robinson

118 · Courtesy the artist. Photo: Michal Strokowski

119 · Courtesy the artist. Photo: M.Shaowanasai

120 · Collection of the artist

121 · Courtesy the artist. Photo: J. Lindsay

124 A · Courtesy the artist; BL · Courtesy the artist; BR · Courtesy the artist. Photo: MOCA London

126 A · Courtesy the artist. Photo: Kikuyama; B · Courtesy the artist. Photo: Kikuyama

127 · Courtesy the artist. Photo: Yohei Yamakami

128 · Courtesy Helsinki Contemporary. Photo: Vanessa Forstén

129 L · Courtesy Helsinki Contemporary; R · Courtesy Helsinki Contemporary. Photo: Jussi Tiainen

130 · Courtesy the artist and Ronald Feldman Fine Arts, NYC

131 A · Courtesy the artists; B · Courtesy the artists

132–133 · Photo: Liliane Lijn

134–135 · Courtesy Germano Montanari. Photo: Gustav Willeit

136 · Courtesy the artist. Photo: Barbara Sutherland

137 · Courtesy the artist. Photo: Mikey Dread777

138 · Courtesy New Tretyakov Gallery, Aristarkh Chernyshev. Photo: Aristarkh Chernyshev

139 · Courtesy the artist and Hannah Barry Gallery; Photo: Damian Griffiths

140 · © the artist. Courtesy Sadie Coles HQ, London

141 A · Courtesy the artist. Photo: Plastiques Ltd; B · Courtesy the artist. Photo: Plastiques Ltd

142 © Archive Mischa Kuball, Düsseldorf / VG Bild-Kunst, Bonn 2018. Photo: Studio Mischa Kuball, Düsseldorf / VG Bild-Kunst, Bonn 2018

143 · Photos: TSANG Kin-Wah

144–145 · © Christian Marclay. Courtesy Paula Cooper Gallery, New York. Photo: Steven Probert

146 · Courtesy the artist. Photo: the artist

147 · Courtesy Shimon Attie, Commissioned by Creative Time, Inc. Photo: Shimon Attie, Image courtesy Jack Shainman Gallery, New York

148 · Courtesy Mikel Glass, (un)SCENE. Photo: Francesca Pagani

149 · Courtesy Kay Rosen. Photo: Elliot Luscombe

150 A · Courtesy the artist. Photo: Pablo Gimenez-Zapiola. Poem by Javier Galarza; C · Courtesy the artist. Photo: Pablo Gimenez-Zapiola. Poem by Felipe Gimenez-Zapiola; B · Courtesy the artist. Photo: Pablo Gimenez-Zapiola.

151 · Photos: Maya Chowdhry

154 AL · Courtesy Hauser & Wirth; AR · Courtesy Hauser & Wirth; R · Courtesy Hauser & Wirth

155 ON WALLS · © Liam Gillick. Courtesy Maureen Paley, London; ON FLOOR · © Liam Gillick. Courtesy Maureen Paley, London

156 · © Carey Young. Courtesy Paula Cooper Gallery, New York

157 · Photo © noshowspace

158 · Courtesy the artist, Galerie Nathalie Obadia (Paris and Brussels) and carlier | gebauer (Berlin). Photo: Benoit Pailley.

159 · Photo: Felipe Barbosa

160 · © the Artist. Courtesy Lisson Gallery. Photo: Dave Morgan

161 · Courtesy the artist and 1301PE, Meessen De Clercq, OMR and Travesía Cuatro. Photo: Bruno Viruete / Estudio Jorge Méndez Blake

162 · Courtesy the artist and Private Swedish Collection. Photo: Patric Leo

163 LA · Courtesy the artist. Photo: Lucian Taylor; LC · Courtesy the artist. Photo: Lucian Taylor; LB · Courtesy the artist. Photo the artist; RA · Courtesy the artist. Photo William Sadowski; RB · Courtesy the artist. Photo William Sadowski

164–166 · Courtesy the artist. Photos: Matthew Clowney

167 · Courtesy the artist. Photo: Andy Keate

168 L · Courtesy CONNERSMITH, Washington, DC. Photo © Joe Ovelman; R · Courtesy CONNERSMITH, Washington, DC. Photo © Joe Ovelman

169 · Courtesy Mier Gallery, Los Angeles

170 · Courtesy the artist

171 · © the artist. Photo © White Cube (George Darrell)

172 · Courtesy the artist. Photos: MOCA London

173 · Courtesy Purdy Hicks Gallery, The Moth House. Photo: @ Edgar Martins (www.edgarmartins.com)

174 · Courtesy Claire Fontaine. Photos: James Thornhill

175 A · Courtesy Mannerheim Gallery. Photo: Robert Montgomery Studio; B · Courtesy Mannerheim Gallery. Photo: Robert Montgomery Studio

176 A · Courtesy Mircea Cantor. Photo Gabriela Vanga; B · Courtesy Mircea Cantor. Photo: Mircea Cantor.

177 · Photos: the artist

178 A · Courtesy the artist & Galerie Krinzinger, Vienna; C · Courtesy the artist & Galerie Krinzinger, Vienna; B: Courtesy the artist & Galerie Krinzinger, Vienna. Photo: Agnese Sanvito

179 A · Photo: MOCA London; B · Courtesy the artist and Cristin Tierney Gallery. Photo: MOCA London

180 · Courtesy Zhang Huan Studio. Photo: Zhang Huan Studio

181 · Courtesy the artist. Photo: Adele Renault

182–183 · Courtesy Shinichi Maruyama and Bruce Silverstein Gallery, New York

186–187 · Courtesy the artist, Lehmann Maupin, New York and Hong Kong, and the Fabric Workshop and Museum, Philadelphia. Photo: Will Brown

188 · Photo: Courtesy MOCA London and Helsinki Contemporary

189 A · Photo: Steve Weinik; B · Photo: Steve Weinik

190 · Courtesy Jack Shainman Gallery, New York. Photo: Shimon Attie, Courtesy Jack Shainman Gallery, New York

191 · Courtesy the artist and Gladstone Gallery, New York and Brussels. Photo: David Regen © Shirin Neshat

192 · Courtesy Galeria Juana de Aizpuru. Photo: Juanjo Pérez Ortiz

193 · © the artist, courtesy Sadie Coles HQ, London

194 · Courtesy the artist and Jack Shainman Gallery, New York. Photo: James Ewing, Courtesy Public Art Fund, NY

195 A · Courtesy the artists and Jack Shainman Gallery, New York. Photo: Jim Ricks; B: Courtesy the artist and Jack Shainman Gallery, New York

196 · Courtesy Mil M2. Photo: Mil M2

197 · Courtesy the artist and The Modern Institute/Toby Webster Ltd, Glasgow. Photo: MOCA London

198 · Courtesy the artist, Peres Projects, Berlin, and Stuart Shave/Modern Art, London. Photo: Pat Bresnan

199 · Courtesy the artist. Photo: Tom Dubrock

200 · Photo: Logan Beck

201 · Photo: Logan Beck

202 · Photo: MOCA London

203 · Courtesy the artist

204–205 · Courtesy Julie Saul Gallery, NYC. Photos: Courtesy the artist

206 · Courtesy Maja Bajevic; Peter Kilchmann gallery, Zurich. Photo: Officine panottiche/nuovostudiofactory

207 A · Photo: Marc Morel; B · Photo: Oliver Clifton

208 · Courtesy the artist and Gavlak Los Angeles. Photo: Lisa Anne Auerbach

209 · Courtesy the artist and Gavlak Los Angeles. Photo: Karl Wolfgang

210 · © Raymond Pettibon. Courtesy David Zwirner, New York/Hong Kong

211 A · Courtesy German AIDS-Foundation, Bonn. Contemporary Collection of Neue Nationalgalerie Berlin/SPK – Staatliche Museen Berlin. Photo: Tom Fecht; B · Courtesy the artist and The FLAG Art Foundation. Photo: Genevieve Hanson, ArtEcho LLC

212–213 · Courtesy the artist and Gavlak Los Angeles. Photo: Jeff McLane

214 · Courtesy Art Collection Telecom. Photo: Zak|Branicka Gallery, Berlin.

215 · Courtesy MKG127 Toronto. Photo: Bill Burns

216 · Photo: Elizabeth Croft

217 · Courtesy: Hannah Barry Gallery & ASHES/ASHES. Photo: Damian Griffiths

218 · Photo: Bob Smith

219 · Courtesy the artist and Grimm Gallery, New York

222 · Courtesy the artist and Blain|Southern. Photo: Peter Mallet

223 · © Harland Miller. Photo: George Darrell © White Cube

224 Courtesy the artist. Photo: T. Ayres

225 · © Ed Ruscha. Courtesy Gagosian

226 · Courtesy Isabelle Schiavi. Photo: Donna Callighan

227 · Courtesy Helsinki Contemporary. Photo: Jussi Tiainen

228 A · Courtesy the artist and October Gallery; B · Courtesy the artist and October Gallery

229 · Photo: MOCA London

230 · Courtesy the artist. Photo: Fabienne Audeoud

231 · Courtesy the artist, Sundaram Tagore Gallery. Photo: Sundaram Tagore Gallery

232 · Courtesy the artist, Galeria Vermelho. Photo: Courtesy the artist

233 · Courtesy Cheim & Read, New York

234–235 · Courtesy the artist and Hauser & Wirth. Photos: Wilfried Petzi

236 A · Courtesy the artist. Photo: Mark Dutcher; B · Private collection. Photo: Mark Dutcher

237 · © Eddie Peake. Photo © White Cube (Jack Hems)

238 · © Dan Colen. Courtesy Gagosian

239 · © Dan Colen. Courtesy Gagosian

240 · Courtesy Spain NOW! Photo: Iris Wakulenko/José Velázquez

241 · © Christopher Wool. Courtesy the artist and Luhring Augustine, New York

242 · Courtesy the artist. Photo: Harvey Opgenorth Studio

243 · Courtesy Harvey Opgenorth/Helsinki Contemporary. Photos: MOCA London

244–245 · Courtesy the artist & ART FIRST. Photos: Justin Piperger.

246 · Courtesy the artist and Simon Lee Gallery

247 · Courtesy the artist and Simon Lee Gallery

248 · Courtesy the artist

249 · Courtesy Schwab Collection, San Francisco. Photo: Johnen Galerie

250 · © Gardar Eide Einarsson, courtesy Maureen Paley, London

251 · Photo: Andy Keate

252 · Courtesy the artist. Photo: Park Chanwoo

253 A · Courtesy the artist and Elizabeth Dee, New York. Photo: Etienne Frossard; B · Courtesy the artist and Elizabeth Dee, New York. Photo: Etienne Frossard

254 · Courtesy the artist and October Gallery. Photo: October Gallery

255 · Courtesy the artist, October Gallery and Sundaram Tagore Gallery. Photo: Golnaz Fathi

256 · Photo: FXP Photography

257 · Photo: FXP Photography

260–61 · Courtesy documenta 14. Photo: Roman März

262 · Courtesy the artist and Casemore Kirkeby gallery, San Francisco. Photo: Charlie Villyard

263 · Courtesy the artist and Utah Museum of Contemporary Art. Photo: Adam Bateman

264 · Courtesy the artist and Caroline Pagès Gallery, Lisbon, Portugal

265 · Courtesy the artist. Photos: Tiago Pinto

266 A · Courtesy the artist and 1301PE, Fundación Jumex Arte Contemporáneo, Meessen De Clercq, OMR and Travesía Cuatro. Photo: Pierre Antoine/MAMVP. Resisting the Present Exhibition, 2011; B: Courtesy: the artist and 1301PE, Fundación Jumex Arte Contemporáneo, Meessen De Clercq, OMR and Travesía Cuatro. Photo: Estudio Jorge Méndez Blake

267 · Photo Paul Hester

268 · Photos: Adrián Villalobos.

269 · Courtesy the artist and Frith Street Gallery, London. Photo: Steve White

270 A · Courtesy the artist. Photo: the artist; B · Courtesy the artist. Photo: the artist

271 · Courtesy Sherman Contemporary Art Foundation, Sydney. Collection: Art Gallery of New South Wales. Photo: Silversalt Photography

272 · Courtesy the artist and Galerie Nordenhake. Photos: Jean-Baptiste Béranger

273 · © Rachel Whiteread. Courtesy the artist and Gagosian

274 · Courtesy Mier Gallery, Los Angeles

275 · Photo: Natasha Rivellini

276–277 · Photo: David Gagnebin-de Bons

278 · Courtesy the artist (Christina Mitrentse). Photo: Hadelin Feront (GNF Brussels)

279 · Courtesy Ordovas. Photo: Mike Bruce.

Index

9/11 terrorist attacks (2001) 170, 174

Active Memory (Sheng) 68
activism 58, 66, 137
advertising 8, 12, 64, 180, 215, 256
Aharoni, Ghiora 76
Aichi Triennale 126
AIDS/HIV 20, 22, 149, 211
air advertising 215
Aitken, Doug 69
Algün, Meriç 273
Ali, Muhammad 180
aluminium 62, 64, 81, 83
Amer, Ghada 64, 232
American history 98, 114, 117, 188, 208
animals 275–7
animation 123–5, 146, 147, 219
Arabic script 76, 89, 97, 230, 232
architecture 268
Argentina 262
Art Delivers People (Horowitz) 140
Arte Povera 18
Artforum magazine 256
artist books 259
Artspeak Incinerator (Claps) 148
Aspen Art Museum, Colorado 208
Attie, Shimon 147, 190
Audéoud, Fabienne 230
Auerbach, Lisa Anne 208–9
Auschwitz 192
Ayres, Tim 224

Bajevic, Maja 206
Balmforth, James 83, 138
Banner, Fiona 42, 107, 268
Basquiat, Jean-Michel 22
Bateman, Adam 259, 263
BAUHAUS No. 1 (Liu) 249
Belfort Citadel, France 44
Belief+Doubt (Kruger) 53
Ben Day technique 16
Bey, Yasiin 180
bicycles 78
Bieniek, Sebastian 30
Bischof, Beni 25, 33
Blank, Irma 20
'BLANKS' exhibition, Elizabeth Dee Gallery, New York 253
Bob and Roberta Smith (Patrick Brill) 218
Bochner, Mel 19, 246
Boetti, Alighiero 13, 18, 166
Bonvicini, Monica 55, 60, 89, 94
book covers 222–3, 252
'Book Paintings' (Morley) 252
books 84, 222–3, 249, 252, 259–79
Booth, Colin 72, 102
bracelet 71
Bracknell and Wokingham

College, Berkshire 40
Braque, Georges 8, 10, 11
breatharianism 202
Breton, Julien (Kaalam) 89, 97
bricks 74, 266
British culture 216
Broken Night (Fathi) 254
bronze 46
Broodthaers, Marcel 18
Brooklyn 62, 194
Brüggemann, Stefan 154
Bruguera, Tania 192
Buckley, Ildikó 55, 59
Buoys Boys (Banner) 42
Burns, Bill 185, 215

Cairo 28
'calligraffiti' 29, 180
calligraphy 8, 29, 68, 89, 97
    conceptual art 180, 182
    paintings 228, 230
    social comment 188, 191
Calovski, Yane 214
Camus, Albert 252
Candiani, Tania 232
'Cantastoria' exhibition, Utah Museum of Contemporary Art 263
Cantor, Mircea 176
carpets 78
Carrick, Benjamin 89, 120
cars 78
Castel, Olivier 141
censorship 83, 262
Center (FORT) 70
ceramic books 84
CGI animation 219
Chance (Messager) 48
Chapman, Jake and Dinos 76
Cheetham, Jack 44
Chernyshev, Aristarkh 138
Chevska, Maria 221, 226
China 74, 101, 106, 113, 180, 270
Chinese Bible (Yang) 270
Chinese characters 68, 74, 106, 113, 180, 228
Chowdhry, Maya 151
Chun Kwang Young 74
Cincinnati 208
cinema 141
circles 182
Claire Fontaine collective 113, 174
Claps, Bill 148
Clifford Chance, London 40, 81
climate change 42
Cobbing, William 84
Colen, Dan 238–9
Coley, Nathan 89, 92
collage 10, 12
Collide (Shaw) 81
colour names 40
'Combines' (Rauschenberg) 12
comic books 16, 146, 210
Community Standards (Flood) 198

computer-generated imagery (CGI) 219
computer programs 132
conceptual art 16, 120, 153–83
concrete 266, 268, 273
concrete poetry 12, 38, 107, 130, 202
Conscientious Objectors (Etchells) 104
consumerism 20
Contemporary Art Museum, Raleigh, North Carolina 35
Coombs, Paul 185, 188, 189
copper 86
Coptic Christians 28
Courbet, Gustave 174
Craig-Martin, Michael 158
Craighead, Alison 130
Creed, Martin 110
cress seeds 151
Croft, Elizabeth 216
Cubism 10
Cullar-Ledford, Thedra 266
Cunningham, David 156
cursive script 245
cut-up technique 11–12, 275
Czerepok, Hubert 89, 118

Dabrowska, Anka 25, 40
Dada movement 10
dance 62, 219
De La Warr Pavilion, Bexhill-on-Sea 42
death 172
Deller, Jeremy 185, 196
Demuth, Charles 9
diaries 270
Dickinson, Emily 81, 160
digital media 123–51
dildos 188
Dipple, Alex 162
'Divided Waters' exhibition, Venice 76
Don't be evil (Segal) 51
Double America (Ligon) 98
drawings 205, 221–57
Drózdz, Stanislaw 16–18
Duchamp, Marcel 10–11, 102, 113, 250
Dunn, Ralph 202
Duravcevic, Aleksandar 46, 278
Dutcher, Mark 87, 237

Eerdekens, Fred 86, 120
Egypt 28
Einarsson, Gardar Eide 250
Ekholm, Roberto 202
el Khalil, Zena 62
eL Seed 28
Elizabeth Dee Gallery, New York 253
embroideries 18, 166–7, 206, 214, 232
environment 42, 130
erotic books 264
    see also sexuality

Etchells, Tim 104
Everson, Ryan 60
Exceptional Suicide (Yahnker) 270
Existenzängste (Bischof) 33
EXIT (LARGE) (Aitken) 69

Fathi, Golnaz 254–5
Fear Expanded (Everson & Garcia) 60
Fecht, Tom 23, 211
Felt (Koh) 117
feminism 18
film 141
    see also video
Finland 37
Finnegans Wake (Joyce) 104
fire 174
Fishman, Louise 13, 18
Flag of Dildosis (Coombs) 188, 189
Fleck, Ludwik 155
Flood, Mark 198–9
Floyer, Ceal 153, 160
Fluxus collective 12
folktales 159
Fonseca, Ana 259, 264, 265
Forever (yellow) (Noble & Webster) 94
FORT collective 70
Foucault, Michel 214
Fountain (Duchamp) 11
Fowler, Eve 168, 274
Foyles bookshop, London 30
Frostenson, Katarina 162
Fuck (Colen) 238
Futurism 11

Galhotra, Vibha 42, 67
Gallery Graffiti (Opgenorth) 242–3
Garcia, Jason 60
gardens 64
gay people 22, 188, 192, 202, 205, 237, 274
Geers, Kendell 110, 170, 248
Genesis (Imhauser) 124
GER/ The Stranger (Aharoni) 76
GIF animation 123, 124, 125
Gilbert and George 20
Gillick, Liam 155
Gimenez-Zapiola, Pablo 150
Giorno, John 12
Glasgow School of Art 44
glass 60, 68, 69, 76, 202
Go Into This Space (Themann) 146
Going to the Gallery (Mackrell) 178
gold 71
Google 51
Göthman, Lukas 221, 227
graffiti 29, 33, 38, 154, 180
    paintings 240, 242–3
    'Senseless Drawing Bots' 126–7
    tags 153, 176
Gran Fury 20–2
Graphics Interchange Format (GIF) 123, 124, 125

Gris, Juan 9, 10
Gysin, Brion 11

Hair Today (Supreme Hold)
    (Longly) 83
'HAME' series (Murdoch) 46
Hamer, Michelle 206
handwriting 147, 168, 191, 245
hate 174
He An 106
Hebrew script 76
Helsinki Contemporary 37, 242
Hi (Rosen) 35
Hidalgo, Alexander 102
Highlanes Gallery, Drogheda 57
Hirshhorn Museum and
    Sculpture Garden,
    Washington DC 53
Hirst, Nicky 40, 172
History Kids (Ruscha) 224
HIV/AIDS 20, 22, 149, 211
Holocaust 140, 192, 273
Holy Shit (Colen) 238
Holzer, Jenny 20, 90
Horn, Roni 23, 81, 234–5
Horowitz, Jonathan 140, 192

I Am a Man (Thomas) 194
IBM 250
Identity (Duravcevic) 46
'If Not Winter' (Booth) 72
Imhauser, Joseph 124
immigration 68, 147, 189, 201
Indiana, Robert 16
inedia 202
'Info-Sculptures' 138
installations 18, 25–53, 92, 133–5,
    142, 146
    books 259–79
    social comment 211, 219
instruction manuals 250
'Interchange Junctions'
    exhibition, London 57
internet 130
    see also social media
Invisible Friend (Takala) 129
iO Gallery, Brighton 162
Iran 191
ISIS flag 188
Islam 191
Israel 190
Italy 78
Ivanoska, Hristina 214

Japanese brush painting 182
Jardim perfumado (Fonseca) 264, 265
Jarman, Derek 20
Jeffrey, Nick 216
Jesus Wept (Booth) 102
Jews 76, 192, 273
Jezik, Enrique 25, 44, 66
Johns, Jasper 12
Joyce, James 104
Judenplatz Holocaust Memorial,

Vienna 273
Jurkiewicz, Zdzislaw 16
Just in Time (Knotek) 125

K (Price) 219
Kaalam (Julien Breton) 89, 97
Kafka, Franz 266
Kanno, So 126–7
Kass, Deborah 55, 62
Kassel 262
Kirton, Travis 137
Kittens (Bateman) 263
knitting 208
    see also embroideries
Knotek, Anatol 25, 48, 125
Koans 18
Koh, Terence 117
Konstakademien, Stockholm 273
Korean culture 74
Korkeila, Jukka 25, 37
Kosuth, Joseph 104
Kruger, Barbara 20, 53
Kruithof, Anouk 259, 262
KUAD Gallery, Istanbul 104
Kuball, Mischa 142
Künstlerhaus Bethanien, Berlin 34
Kusho #1 (Maruyama) 182

laminate panels 84
laser projections 132, 147
Latin script 107–9, 156, 172, 228
Lauster, Darryl 55, 72, 117
LED lights 60, 90, 106, 138
Leitão, Sofia 264, 265
Lemu, Massa 185, 201
Lennon, John 185
Lesick, Kurtis 137
Lewty, Simon 245
Lexier, Micah 25, 33
LGBTQ+ people 22, 188, 192, 202,
    205, 237, 274
'Libation to Eros' series (Petry) 38
libraries 259, 273
Lichtenstein, Roy 16
light 20, 86, 89–121
    LED lights 60, 90, 106, 138
    spotlights 156
light bulbs 89, 94
'light poems' 90
lighter, etched 76
Ligon, Glenn 98
Lijn, Liliane 18–20, 123, 132–3
Linke, Simon 22, 256–7
Liu Ye 249
'Live Action Painting' 240
live art (performance) 137, 153–83
Logan, Zachari 205
Longly, George Henry 83
Luxemburg, Rosa 226
Lyon Biennale 38

Mackrell, William 153, 178
Magee, Alan 57
Magritte, René 11

Manchester Mega Mela 151
Manhattan 62
manuals, instruction 250
marble 72, 83
Marclay, Christian 146, 170
Martins, Edgar 172
Maruyama, Shinichi 182
Mary, Virgin 37
Massoudy, Hassan 17, 230
Mastrovito, Andrea 259, 275–7
Mater et Magistra (Korkeila) 37
Maynou, Josep 78
memento mori 176
memory 46
Méndez Blake, Jorge 160, 266
Merz, Mario 20
Messager, Annette 25, 48
Metropolitan Museum of Art,
    New York 149
Meulman, Niels 29, 180
Mil M2 collective 185, 196
Miller, Harland 222–3
Millerntor Gallery, Hamburg 30
minimalism 140
Minujín, Marta 262
mirrors 69, 102
Mitrentse, Christina 259, 278
Mondrian, Piet 249
Mongolia 42
Montgomery, Robert 89, 90, 174
moonneme project (Lijn) 132–3
Moreau de Justo, Alicia 66
Morgan, Lisa Z. 166
Morley, Simon 252
Morse code 148
mulberry paper 74
Mulvihill, Bryan 221, 228
murals 29
Murdoch, Kate 25, 46
museums 8, 18
music 62, 141
mythology 159

'N-N-N Paintings' (Ayres) 224
Nameless Library (Whiteread) 273
'Names and Stones' series
    (Fecht) 211
Nannucci, Maurizio 20, 107
Nazis 11, 44, 76, 192, 262, 273
Neo Deo (Eerdekens) 120
neon art 20, 89, 98–102, 104–21
Neshat, Shirin 23, 191
New Delhi 29
new media 123–51
New Objectivity 11
New York 62, 147, 149, 170, 188,
    194, 253
newsfeeds 130
newsprint 10, 12, 162
Nietzsche, Friedrich 142
'NO, Global Tour' (Sierra) 58
'Noah's Yacht' show, Zevitas
    Marcus, Los Angeles 270
Noble, Tim 94

Nothing Last Forever (Knotek) 48
novels 178, 266
nuclear waste 130

Ono, Yoko 185
Opgenorth, Harvey 242–3
Ortiz, Michelle Angela 189
Ostendarp, Carl 253
otherness 76
Ouairy, Alexandre 101
Ovelman, Joe 168
Ovid 71
OY/YO (Kass) 62

paintings 160, 194, 216, 221–57
    Japanese brush painting 182
    on large canvas 180
Palace Liquorsoul (Ward) 114
Palestine 190
palindromes 98
Palmer, Jane 55, 59
paper, mulberry 74
The Parthenon of Books
    (Minujín) 260–2
patriarchy 18
Peake, Eddie 237
'The Penguin Books Series'
    (Miller) 222–3
Perception (eL Seed) 28
'Perfect Circle' series (Bieniek) 30
performance 137, 153–83
Persian script 254
Petry, Michael 38
Pettibon, Raymond 23, 210
photography 53, 97, 150, 172
photomontage 53
Picabia, Francis 10
Picasso, Pablo 10, 11
Pierson, Jack 64
Pink Investigator (Lisa Z. Morgan)
    166
plastic 81
'poetic sculpture' 151
poetry 64, 68, 71, 113, 150, 151
    conceptual art 160, 162, 168,
    174, 180
    concrete poetry 107, 130, 202
    'light poems' 90
Poland 118, 226
political campaigns 208, 218
political systems 100
Polonsky, Nicole 84
polythene 250
Pop art 12, 16
porcelain 228
'Post-It Notes' series
    (Ovelman) 168
posters 8–10, 37, 129, 137,
    141, 149, 168
postmodern art 20
Power Plant gallery, Toronto 107
Price, Elizabeth 219
Prince, Richard 22
projections 90, 123, 132, 141–50

Prouvost, Laure 153, 158
proverbs 71
punctuation marks 160, 162
puns 10, 11, 188

QR (Quick Response) codes
    123, 124
Queens Museum of Art,
    New York 64

racism 98, 114, 118, 168, 194
Rainbow Aggregator (Salavon) 130
Randall Weeks, Ishmael 259, 268
Rauschenberg, Robert 12
'readymades' 10, 11
receipt, artful 160
religion 92, 142, 191
'reliques' 158
'Remembered Words'
    (Horn) 234–5
Ricalde, Rosana 71, 159
Riello, Antonio 55, 78
Robertson, John 221, 250
Robilliard, David 20
Rosen, Kay 35, 149
Rossi, Luca 133–5
rotten (Göthman) 227
Royal Academy of Arts, London 94
Rriippp (Marclay) 170
RUN (Bonvicini) 60
Ruscha, Ed 14–15, 16, 224

Salavon, Jason 123, 130
Sappho 72
Scotland 46
Scott, Sheldon 89, 114
sculptures
    books 262–4
    cardboard letters 44
    'Info-Sculptures' 138
    'poetic sculpture' 151
    text sculptures 55–87
Segal, Miri 51
Self-Portrait as a Wall (Lexier) 33
'Senseless Drawing Bots' (Kanno
    & Yamaguchi) 126–7
Sensorium – Go Into This Space
    (Themann) 34
September 11 (2001) terrorist
    attacks 170, 174
Serra, Richard 140
sexuality 87, 166, 168, 188, 237, 264
shamans 153
Shaowanasai, Michael 89, 119
Shaw, Fiona 81
Sheng, Shan Shan 68
Shenzhen 106
Shi Yong 113
shoelaces 188, 189
Sierra, Santiago 58
silver 71
SMACH Biennale, San Martin
    de Tor 133
social comment 185–219

social media 129, 133, 137, 198
song titles 60
SORRY (Magee) 57
'Sorry!' paintings (Jeffrey) 216
sound and video installations 142
speech-balloons 194–5
spotlights 156
steel 60, 64, 67–9, 69, 81, 83, 138
Stein, Gertrude 168
stencils 38, 40, 66, 198, 240
street performance 201
Styrofoam 62
suicide notes 172
Surrealism 11
Surround Sounds (Marclay) 146
SUSO33 240
Sweat (Peake) 237
symbolism 8, 10

'Tag Clouds' series (Tremblin) 176
Takala, Pilvi 129
Takk (Thanks) (Croft) 216
Tao Hongjing (Alexandre Ouairy)
    101
tapestries *see* embroideries
Tate Triennial 98
Tempelhof Poem (Montgomery) 90
Terminal Velocity (Young) 156
textiles 78
    see also embroideries
texting 129, 196
Thailand 119
Themann, Mark 34, 146
Thomas, Hank Willis 194–5
Thomson, Jon 130
three-dimensional works 55–87
Thulin, Anne 162
Tian Wei 228
till receipt 160
time 125, 130
Tiravanija, Rirkrit 74
Titchner, Mark 25, 30
Tompkins, Betty 211–13
Torah 76
Touch Me Not (Duravcevic) 278
Toulouse-Lautrec, Henri de 8
'Trace' series (Lauster) 72
The Treachery of Images (Magritte) 11
Tremblin, Mathieu 153, 176
True Girl (Maynou) 78
'Truism' series (Holzer) 90
Tsang Kin-Wah 38, 142
Tur, Nasan 100
Turk, Gavin 166
Twombly, Cy 12, 254
typefaces 40, 42, 58, 64
typewriters 71, 178

United States 98, 114, 117, 129,
    188, 208
US Constitution 188
Utah Museum of Contemporary
    Art 263

Venetian glass 68
Venice Biennale 46, 74, 142, 196,
    206, 214
video
    Horowitz, Jonathan 140
    installations 142, 146, 219
    Takala, Pilvi 129
vinyl text 154–6
Violin and Newspaper (Braque) 8, 10
Virgin Mary 37

wall-based installations 25–53
'wallpaper' works 38
Ward, Nari 114, 188
Warhol, Andy 12
weaving 78
    see also embroideries
Webster, Sue 94
Weiner, Lawrence 16, 25, 28, 256
Welcome (Floyer) 160
Whiteread, Rachel 273
Who Owns the Earth? (Galhotra) 42
Who's Hot Now? (Hidalgo) 102
Wild Blue Yonder (Hirst) 40
Wilde, Aida 137
women 18, 66, 211–13, 216, 232
'WOMEN Words, Phrases, and
    Stories' exhibition, FLAG Art
    Foundation, New York 211–13
wool 78
Wool, Christopher 22, 240–1
workers' contracts 196
Wyn Evans, Cerith 98

Yahnker, Eric 259, 270
Yamaguchi, Takahiro 126–7
Yang Zhichao 270
YES (Buckley & Palmer) 59
You Don't Own Me (Pierson) 64
Youd, Tim 178
Young, Carey 153, 156

zero-hour contracts 196
Zhang Huan 180
Zippo lighter, etched 76
Zobernig, Heimo 246

Michael Petry is an artist, author and Director of the Museum of Contemporary Art (MOCA), London. His books include *Nature Morte* and *The Art of Not Making*, both published by Thames & Hudson.

FRONTISPIECE · Chun Kwang Young
Aggregation 17-FE014 (detail), 2017
Mixed media with Korean
mulberry paper
163 × 228 cm (64⅛ × 89¾ in.)

PAGE 4 · Lukas Göthman
yours again tomorrow morning (detail), 2016
Oil on canvas
165 × 136 cm (65 × 53½ in.)

With 305 illustrations

First published in the United Kingdom
in 2018 by Thames & Hudson Ltd,
181A High Holborn, London WC1V 7QX

First paperback edition 2021

The Word is Art © 2018 Thames & Hudson Ltd
Text © 2018 Michael Petry

Designed by Jonathan Abbott

British Library Cataloguing-in-Publication Data
A catalogue record for this book is available from
the British Library

ISBN 978-0-500-29597-7

Printed and bound in China by Imago Publishing Limited

Be the first to know about our new releases, exclusive content and author events by visiting
thamesandhudson.com
thamesandhudsonusa.com
thamesandhudson.com.au